Women Bishops in the Church of England?

Women Bishops in the Church of England?

A report of the House of Bishops' Working Party
on Women in the Episcopate

 CHURCH HOUSE
PUBLISHING

Church House Publishing
Church House
Great Smith Street
London
SW1P 3NZ
Tel: 020 7898 1451
Fax: 020 7989 1449

ISBN 0 7151 4037 X

GS 1557

Printed in England by
The Cromwell Press Ltd,
Trowbridge, Wiltshire

Published 2004 for the House of Bishops
of the General Synod of the Church of
England by Church House Publishing.

Contents

Membership of the Working Party on Women in the Episcopate

Members of the Working Party
The Bishop of Rochester, the Rt Revd Dr Michael Nazir-Ali (Chair)
The Bishop of Stafford, the Rt Revd Christopher Hill (Vice-chair)
Dr Christina Baxter (Principal, St John's College, Nottingham)
The Bishop of Lewes, the Rt Revd Wallace Benn
The Dean of Leicester, the Very Revd Vivienne Faull
The Bishop of Bolton, the Rt Revd David Gillett
The Revd Deacon Christine Hall (Director, Bishop Otter Centre for
   Theology and Ministry, Chichester to 2003)
The Bishop of St Albans, the Rt Revd Christopher Herbert (member
   until September 2002)
Professor Ann Loades (University of Durham to 2003)
The Bishop of Gibraltar in Europe, the Rt Revd Dr Geoffrey Rowell
The Archdeacon of Worcester, the Ven. Dr Joy Tetley

Ecumenical representatives
The Revd Dr Anthony Barratt – The Roman Catholic Church
   (Ecumenical Representative on General Synod. Formerly: Vice
   Rector, St John's Seminary, Wonersh. Latterly: Our Lady of
   the Annunciation Church, New York)
The Revd Dr Richard Clutterbuck – The Methodist Church (Chair
   of the British Methodist Faith and Order Committee. Formerly:
   Principal of The West of England Ministerial Training Course.
   Latterly: Principal of Edgehill Theological College, Belfast)

Consultants
The Revd Canon Dr Nicholas Sagovsky (Westminster Abbey)
The Revd Canon Professor Anthony Thiselton (University of
   Nottingham)

Staff assessors
The Revd Preb. Dr Paul Avis (General Secretary, Council for Christian
   Unity, Archbishops' Council)

Mr William Fittall (Secretary General of the Archbishops' Council and the General Synod)

Mr Stephen Slack (Head of Legal Office, Archbishops' Council)

In attendance

Dr Martin Davie (Theological Consultant, House of Bishops, Secretary to the Working Party)

Mr Jonathan Neil-Smith (Secretary, House of Bishops)

Mr Adrian Vincent (Executive Officer, House of Bishops)

Preface

We are most grateful to the Bishop of Rochester and his working party for producing this comprehensive report. It has been the subject of extensive discussion both within the House of Bishops and the Bishops' Meeting (consisting of all diocesan, suffragan and full time assistant bishops in the Church of England), and it is now published under the authority of the House.

We are happy to commend it for prayerful study within the dioceses of the Church of England and to invite other Churches in the Anglican Communion and our ecumenical partners to let us have their reflections on it.

On behalf of the House of Bishops
✠ Rowan Cantuar
✠ David Ebor

November 2004

Foreword by the Chair of the Working Party

From the very beginning, I have understood the Working Party's mandate to have been further study of episcopacy so that the issues relevant to the admission of women to the episcopate in the Church of England are raised and addressed. We have tried to do this as comprehensively as possible and hope that our report will prove to be a useful resource for discussion and debate in the Church as a whole, as well as in General Synod.

The Working Party was set up by the House of Bishops in response to a request from General Synod and consisted of bishops, ordained and lay women, expert consultants and ecumenical participants. A wide range of views on the subject was to be found among the members – and we have struggled, in the course of our meetings, to understand what each member has been trying to say to us all. Our meetings have demonstrated a basic unity, not only in faith, but quite often in theological approach and commitment to scholarship. It would be wrong to pretend that there has been no pain involved in working together. Members have, however, realized the necessity of this difficult task for the sake of the Church, its mission and its unity.

We received over seven hundred submissions in writing. They were from a variety of points of view. Each was read and evaluated in the light of our mandate. We saw a large number of those who had made submissions though, regrettably, we could not see them all. We were able to consult a number of our partner churches in the Anglican Communion, among the Porvoo churches and also some of our ecumenical partners. We hope that many of the views expressed in the submissions and the consultations are reflected in the report.

Our approach has been to consider the emergence of episcopacy in the light of the Bible and the experience of the earliest Christian communities. We have also taken account of specifically Anglican emphases in this regard, especially from the sixteenth century onwards.

We hope that this work will have value more widely than in just the context of our present discussion.

We have considered the place of women in Church and society and have attempted to relate this to an account of women's ministries down the centuries. Once again, we have done this with our Bibles open before us. Whilst we have not shied away from detailed exegesis of the so-called 'difficult' texts, on the one hand, or of the 'egalitarian' ones, on the other, our basic approach has been to situate the questions about the place of women in society, and their ministry in Church, within the whole trajectory of a properly biblical anthropology. We have also, of course, reflected on how women have actually exercised ministry since biblical times.

Many of the theological arguments involved in the question about women bishops were also raised during the debate about the admission of women to the priesthood. Some of them have, however, been raised in a new way or with fresh force. There are others, of course, which are wholly new. Each has been given attention in the light of the decision which the Church has to make about women bishops. We have set out our views on reception and development not simply in terms of process but as theological ideas. This is important for a living tradition which seeks to be faithful to what has been handed on but seeks also to engage with changing circumstances and new situations. Once again, we hope that the material will have some use beyond the present context.

We have examined the possible options for maintaining as much unity as possible, if the Church were to decide that it would be appropriate to admit women to the episcopate. The theological implications for each option have also been outlined. It may well be that theological tidiness has to be balanced, in this context, with the need to maintain as much unity as is possible and to go as far as we can in respecting conscience. The manner in which this is done should be such that the effectiveness of the Church's mission and ministry is not unnecessarily jeopardized.

Beyond its immediate use in a General Synod debate, we are hoping that an appropriate educational process can be developed and made available so that the report can be studied more widely by individuals and groups in dioceses, deaneries and parishes.

I am very grateful to the members of the Working Party for all their hard work over the last three years. We are greatly in the debt of the secretary of the Working Party, Dr Martin Davie, and his assistant, Mr Adrian Vincent.

✠ Michael Roffen:
Bishop of Rochester
Chair of the House of Bishops' Working Party on Women in the Episcopate

June 2004

chapter 1

Introduction

1.1 The background to the current report

1.1.1   The twentieth century saw many changes in British society and one of the biggest of these was the change in the status of women within it. At the beginning of the century women did not have the vote and their educational and employment opportunities were limited compared with those enjoyed by men. By the end of the century women had obtained the same political, educational and employment rights as men.

1.1.2   As we shall explain in more detail in Chapter 4, there is a continuing debate about how deeply these changes have affected ingrained attitudes about the respective roles of men and women and whether Britain is still a society in which women are disadvantaged. What is clear, however, is that in society at large there is, in theory at least, general acceptance of the idea that women should enjoy the same opportunities as men in all spheres of life.

1.1.3   The changes that have taken place in wider society have also been paralleled by changes within the Church of England. As we shall also explain in more detail in Chapter 4, during the twentieth century women took a continually increasing part in the government of the Church of England and the exercise of authorized public ministry. The clearest symbols of this process of change were the vote by General Synod in November 1992 to ordain women as priests and the subsequent ordination of the first women to the priesthood at Bristol Cathedral on 12 March 1994.

1.1.4   Nevertheless, in spite of this development of the role of women within the Church there is still a lack of consensus within the Church of England on the issue of women's ministry. The decision to ordain women as priests was taken in the face of strong opposition from many in the Church and in the years since the decision was taken this opposition has not died away. The division between those who believe that it is right for women to exercise the same forms of public ministry as men and those who do not remains, and there is at present no sign of its ceasing to exist.

1.1.5   One sign of this continuing division is that, although the pressure for a debate on the ordination of women as bishops has grown in the years since women were first ordained as priests, there are those in the Church of England who cannot see why a debate on episcopacy is needed. This is because for them the answer to the question of whether or not women should be bishops is so clear that there is nothing to debate.

1.1.6   As we shall see in more detail in Chapter 5 of this report, there are those who hold strongly that women obviously should be bishops. As they see it, it is only when all ministerial offices in the Church of England are open to both women and men that the Church will be able to bear consistent witness to the equality between women and men as those made in the image and likeness of God and will be able to make most effective use of the talents that God has given to his people.

1.1.7   On the other hand there are also those who hold strongly that women obviously should not be bishops. This is either because they hold that the introduction of women bishops would be contrary to the witness of Scripture and tradition, or because they hold the Church of England does not have the authority to make such an innovation, or because they feel that it would cause grave disunity within the Church of England and between the Church of England and the Roman Catholic and Eastern Orthodox Churches.

1.1.8   However, it is precisely because there is this strong disagreement that the issue needs to be debated. In the earliest days of the Christian Church there was passionate disagreement on the question of whether Gentiles who became Christians needed to be circumcised and obey the Jewish law in its entirety. St Luke tells us that in order to resolve this issue, which was threatening to divide the Church, a council was held in Jerusalem (Acts 15.1-35) at which the issue was debated and the will of God was discerned.

1.1.9   What the story of the council of Jerusalem points us to is the truth that if collective discernment of the will of God is to be achieved then there needs to be prayerful discussion of contentious issues. As the ARCIC report *The Gift of Authority* notes:

> In changing situations producing fresh challenges to the Gospel, the discernment, actualization and communication of the word of God is

the responsibility of the whole people of God. The Holy Spirit works through all members of the community, using the gifts he gives to each for the good of all.[1]

1.1.10   In order that the people of God can discharge this responsibility it is necessary for adequate debate to take place so that there is the opportunity for the voice of the Holy Spirit to be heard through the different contributions made by those taking part. Without such discussion in the light of Scripture, tradition and reason decisions will be made simply on the basis of the beliefs held by those exercising positions of power and authority in the Church and the opportunity for wider discernment will be lost.

1.1.11   However, for debate to be fruitful it needs to be *informed* debate. The voice of the Holy Spirit is heard not in spite of, but most often on the basis of, careful study and reflection of matters under discussion. Acts 15 is the classic New Testament model of the Early Church debating a contentious issue. What we see in that chapter is a decision being made after careful consideration on the basis of three factors: the theological argument from St Peter that the basis of salvation was by grace through faith and not through observance of the Jewish law (Acts 15.6-11), the testimony of St Barnabas and St Paul as to what they had seen God doing among the Gentiles (Acts 15.12) and the exposition of Amos 9.11-12 by St James (Acts 15.13-21). There is an interplay between a general theological argument, the testimony of experience, and an exploration of the meaning of specific biblical texts and it is on this basis that a letter was sent out saying '. . . it has seemed good to the Holy Spirit and to us' (Acts 15.28).

1.1.12   It was a concern that the debate about women bishops should be a properly informed one that underlay the motion by the Archdeacon of Tonbridge, Judith Rose, which was passed by General Synod in July 2000:

> That this Synod ask the House of Bishops to initiate further theological study on the episcopate, focusing on the issues that need to be addressed in preparation for the debate on women in the episcopate in the Church of England, and to make a progress report on this study to Synod in the next two years.

The Working Party that has produced this report was set up to carry out this further theological study.

1.2 The nature of the current report

1.2.1   As requested by the General Synod motion, the Working Party made a progress report to General Synod in July 2002 [2] and this final report now completes the Working Party's work. In order to understand the character of this final report there are three issues that need to be noted.

1.2.2   The first issue is precisely what was asked for in the motion passed by General Synod. Synod did not ask the Working Party to make a recommendation as to whether women should or should not be ordained as bishops in the Church of England. What it did ask for was further study on the episcopate, focusing on the issues that would need to be considered in any future debate on the issue of whether women should be bishops.

1.2.3   The nature of the remit given to the Working Party explains the nature of this current report. The Working Party has attempted to set out as clearly and as even-handedly as possible the issues that will need to be considered in any future Synod debate while refraining from making any suggestions as to what the outcome of that debate should be.

1.2.4   The members of the Working Party reflect the impasse that exists in the Church of England as a whole in that they disagree about whether women should be bishops, and whether there should be women bishops now. However, they agree on what they think the issues are that need to be debated and it is this agreement that is reflected in this report.

1.2.5   The second issue is the complexity of the topic under consideration in this report. At first sight the question that General Synod will need to consider in any future debate seems to be a very simple one. Is it right for women to be ordained as bishops? However, further reflection reveals that this simple question needs to broken down into four further questions if it is to be tackled properly.

(a) What is the nature of the episcopate as the Church of England understands it?

1.2.6   Any debate on whether women should be bishops in the Church of England needs to be informed by a clear understanding of the nature of episcopal ministry. If this clarity is lacking Synod will not be able to make a properly informed decision about whether this ministry is one that may legitimately be discharged by a woman.

(b) Can it be right in principle for a woman to be a bishop?
1.2.7   As has already been indicated, this is the fundamental question that needs to be discussed. For the purposes of this report and of any future Synod debate it needs, however, to be nuanced slightly. This is because the question that Synod will have to consider is not just the abstract question of whether it would be right for a woman to be a bishop in some hypothetical Church, but the concrete question of whether it would be right for a woman to be a bishop in the Church of England given the Church of England's present understanding of episcopacy.

(c) Would this be an appropriate time for the Church of England to move towards appointing women as bishops?
1.2.8   As well as the basic issue of whether it would be right for a woman to be a bishop in the Church of England, Synod will also need to consider the question of timing. It might be right to appoint women bishops in the Church of England at some point in the future but wrong to do so now. As we have noted, it might be argued, for example, that there was insufficient consensus within the Church of England or ecumenically on the issue, or that a longer period of time was needed for the reception of the 1992 decision to ordain women as priests.

1.2.9   On the other hand, it might also be argued that not only was it right for women to be appointed as bishops in the Church of England, but that this was something that should be done now. It might be argued, for example, that there were senior women priests whose God-given talents should now be exercised in the college of bishops, or that the Church's witness to the Gospel was rendered incredible in our society by its continuing discrimination against women.

(d) If it were the appropriate time to appoint women as bishops in the Church of England, how should the Church of England go about implementing this change and what provision, if any, should be made for those who would be unable to accept women bishops?
1.2.10   If it were felt to be the appropriate time to appoint women as bishops, Synod would also need to consider how to make this change.

- The most straightforward way of doing this would be a simple alteration to Canon Law and the 1993 measure in order to remove all restrictions to women being bishops. However, there would be consequences that would need to be addressed in relation to resolutions A and B under the 1993 measure, and in relation to the provision of extended episcopal care under the 1993 Act of Synod. It seems probable that either further consequential legislation or a code of practice would be required in order to deal with these issues.

• In order to meet the concerns of those opposed to the ordination of women as bishops, Synod might want to consider the ways in which the ministry of women bishops might be restricted, a development of the present scheme of extended episcopal oversight, or the more radical option of the establishment of some kind of third province that would retain an exclusively male episcopate.

• The question of other provisions for those unable to accept women bishops would also need consideration. When the Church of England agreed to proceed with the ordination of women as priests, provision was made under the *Priests (Ordination of Women) Measure 1993*, the *Ordination of Women (Financial Provisions) Measure for 1993* and the *Episcopal Ministry Act of Synod* for those who were unable to accept women priests. Since it is clear that in the event of there being legislation to enable women to be bishops there would also be those who would be unable to accept women bishops, the question then arises as to whether appropriate provision should be made in their case and, if so, how.

1.2.11 The issues involved here are both theoretical and practical. Would it be right in principle to make any such restriction or provision and, if it were right, what sort of restriction or provision would be both in accord with Anglican ecclesiology and also workable in practice?

1.2.12 The intention of this report is to help Synod explore these four questions. In order to do this the report will consider each question in turn, looking in more detail at the issues which have just been noted in the light of the Working Party's own discussions and the points made by those groups and individuals who submitted evidence to it. Before moving on to consider the questions themselves, however, the report will begin by looking at the nature of the episcopate as the Church of England currently understands it.

1.2.13 Episcopal ministry has been exercised in many different ways down the centuries and across the world. This report, however, focuses on the way in which episcopal ministry is understood and practised in the Church of England. This is because what is under consideration in this report is the issue of whether it is right for women to become bishops in the Church of England. The teaching and practice of other churches is noted when it is relevant to the consideration of this issue.

chapter 2
Episcopacy in the Church of England

2.1 Ecumenical agreement on ministry

2.1.1 There is now a growing ecumenical consensus on the issue of ministry which is reflected in the World Council of Churches Faith and Order report, *Baptism Eucharist and Ministry* (*BEM*)[1] and also in recent ecumenical agreements into which the Church of England has entered. Examples of such agreements are *The Meissen Agreement* with the Evangelical Church in Germany,[2] *The Porvoo Agreement* with the Nordic and Baltic Lutheran Churches,[3] *The Fetter Lane Agreement* with the Moravian Church in Great Britain and Ireland,[4] *The Reuilly Agreement* with the French Lutheran and Reformed Churches[5] and the recently agreed *Anglican–Methodist Covenant.*[6]

2.1.2 The statements *Ministry and Ordination* and *Authority I* contained in the ARCIC *Final Report,*[7] which were declared by General Synod and Resolution 8:1 of the Lambeth Conference of 1988 to be 'consonant in substance' with Anglican belief, reflect this same ecumenical consensus about the nature of ministry.

2.1.3 The discussion about ministry in the *Dublin Agreed Statement* of the Anglican-Orthodox dialogue[8] focuses on the issue of primacy and does not therefore reflect the same wide-ranging agreement about the theological understanding of ministry that is found in *BEM* and these other agreements.

2.1.4 The basic points of agreement in *BEM* and the ecumenical agreements are as follows:

● The corporate priesthood of all the baptized and the ministry of the whole people of God:

> We believe that all members of the Church are called to participate in its apostolic mission. All the baptized are therefore given various gifts and ministries by the Holy Spirit. They are called to offer their being

as 'a living sacrifice' and to intercede for the Church and the salvation of the world. This is the corporate priesthood of the whole people of God and the calling to ministry and service (1 Peter 2.5).[9]

● The ordained ministry of word and sacrament as a divine institution which exists to serve the ministry of the whole people of God.

> Within the community of the Church the ordained ministry exists to serve the ministry of the whole people of God. We hold the ordained ministry of word and sacrament to be a gift of God to his Church and therefore an office of divine institution.[10]

● The need for a ministry of *episcope* (oversight)[11] to safeguard the apostolicity and unity of the Church.

> We believe that a ministry of oversight (*episkope*), exercised in personal, collegial and communal ways, at all levels of the Church's life, is necessary to witness to and safeguard the unity and apostolicity of the Church.[12]

2.2 The emergence of episcopacy in the Early Church

2.2.1   As well as accepting these general ecumenical principles about ministry, the Church of England holds that the ordained ministry of word and sacrament and the ministry of *episcope* should be exercised within the framework of the ancient threefold order of ministry consisting of bishops, priests and deacons. This threefold order emerged in the first centuries of the Church's existence and, as we shall see later in the chapter,[13] it was deliberately maintained in the Church of England by the Anglican Reformers in order to retain continuity with the teaching and practice of the Early Church.

2.2.2   In what follows we shall give an Anglican reading of the development of episcopacy in the Early Church as part of the emergence of the threefold order of ministry and explain how this eventually led to the development of the pattern of episcopal ministry that we have in the Church of England today. This is not a scholastic attempt to justify the episcopal ministry of the Church of England by an appeal to patristic precedent. It is, instead, an attempt to explain the historical and theological roots of contemporary Church of England practice.

2.2.3   *Baptism, Eucharist and Ministry* explains the origins of the threefold order of ministry as follows:

The New Testament does not describe a single pattern of ministry which might serve as a blueprint or continuing norm for all future ministry in the Church. In the New Testament there appears rather a variety of forms which existed at different places and times. As the Holy Spirit continued to lead the Church in life, worship and mission, certain elements from this early variety were further developed and became settled into a more universal pattern of ministry. During the second and third centuries, a threefold pattern of bishop, presbyter and deacon became established as the pattern of ordained ministry throughout the Church.[14]

2.2.4   Scholars such as J. B. Lightfoot in his *Commentary on St Paul's Epistle to the Philippians* (1868), Charles Gore in *The Church and the Ministry* (1919), W. H. C. Frend in *The Early Church* (1982), and R. A. Campbell in *The Elders* (1994) give different historical accounts of how the threefold order emerged, but they all support the basic correctness of what *BEM* says about the origins of the threefold pattern of bishops, priests and deacons. Developing out of the variety of forms of ministry to be found in the New Testament this threefold order became established as *the* accepted pattern of ministry in the Church during the second and third centuries and was universal thereafter. In the words of the sixteenth-century theologian Richard Hooker:

> Nor was this order peculiar unto some few churches, but the whole world universally became subject thereunto; insomuch as they did not account it to be a church which was not subject unto a bishop.[15]

2.2.5   During the later patristic period there were writers such as Ambrosiaster, St Jerome, St John Chrysostom and Theodore of Mopsuestia, who emphasized that the offices of bishop and presbyter were, originally, if not identical, then certainly not very different.[16] In Epistle CXLVI to Evangelus, St Jerome declares, for example, that it is wrong for deacons to take precedence over presbyters because St Paul teaches in passages such as Acts 20.28, Philippians 1.1 and Titus 1.5-7 that 'presbyters are the same as bishops'.[17] St John Chrysostom likewise comments on the way in which St Paul moves from the office of bishop to that of deacon in 1 Timothy 3.8 while omitting to mention presbyters:

> The reason for this omission was that between Presbyters and Bishops there was no great difference. Both had undertaken the office of Teachers and Presidents in the Church, and what he has said

concerning Bishops is applicable to Presbyters. For they are only superior in having the power of ordination, and seem to have no other advantages over Presbyters.[18]

2.2.6   It is important not to misrepresent what these writers were saying. Although they emphasized the similarity that had originally existed between bishops and presbyters, and saw the contemporary difference between them as being restricted to the bishop's exclusive right to ordain, there is no evidence that they held that the Church should abandon the threefold order of ministry.

2.2.7   In the letter from which we have just quoted, for instance, St Jerome argues that the existence of the threefold order of ministry reflects an Old Testament precedent:

> In fact as if to tell us that the traditions handed down by the apostles were taken by them from the old testament, bishops, presbyters and deacons occupy in the church the same positions as those which were occupied by Aaron, his sons and the Levites in the Temple.[19]

2.2.8   In this same letter he maintains that the episcopate emerged to prevent schism:

> When subsequently one presbyter was chosen to preside over the rest, this was done to remedy schism and to prevent each individual from rending the church of Christ by drawing it to himself.[20]

And in a tract against the schismatic Luciferians he declares that this same principle of the maintenance of unity requires a continuing distinction between bishops on the one hand and presbyters and deacons on the other:

> The well being of a Church depends upon the dignity of its chief-priest, and unless some extraordinary and unique functions be assigned to him, we shall have as many schisms in the Churches as there are priests.[21]

2.2.9   To put the matter simply, writers such as Ambrosiaster, St Jerome, St John Chrysostom and Theodore of Mopsuestia held that there was originally no great distinction between bishops and presbyters, but they accept that a clear distinction later emerged in the Church and they showed no wish to try to turn back the clock. When a fourth-century writer called Aerius[22] argued that there was no difference at all between bishops and presbyters in the Church of his own time his opinions were condemned as heretical.[23]

2.2.10   In addition, it should be noted that the evidence presented by Lightfoot strongly indicates that, although the threefold order only gradually became universal during the second and third centuries, nevertheless the origins of this order can be traced back into the first century and specifically to the actions of the apostle John in ordaining bishops for the churches in Asia Minor. In Lightfoot's words:

> the institution of an episcopate must be placed as far back as the closing years of the first century, and ... cannot, without violence to historical testimony, be dissevered from the name of St John.[24]

2.2.11   Direct evidence for this is provided by Clement of Alexandria[25] and Tertullian,[26] who specifically testify to the episcopate in Asia Minor having been founded by St John, and by the *Muratorian Fragment* which talks about his 'fellow disciples and bishops' being gathered about him.[27] Indirect evidence is provided by what we learn of the antiquity and wide extension of episcopacy in Asia Minor in the second century from the letters of St Ignatius,[28] the account of the martyrdom of St Polycarp[29] and the testimony of those early Christians sources cited by Eusebius in his *Ecclesiastical History*.[30] Such evidence shows that episcopacy was widespread early in the second century in precisely those regions where St John is said to have appointed bishops, and to this extent it supports what the direct evidence tells us.

2.2.12   The importance of Lightfoot's argument is that it points to the apostolic origin of the threefold order. In his own words:

> The result has been a confirmation of the statement in the English Ordinal, 'It is evident unto all diligently reading the Holy Scripture and ancient authors that from the Apostles' time there have been these orders of Ministers in Christ's Church, Bishops, Priests and Deacons.'[31]

2.2.13   It is indeed possible to argue that that the origins of episcopacy can be traced even further back than the ministry of St John. In 1 and 2 Timothy and Titus we find St Timothy and St Titus, acting as apostolic delegates on behalf of St Paul, exercising what would later be described as episcopal oversight over the churches of Ephesus and Crete, and patristic tradition specifically calls them bishops.[32] The New Testament also tells us that St James exercised leadership in the church in Jerusalem (Acts 12.17, 15.13-21, 21.18, Galatians 1.18-19, 2.9 and 12) and the second-century writers St Clement of Alexandria and St Hegesippus describe him as the first bishop of Jerusalem.[33]

2.2.14   If St James did exercise an episcopal role in Jerusalem this would take episcopacy back to the very earliest days of the Church. The model provided by the Church in Jerusalem may, as Lightfoot suggests, have been followed subsequently when episcopacy was introduced into Asia Minor.[34]

2.3 The role of the bishop in the patristic period

2.3.1   The role of a bishop in the patristic period can be summarized under five basic headings.

Minister of the local church

2.3.2   First, and primarily, the bishop was the chief minister of the local church. This point comes across clearly in the earliest ordinal we possess, which is contained in a treatise known as the *Apostolic Tradition*. This work is an early church order, made up of various different layers of material of uncertain date. It was once thought to be the work of St Hippolytus and therefore reflecting early third century practice in Rome, but it is now increasingly regarded as more eastern than western, partly because of the provenance of its manuscripts and partly because of its influence on subsequent eastern liturgies of ordination. It has been influential in recent liturgical revision, Roman, Anglican and other, largely because of its earlier attribution to Hippolytus.[35]

2.3.3   In the *Apostolic Tradition* the prayer for the consecration of a bishop contains the following account of the bishop's role:

> Father who knowest the hearts of all grant upon this Thy servant whom Thou hast chosen for the episcopate to feed Thy holy flock and serve as Thine high priest, that he may minister unceasingly by night and day, that he may increasingly behold and propitiate Thy countenance and offer to Thee the gifts of Thy holy Church.

> And that by the high priestly Spirit he may have authority 'to forgive sins' according to Thy command, 'to assign lots' according to Thy bidding, to 'loose every bond' according to the authority Thou

> gavest to the Apostles, and that he may please Thee in meekness and a pure heart, 'offering' to Thee a 'sweet-smelling savour'.[36]

2.3.4   What we find in this prayer is an emphasis on the pastoral and priestly role of the bishop. In the words of Casimir Kucharek, this prayer

> explains why this divine power and authority are needed: to shepherd God's holy flock, to serve as God's high-priest, to offer him the gifts of the Church (i.e. to offer the Eucharistic sacrifice), to forgive sins, to ordain others ('to assign lots'), to exorcise and heal ('to loose every bond') according to the same authority which God gave the apostles themselves.

> All these functions indicate a twofold relation of the bishop's office: the bishop is God's representative or *shaliach* to the *ecclesia* (as God's 'servant', he exercises the Lord's place as Good Shepherd); and he is the *ecclesia*'s representative before God (as high priest offering sacrifice before God, ceaselessly propitiating him, etc.).[37]

2.3.5   The Hermeneia edition of the *Apostolic Tradition* notes that its comprehensive account of the powers and functions of the episcopate makes it unique among the ordination rites of the ancient Church. It suggests that this indicates that the *Apostolic Tradition* emerged

> in a particularly difficult situation in which the status of the bishop's office and his authority in the local Christian community were under attack from some quarters.[38]

However, there is no external evidence to support this suggestion and, although the *Apostolic Tradition* is unique in bringing together the different powers and functions of a bishop in the way that it does, everything it says about the bishop's role is paralleled elsewhere in the patristic tradition. What is said in this ordination prayer is therefore representative rather than idiosyncratic.

2.3.6   Elsewhere in the *Apostolic Tradition* we find the bishop presiding at baptism, exorcising those about to be baptized and then confirming them immediately afterwards.[39] He also exercises a teaching role by giving exhortation and answering (or possibly asking) questions at the agape meal.[40]

2.3.7   As T. W. Manson notes, in the *Apostolic Tradition* the bishop is still the chief minister of a particular congregation.[41] As we shall see, the growth of the Church during the later patristic period meant that bishops gradually became responsible for a number of local congregations each with their own ministers. However, the basic model remained in place, and throughout the patristic period the bishop remained the chief minister of teaching, sacrament and pastoral care for all the congregations in his charge. The *Apostolic Tradition* exemplifies the conviction that in each area there shall be one local church led by one bishop.[42]

Instrument of unity

2.3.8   This last point brings us to the second role played by the bishop, which was his role as an instrument of the Church's unity.

2.3.9   We have already noted the argument of St Jerome that bishops emerged out of the presbyterate in order to prevent schism, and it is generally accepted that in the first texts which discuss the role of the episcopate, namely the letters of St Ignatius of Antioch, there is a strong link between the office of bishop and the maintenance of the unity of the Church.

2.3.10   Lightfoot notes that at the beginning of the second century, the time when these letters were written, the Church was facing a grave threat to its unity:

> The withdrawal of the authoritative preachers of the Gospel, the personal disciples of the Lord, had severed one bond of union. The destruction of the original abode of Christendom, the scene of the life and passion of the Saviour and of the earliest triumphs of the Church had removed another. Thus deprived at once of the personal and the local ties which had hitherto bound individual to individual and church to church, the Christian brotherhood was threatened with schism, disunion, dissolution.[43]

2.3.11   The response of St Ignatius to this crisis was to encourage the churches with which he corresponded to maintain their unity by being united with their bishops and clergy, particularly in the celebration of the Eucharist. For example, in his letter to the church in Magnesia he writes as follows:

And now, since I have already seen with the eyes of faith and embraced your whole congregation, in the persons of the men I named, let me urge on you the need for godly unanimity in everything you do. Let the bishop preside in the place of God, and his clergy in place of the Apostolic conclave, and let my special friends the deacons be entrusted with the service of Jesus Christ, who was with the Father from all eternity and in these last days has been made manifest. Everyone should observe the closest conformity with God; you must show every consideration for one another, never letting your attitude to a neighbour be affected by your human feelings, but simply loving one another consistently in the spirit of Jesus Christ. Allow nothing whatever to exist among you that could give rise to any division; maintain absolute unity with your bishop and leaders, as an example to others and a lesson in the avoidance of corruption.

In the same way as the Lord was wholly one with the Father, and never acted independently of Him, either in person or through the Apostles, so you yourselves must never act independently of your bishop and clergy. On no account persuade yourself that it is right and proper to follow your own private judgement; have a united single service of prayer which everybody attends; one united supplication, one mind, one hope, in love and innocent joyfulness. All of you together, as though you were approaching the only existing temple of God and the only altar, speed to the one and only Jesus Christ – who came down from the one and only Father, is eternally with that One, and to that One is now returned.[44]

2.3.12   This emphasis on the relationship between the bishop and the unity of the Church is also to be found in the writings of St Cyprian in the middle of the third century. Like St Ignatius, St Cyprian, who was Bishop of Carthage in North Africa, was faced with the issue of division in the Church in the aftermath of the Decian persecution, and like his predecessor he placed the role of the bishop at the centre of his account of the Church's unity. His argument is helpfully summarized by Gore:

The Church is one, then, – this is his position – with a visible external unity. The essence of that unity lies indeed in a spiritual fact – the life of Christ which is communicated to the Church: but this life is communicated to a visible society, bound together by visible bonds of external association. To this visible society he that would be Christ's must belong; 'he cannot have God for his Father who has not the Church for his mother.' The sin of schism separates from Christ in such completeness that not even martyrdom can expiate it. Of this unity the bishop is in each community at once the symbol, the guardian and the instrument. He is the instrument of it because 'the bishops, who succeed to the Apostles by an ordination which makes them their representatives,' are the possessors of that sacerdotal authority and grace with which Christ endowed His Church, and which is necessary for her existence. This plenitude of priesthood is in every bishop, and in every bishop equally, just as every one of the Apostles was 'endowed with an equal fellowship of honour and power.' But the apostolate, which was finally given to all equally, was given first to St. Peter, that by being first given to one man, there might be emphasized forever the unity which Christ willed to exist among the distinct branches or portions of His Church. The episcopate which belongs to each bishop belongs to him as one of a great brotherhood linked by manifold ties into a corporate unity.[45]

2.3.13 Two points that are important to note from St Ignatius and St Cyprian are that the bishop was not an isolated figure and that in the patristic period the bishops expressed their unity by meeting to take counsel together.

2.3.14 As can be seen in the quotation given above, St Ignatius' argument is that the unity of the Church is rooted not only in the unity of the people with their bishop but also in their unity with their presbyters and deacons. In his view the government of the Church has been committed by God to the bishop *together with* his presbyters and deacons. This view of the government of the Church was accepted throughout the patristic period. It was not the bishops alone who governed the Church. Rather, the bishops governed the Church together with their presbyters who shared in their priestly ministry and formed their governing council and with the assistance of their deacons.

2.3.15 While St Ignatius focuses on the local church and stresses the unity of the bishop with his presbyters and deacons, St Cyprian stresses the unity of the bishops of the universal Church with each other and sees this as being manifested when bishops meet together in council. In the words of Kallistos Ware, for St Cyprian the

> solidarity of the episcopate is manifested precisely through the holding of a council; in reaching a common mind at a council, the bishops are in an explicit manner exercising their episcopate *in solidum*.[46]

The tradition of bishops meeting together in council reflected by St Cyprian went back to the middle of the second century and was to find expression in the great ecumenical councils of the patristic period such as the Councils of Nicaea and Chalcedon.

2.3.16 As well as emphasizing the importance of bishops meeting together in council, St Cyprian also stressed the importance of bishops, clergy and laity taking council together. Thus in a letter to his presbyters and deacons written in 250 and concerned with the reconciliation of those who had lapsed during the persecution under the Emperor Decius he writes:

> For this is suitable to the modesty and the discipline, and even the life of all of us, that the chief officers [bishops] meeting together with the clergy in the presence also of the people who stand fast, to whom themselves, moreover, honour is to be shown for their faith and fear, we may be able to order all things with the religiousness of a common consultation.[47]

2.3.17 We can see this principle of consultation involving the whole people of God being put into practice in St Cyprian's account of the council held at Carthage in 258. In this account he describes how

> a great many bishops from the provinces of Africa, Numidia and Mauretania had met together at Carthage, together with the presbyters and deacons, and a considerable part of the congregation who were also present.[48]

Guardian of apostolic tradition

2.3.18 The third role of the bishop was as a guardian of apostolic tradition. This was a point that was particularly emphasized by St Irenaeus and by Tertullian at the end of the second century.

2.3.19 In response to the claims made by the heretical groups known collectively as the Gnostics that they possessed teaching secretly handed down by Christ and the apostles, St Irenaeus maintains in *Against Heresies* that the true apostolic teaching was passed on by the apostles to the bishops whom they appointed to succeed them.

> It is within the power of all, therefore, in every Church, who may wish to see the truth, to contemplate clearly the tradition of the apostles manifested throughout the whole world; and we are in

a position to reckon up those who were by the apostles instituted bishops in the Churches, and [to demonstrate] the succession of these men to our own times; those who neither taught nor knew anything like what these [heretics] rave about. For if the apostles had known hidden mysteries, which they were in the habit of imparting to 'the perfect' apart and privily from the rest, they would have delivered them especially to those to whom they were also committing the Churches themselves. For they were desirous that these men should be very perfect and blameless in all things, whom also they were leaving behind as their successors, delivering up their own place of government to these men.[49]

2.3.20   In order to illustrate the way in which the apostolic tradition was handed down by an unbroken succession of bishops St Irenaeus appeals to the example of the churches of Rome and Asia in both of which there was a publicly known list of bishops going back to the apostles and in both of which the 'tradition of the apostles' had been preserved.[50] In addition he argues in Book IV of *Against Heresies* that the bishops who had been entrusted with the apostolic tradition had also been given the gift of truth in order to transmit it faithfully:

> it is incumbent to obey the presbyters who are in the Church,
> – those who, as I have shown, possess the succession from the apostles; those who together with the succession of the episcopate have received the certain gift of truth, according to the good pleasure of the Father.[51]

2.3.21   Tertullian puts forward a similar argument in his work *On Prescription Against Heretics* in which he challenges the heretical groups to produce a succession of bishops going back to the apostles.

> But if there be any [heresies] which are bold enough to plant themselves in the midst of the apostolic age, that they may thereby seem to have been handed down by the apostles, because they existed in the time of the apostles, we can say: Let them produce the original records of their churches; let them unfold the roll of their bishops, running down in due succession from the beginning in such manner that [that first bishop of theirs] ... shall be able to show for his ordainer and predecessor some one of the apostles and apostolic men, – a man, moreover, who continued steadfastly with the apostles. For this is the manner in which the apostolic churches transmit their registers: as the church of Smyrna which records that Polycarp was placed therein by John; as also the church of Rome, which makes

Clement to have been ordained in like manner by Peter. In exactly the same way the other churches likewise exhibit (their several worthies) whom, having been appointed to their episcopal places by apostles, they regard as transmitters of the apostolic seed.[52]

2.3.22   It should be noted, however, that neither St Irenaeus nor Tertullian envisages the teaching of the bishops of their day as the only or primary source of Christian doctrine. Both of them, and the patristic tradition as a whole, held that there was a threefold source of Christian doctrinal authority:

- First and foremost there were the Scriptures of the Old Testament and the works of the apostles and those associated with them that were eventually brought together as the New Testament. These writings had divine authority because they were inspired by the Holy Spirit.

- They had to be interpreted, however, and the guide to authoritative interpretation was the Church's 'rule of faith', the basic orthodox interpretation of the biblical revelation that became the basis of the Catholic Creeds.

- The authority of the rule of faith was in turn guaranteed by the succession of bishops from the apostles as described above.

2.3.23   A bishop was therefore regarded as having teaching authority because he had been appointed in an unbroken succession of bishops stretching back to the apostles themselves. Consequently, he had both knowledge of the true interpretation of the Scriptures handed down by the apostles and the gift of the Spirit both to uphold him in the truth and to enable him to pass it on correctly to others.

2.3.24   In the patristic period the bishops exercised their role as guardians of the apostolic tradition in a number of different ways. They taught the apostolic faith and challenged deviations from it through their preaching, their catechetical instruction, and their writings and by meeting together in council to draw up definitions of the true faith in the face of heresy.

2.3.25   In much recent writing about the patristic period the role of the bishop as the president at the Eucharist has been emphasized,[53] but the importance of the bishop's preaching role should not be overlooked. The office of preaching was at first reserved to the bishop[54] and his *cathedra* or bishop's chair was the place from which he preached, since in the Early Church, as in the synagogue (Luke 4.20), teaching was originally given sitting down. In his treatise *On the Priesthood*, which is about the office of bishop, St John Chrysostom emphasizes the importance of preaching by arguing that it is the sole method by which the soul may be healed:

> there is but one method and way of healing appointed, after we have gone wrong, and that is, the powerful application of the Word. This is the one instrument, the only diet, the finest atmosphere. This takes the place of physic, cautery and cutting, and if it be needful to sear and amputate, this is the means which we must use, and if this is of no avail, all else is wasted: with this we both rouse the soul when it sleeps, and reduce it when it is inflamed; with this we cut off excesses, and fill up defects, and perform all manner of other operations which are requisite for the soul's health.[55]

Minister of ordination

2.3.26 The fourth role of the bishop was as the minister of ordination. This was seen as a key distinction between the offices of bishop and presbyter.

2.3.27 In the *Apostolic Tradition* a bishop is ordained by means of the laying on of hands by other bishops, one of whom says the ordination prayer.[56] In the same work we are told that 'when a presbyter is ordained the bishop shall lay his hand upon his head, the presbyters also touching him',[57] and it is the bishop who says the ordination prayer. When a deacon is ordained it is the bishop alone who lays on hands and then says the ordination prayer.[58]

2.3.28 The pattern here is clear. It was the bishops alone who ordained and the reason given for this was that only a bishop and not a presbyter had the authority to confer orders:

> For the presbyter has authority only for this one thing, to receive. But he has no authority to give holy orders. Wherefore he does not ordain a man to orders, but by laying on hands at the ordination of a presbyter he only blesses while the bishop ordains.[59]

2.3.29 The pattern that we find in the *Apostolic Tradition* is also the pattern that we find almost unvaryingly in the patristic Church.

A possible exception is provided by the church in Alexandria. Ambrosiaster and the Alexandrian patriarch Eutychius, writing much later, have been understood as providing evidence that presbyteral ordination was practised in the Egyptian church until as late as the fourth century.[60] This interpretation of their testimony has been disputed,[61] but even if it is correct and presbyteral ordination of presbyters and bishops was practised in the Egyptian church this would be an example of the exception that proves the rule since there is no evidence that presbyteral ordination was practised elsewhere.

2.3.30 Canon IV of the Council of Nicaea laid down some specific rules about the appointment and ordination of bishops. It ruled that:

> It is by all means proper that a bishop should be appointed by all the bishops in the province; but should this be difficult, either on account of urgent necessity or because of distance, three at least should meet together, and the suffrages of the absent [bishops] also being given and communicated in writing, then the ordinations should take place. But in every province the ratification of what is done should be left to the Metropolitan.

2.3.31 This canon was interpreted differently by the churches of the East and the West. In the East it was seen as ruling out either the popular election of bishops or their selection by princes.[62] As the East saw the matter, Canon IV of Nicaea meant that henceforth bishops should only be chosen by other bishops. In the West the canon was taken to mean that three bishops were necessary for a valid episcopal ordination and that the election of a bishop had to be confirmed by the senior bishop of the province concerned (the Metropolitan).

2.3.32 This disagreement apart, the canon clearly embodies the principle implicit in the provision that had always been made for the ordination of bishops by other bishops, namely that a bishop was not an isolated figure but part of a wider episcopal college whose approval was necessary if a valid ordination was to take place. Furthermore, because a bishop was the representative of his church the approval of an episcopal appointment by other bishops and their ordination of the bishop concerned was also a sign that his church was regarded as part of the Catholic Church rather than as an heretical or schismatic sect.

Leader in mission

2.3.33   A fifth and final role of the bishop was that of leader in mission. The four roles noted thus far might seem to suggest bishops in the patristic period had a ministry that was exclusively oriented towards those who were already part of the Church. However, throughout that period bishops were constantly engaged in mission to those outside the Church. Three examples will serve to illustrate this point.

2.3.34   The first example comes from the account of the martyrdom of St Polycarp, Bishop of Smyrna, which took place in about 155. We are told that after it was announced that St Polycarp had confessed to being a Christian,

> the whole audience, the heathens and the Jewish residents of Smyrna alike, broke into loud yells of ungovernable fury: 'That teacher of Asia! That father-figure of the Christians! That destroyer of our gods, who is teaching the multitudes to abstain from sacrificing to them or worshipping them!'[63]

2.3.35   It was because Bishop Polycarp was regarded as the person who had been at the forefront of the Christian missionary activity in Asia Minor in the first half of the second century that the crowd was so keen to see him killed.

2.3.36   Another example is the missionary work of St Martin, Bishop of Tours, in the fourth century. In the words of the mission historian K. S. Latourette:

> As bishop, Martin was an active missionary, especially in his own diocese. In this he was in accord with the imperial policy of Gratian and Theodosius and was merely paralleling, although possibly more zealously than most, what many other bishops were doing in their domains. At the time of his accession to the see, Christianity appears to have been restricted chiefly to the city of Tours, then probably a place of only a very few thousand inhabitants. The surrounding countryside seems to have been pagan. Martin led his monks in preaching, in destroying temples, and in baptizing.[64]

2.3.37   A third example, which comes from the seventh century, is the account given by Bede of the work of Paulinus, Bishop of York and later Rochester. Bede tells us that Paulinus was determined to bring the nation to which he was sent the knowledge of the Christian truth, and to fulfil the Apostle's saying, 'to espouse her to one husband, that he might present her as a chaste virgin to Christ'. Therefore, directly he entered the province he began to toil unceasingly not only by God's help to maintain the faith of his companions unimpaired, but if possible to bring some of the heathen to grace and faith by his preaching.[65]

2.3.38 Initially Paulinus' missionary efforts were unfruitful, but after the baptism of the Northumbrian king, Edwin, his people began to turn to Christianity as well:

> Indeed, so great was the fervour of faith and the desire for baptism among the Northumbrian people that Paulinus is said to have accompanied the king and the queen to the royal residence at Ad-Gefrin and remained there thirty-six days constantly occupied in instructing and baptizing. During this period, he did nothing from dawn to dusk but proclaim Christ's saving message to the people, who gathered from all the surrounding villages and countryside; and when he had instructed them, he washed them in the cleansing waters of baptism in the nearby River Glen.[66]

2.3.39 Many more examples could have been given, but these three make the point that in the patristic period bishops were involved in leading the Church's missionary outreach.

2.4 The development of the episcopal office

2.4.1 Although these five episcopal roles remained constant throughout the patristic period the episcopal office also developed in a number of ways during that time.

2.4.2 As we have already mentioned, the bishop of the *Apostolic Tradition* would have exercised episcopal oversight over a single congregation in one of the cities of the empire. However, as the Church continued to grow the local churches became larger and spread beyond the cities to the outlying rural areas. It became impossible for a single individual to exercise effective day-to-day pastoral oversight over all the Christians involved.

2.4.3 Two developments emerged to address this problem. First, we find reference to the existence of *chorepiscopi* in the rural areas. These are first mentioned in the thirteenth canon of the Council of Ancyra in 314, and although their origins and the precise nature of the ministry they exercised has been disputed, in certain ways they appear to have been what we would today call suffragan bishops, exercising episcopal ministry in the rural areas under the authority of the bishop of the local city.[67] Secondly, originally in the cities but later in the rural areas, we find presbyters exercising a ministry of word and sacrament in local congregations as delegates of their bishop, thus paving the way for the parochial system as we know it today.

2.4.4   In addition to the roles mentioned above, bishops were responsible for taking care of the Church's revenues and taking care of the needs of the poor.[68] As the Church grew in size and acquired wealth and property this meant that the bishop came to have an increasing administrative role assisted by his deacons led by the head or 'arch' deacon. After the official recognition of Christianity by the Roman state in the fourth century the bishop frequently came to play a prominent role in wider society as well.[69]

2.4.5   Another development was the beginning of a differentiation between episcopal sees. The bishop of the capital city of a Roman province (the Metropolitan bishop) came to exercise authority over the province as a whole. As we have seen, the Metropolitan ratified the selection of new bishops within the province. He also had the right to summon a provincial council. The Metropolitical system also developed, *mutatis mutandis*, beyond the Roman empire, being found, for example, in the churches of the Persian empire.

2.4.6   A further differentiation was the distinctive role given to the bishops of the principal cities of the empire such as Rome, Alexandria, Antioch and Carthage, who exercised authority in terms of the appointment of bishops and the calling of councils over an area encompassing several provinces. Eventually, this kind of authority (which came to be known as 'patriarchal' authority) was assigned to the five cities of Rome, Alexandria, Antioch, Jerusalem and Constantinople. The first three cities on this list had long been recognized as exercising patriarchal authority. Jerusalem was added to the list because it was the mother church and Constantinople was added because Constantine had made it the capital of the empire (the 'New Rome' as Canon II of the Council of Constantinople put it).

2.4.7   The fact that different sees varied in authority and in wealth meant that there was a temptation for bishops to seek to move from one see to another. This was forbidden by the fifteenth canon of the Council of Nicaea which declares that 'neither bishop, presbyter, or deacon shall pass from city to city'. It was felt that such movement was normally due to illegitimate ambition and would lead to an invidious distinction between sees. There was also the strongly held theological principle that a bishop was married to his see and so moving see was the spiritual equivalent to divorce and adultery. In practice this canon came to be ignored, however, because it was felt to be useful to the Church to be able to move bishops from one see to another.

2.4.8   The final development that we need to consider is the claim made for the universal authority of the bishop of Rome. Rome had always enjoyed great prestige and authority. It was the site of the martyrdom of Saints Peter and Paul, St Peter was believed to have been its first bishop, it had a reputation for doctrinal purity, and it was the chief city of the empire. The Roman church was unhappy about the authority given to the church of Constantinople because it felt that this undermined its own position and was based on a mistaken identification of political and spiritual authority.

2.4.9   Partly in response to this, and partly as a development of a claim to jurisdiction over other churches that can be traced at least as far back as Pope Victor's intervention in the dispute about the dating of Easter at the end of the second century, and possibly as far back as the letter of St Clement of Rome to the church in Corinth at the end of the first century, the popes of the fourth century came to make increasingly strong claims for a universal primatial authority on the basis that their authority derived from the commission given to St Peter and that this commission gave them continuing authority over the Christian Church as a whole.[70]

2.5 A brief history of episcopacy in the Church of England

2.5.1   As Bede's *A History of the English Church and People* makes clear, the English church adhered to the normative threefold pattern of bishops, presbyters and deacons from the earliest days of its history. In common with the entire Catholic Church it retained this pattern throughout the Middle Ages. As Hooker put it in the sixteenth century:

> In this realm of England, before Normans, yea before Saxons, there being Christians, the chief pastors of their souls were bishops . . .

Under the selfsame form it remained till the days of the Norman conqueror. By him and his successors thereunto sworn, it hath from that time till now by the space of five hundred years more been upheld.[71]

2.5.2 The so-called 'Celtic' church of northern and south-west England, Wales, Scotland and Ireland was in some respects theologically and liturgically conservative.[72] It was characterized by a monastic tradition somewhat different from that developing under the impetus of the Benedictine movement which was introduced into England by the mission sent by Pope Gregory and led by St Augustine of Canterbury (597). Nevertheless, the difference between 'Roman' and 'Celtic' Christianity should not be overemphasized. There was more diversity in *all* forms of Western Christianity than later 'romantic' Celtic and 'romanicized' Latin retelling would suggest. Nevertheless, the Roman emphasis on the bishop and jurisdiction was probably a significant difference between the two Christian traditions in these islands. However, as a result of increasing mutual contact and a number of local synods, the Synod of Whitby (664) in particular, the unified identity of the *Ecclesia Anglicana* emerged as a church fully assimilated into the mainstream of the Western Church. This meant that it recognized the primacy of the pope, and papal authority continued to be accepted by the English Church until the Reformation.[73]

2.5.3 As *BEM* notes:

> At some points of crisis in the history of the Church, the continuing functions of ministry were in some places and communities distributed according to structures other than the predominant threefold pattern. Sometimes appeal was made to the New Testament in justification of these other patterns. In other cases, the restructuring of ministry was held to lie within the competence of the Church, as it adapted to changing circumstances.[74]

2.5.4 One such point of crisis was the Protestant Reformation in the sixteenth century, in the course of which some churches that were reformed in line with Protestant thinking, such as the Lutheran churches in Germany or the Reformed Church in France, did not retain the threefold pattern.[75] The Church of England, however, while accepting many aspects of the Reformation, consciously retained the traditional pattern of ministry in order to retain continuity with the Early Church.

2.5.5   In his *Apology for the Church of England*, for example, John Jewel seeks to counter the charge of heretical innovation brought against the Church of England by its Roman Catholic opponents by setting out the beliefs of the Church of England, beliefs which he says are confirmed

> by the words of Christ, by the writings of the apostles, by the testimonies of the catholic fathers, and by the examples of many ages.[76]

2.5.6   Among the beliefs that he lists is the belief

> that there be divers degrees of ministers in the church; whereof some be deacons, some priests, some bishops; to whom is committed the office to instruct the people, and the whole charge and setting forth of religion.[77]

2.5.7   For Jewel, therefore, the retention of the threefold order of ministry signifies the commitment of the reformed Church of England to maintaining historic orthodox Christianity. The threefold order is what is found in the New Testament and the Fathers, and the Church of England has simply maintained this inheritance.

2.5.8   This emphasis on historical continuity is even more evident in the Preface to the Ordinal attached to the *Book of Common Prayer*, first published in 1550, from which we have already quoted. This states in full:

> It is evident unto all men diligently reading holy Scripture and ancient Authors, that from the Apostles' time there have been these Orders of Ministers in Christ's Church: Bishops, Priests and Deacons. Which Offices were evermore had in such reverend Estimation, that no man might presume to execute any of them, except he were first called, tried, examined, and known to have such qualities as are requisite for the same; and also by publick Prayer, with Imposition of Hands, were approved and admitted thereunto by lawful authority. And therefore, to the intent that these Orders may be continued, and reverently used and esteemed, in the Church of England; no man shall be accounted or taken to be a lawful Bishop, Priest, or Deacon in the Church of England, or suffered to execute any of the said Functions, except he be called, tried, examined and admitted thereunto, according to the Form hereafter following.

2.5.9   What these words make clear is both the conviction that the threefold order of ministry goes back to the time of the apostles and the intention that it should continue in the Church of England, an intention which the Ordinal is intended to make a reality. In the words of Stephen Neill:

> In many things the Church of England may be accused of ambiguity; these sentences are marked by a superb lucidity, and leave no doubt at all that the intention of their authors, and of those who used this service, was to continue in the Church of England those orders of bishop, priest, and deacon which had existed in the Church since the time of the Apostles, *and no others*.[78]

2.5.10   As Neill also points out, the desire to maintain continuity of orders was also clearly demonstrated at the consecration of Matthew Parker as Elizabeth I's first Archbishop of Canterbury on 17 December 1559:

> In the consecration of Matthew Parker the greatest care was taken to maintain continuity with the past, and above all to ensure that the succession of episcopal consecration was unbroken. Four bishops performed the consecration according to the form in the Edwardian Ordinal, and of these, two had been consecrated in the reign of Henry VIII under the old order.[79]

2.5.11   Alongside this continuity there were, however, two significant points of discontinuity.

2.5.12   The first of these was the rejection of the authority of the pope. This was not simply due, as is often implied, to Henry VIII's dispute with the papacy over his marriage to Catherine of Aragon. There were more fundamental issues that shaped the thinking of the English Reformers on this issue. They objected to what they saw as the moral and doctrinal corruption which they believed to be either tolerated or supported by the papacy, and they felt as a matter of theological principal that it was wrong for one bishop to exercise authority over the Church as a whole.[80]

2.5.13   As Eamon Duffy notes, in spite of the Church of England's rejection of papal authority, 'it retained totally unchanged the full medieval framework of episcopal church government'.[81] What happened at the Reformation was that the Church of England retained the pattern of church government that had developed in England in the early Middle Ages on the basis of the patristic legacy minus those elements of papal oversight and control that had developed in the later medieval period.

2.5.14   A clear example of this is provided by 1534 *Act for the Submission of the Clergy and Restraint of Appeals.* This laid down that a bishop should be elected by a cathedral chapter after it had received from the king permission to elect and a 'letter missive' containing the name of the person the chapter 'shall elect and choose', and that when the election had taken place the result would be confirmed by the metropolitan bishop of the province.[82] As Colin Podmore explains, the procedure laid down in the Act was a restoration of traditional practice, with the confirmation of the election by the archbishop being restored, after this procedure had been made redundant by the introduction of direct appointment of bishops by the pope in the fourteenth century.[83]

2.5.15   With the abolition of papal authority the Church of England became a church operating under the authority of the Crown in which there were two provinces, Canterbury and York, each with its own Metropolitan, with the Archbishop of Canterbury being *primus inter pares* (first among equals).

2.5.16   As Neill explains, the reason that the royal authority of Henry VIII replaced papal authority was the conviction set out in the preamble to the 1532 *Act in Restraint of Appeals* that England was an 'empire':

> What is an empire? It is a realm, which is wholly independent legally (and that meant to Henry and his advisers, in the law of both Church and State) of every other realm. But if that was so, if Henry was the new Justinian, what became of the Pope's claim that he was the supreme judge of Christendom, and that he alone had the final voice in all ecclesiastical causes? Henry answered roundly that this was a usurped jurisdiction; former Popes had made no such claim, and it had not been admitted by earlier English kings; it was an abuse that had crept in in the times of ignorance – but now the times of ignorance had passed away.[84]

It is this conviction that is reflected in the statements in Article XXXVII of the Thirty-Nine Articles to the effect that:

> The King's Majesty hath the chief power in this Realm of England, and other his Dominions, unto whom the chief Government of all Estates of this Realm, whether they be Ecclesiastical or Civil, in all cases doth appertain, and is not, nor ought to be, subject to any foreign jurisdiction.

and that:

> The Bishop of Rome hath no jurisdiction in this Realm of England.

2.5.17 The second point of discontinuity was a willingness to recognize the presence of the Church of Jesus Christ in Christian communities that did not have bishops. In the patristic and medieval periods a church without bishops in historic succession would simply not have been seen as a church, but the newly reformed English church was unwilling to take this view. As Article XIX of the Thirty-Nine Articles makes clear, the marks of the visible Church were the right preaching of the word and the right administration of the two dominical sacraments and not a particular form of church government. As Archbishop John Whitgift put it:

> the essential notes of the church be these only: the true preaching of the word of God, and the right administration of the sacraments ... so that, notwithstanding government, or some kind of government, may be a part of the church ... yet it is not such a part of the essence and being, but that it may be the Church of Christ without this or that kind of government.[85]

2.5.18 While the Church of England was careful to retain the traditional episcopal form of church government it was unwilling to refuse ecclesial recognition to those continental Lutheran and Reformed churches that did not do so.

2.5.19 The retention of the historic threefold order was not universally accepted within the Church of England. During the reign of Elizabeth I certain of the more radical members of the Puritan party began to advocate the abolition of bishops and the adoption of a presbyterian system of church government instead. As John Moorman puts it:

> That the Church of England should preserve episcopal government had never for a moment been doubted by the framers of the

Elizabethan settlement, but to the Puritans it was anathema; and they set themselves to work for the abolition of episcopacy and the establishment of a presbyterian type of church government with a form of worship which gave complete liberty to the minister.[86]

2.5.20 Moorman's statement needs qualification in that there were moderate Puritans who were prepared to accept episcopacy, but his overall picture is an accurate one.[87]

2.5.21 The presbyterian position was set out with great vigour in a series of Puritan manifestos, the most important of which was the *Admonition to Parliament* of 1572, published anonymously, but in fact the work of the Puritan writer Thomas Wilcox.[88]

2.5.22 In response, upholders of the Elizabethan settlement mounted an equally vigorous defence of episcopacy. Thus Richard Hooker notes in Book VII of the *Laws of Ecclesiastical Polity* that the 'sacred regiment of bishops' has been the universal form of church government in the history of both the universal Church and the Church in England and declares:

> O nation utterly without knowledge, without sense! We are not through error of mind deceived, but some wicked thing hath undoubtedly bewitched us, if we foresake that government, the use whereof universal experience hath for so many years approved, and betake ourselves unto a regiment neither appointed of God himself, as they who favour it pretend, nor till yesterday ever heard of among men.[89]

Hooker argues that episcopacy is of apostolic origin, and he also defends the way that episcopacy is structured in the Church of England, including government by Metropolitans, on the grounds that this is necessary for the good governance of the Church.

2.5.23 There were those who sought to bridge the gap between the two positions. For example, James Ussher, Archbishop of Armagh, published in 1640 a work entitled the *Reduction of Episcopacy unto the Form of Synodical Government* which proposed a way of combining episcopacy with a presbyterian form of church order. However, in spite of the efforts of Ussher and others, the seventeenth century saw the Church of England polarize as bitterness grew on all sides, due on the one hand to the attempt by Charles I and Archbishop Laud to suppress

Puritan dissent and on the other to the execution of Charles I and, during the period of the Commonwealth, the official abolition of episcopacy and the use of the Prayer Book from the English Church.

2.5.24 This polarization meant that after the restoration of the monarchy in 1660 agreement proved impossible to achieve at the Savoy Conference in 1661; on St Bartholomew's day 1662 approximately 1,760 Puritan clergy who would not accept the exclusive use of the 1662 Prayer Book and, where necessary, receive episcopal re-ordination were expelled from their livings.

2.5.25 Thereafter the issue of episcopacy has been a closed question as far as the Church of England is concerned. The historic threefold order of ministry headed by bishops ordained in historic succession has been the universal norm. As the Anglican Communion gradually evolved from the seventeenth century onwards what was the norm for the Church of England became the norm for the Anglican tradition worldwide. Following the adoption of the 'Lambeth Quadrilateral' by the Lambeth Conference of 1888, Anglicans have remained committed to four cornerstones for a reunited Church: Scripture, the Catholic Creeds, the sacraments of Baptism and the Eucharist, and 'the Historic Episcopate locally adapted to the needs of various regions and peoples'. In the words of the Reuilly Common Statement:

> Anglicans hold that the full visible unity of the Church includes the historic episcopal succession.[90]

2.6 Differing understandings of episcopacy in the Church of England

2.6.1 Although there has thus been agreement on the requirement for episcopacy as a matter of agreed church polity, where Anglicans have continued to disagree is on the significance of episcopacy. This is a disagreement that goes back to the sixteenth and seventeenth centuries.

2.6.2 In his essay 'Developments in the Understanding and Practice of Episcopacy in the Church of England' John Findon sketches out 'four views of the place of episcopacy in the life of the Church which were held by Anglicans in the years from 1559–1689.'[91]

2.6.3 First, there was what he calls the 'Adiaphorist' position, a position which held that on the issue of church polity: 'God had given no commands and it was right that local circumstances should be allowed to dictate the most appropriate pattern.'[92] The quotation from Archbishop Whitgift given above (p.31) is a good example of this approach. As we have seen, his response to the claim that the presbyterian system was the one ordained by God and therefore necessary for the Church is to say that no one system of government (whether episcopal or presbyterian) is required in order for the Church to be the Church.

2.6.4   Secondly, there was what Findon calls the 'Bancroftian' position (so named after Richard Bancroft the future Archbishop of Canterbury who advocated it in a famous sermon in 1589) which combined 'an unashamed assertion of the divine right of the [episcopal] order, coupled with a refusal to insist on its necessity at all times and in all places'.[93]

2.6.5   A classic example of this approach is found in Hooker. On the one hand, as we have already indicated, Hooker strongly asserts the apostolic and God-given origin of episcopacy. On the other hand he does not hold that it is an absolutely necessary part of the life of the Church:

> On the other side, bishops, albeit they may avouch with conformity of truth that their very authority hath thus descended even from the very apostles themselves, yet the absolute and everlasting continuance of it they cannot say that any commandment of the Lord doth enjoin; and therefore must acknowledge that the Church hath power by universal consent upon urgent cause to take it away, if thereunto she be constrained through the proud, tyrannical and unreformable dealings of her bishops, whose regiment she hath thus long delighted in, because she hath found it good and requisite to be so governed.[94]

2.6.6   Thirdly, there was the 'Laudian' position (named after Archbishop Laud). This placed strong emphasis on the importance of the teaching and practice of the ancient Church, and held that bishops belonged to a different order of ministry from priests (rather than being a different degree of the same order of ministry as some held). It also held that episcopal ordination was absolutely necessary if someone was to minister in the Church of England. It seems that there had been a few isolated examples of people serving as ministers in the Church of England on the basis of presbyteral ordination, even though there was opposition to the appointment of such ministers and uncertainty on the part of some as to whether their appointment was legal.

2.6.7   The influence of the Laudian position can be seen in the alterations to the 1550 ordinal in the version produced in 1662. First, the words 'Receive the Holy Ghost for the office and work of a Bishop in the Church of God' were added to the ordination service for bishops clearly to differentiate their ordination from the ordination of priests. Secondly, the words 'or hath had formerly Episcopal Consecration or Ordination' were added to the statement in the Preface to the Ordinal that no one should serve as a minister in the Church of England unless ordained according to the form of ordination set out in the Ordinal. This latter addition was intended to close a potential loophole whereby those with foreign presbyterian orders could claim that they had been validly ordained already according to a parallel albeit non-episcopal rite.

2.6.8   Fourthly, there was what Findon refers to as the 'Dodwellian' position (named after the late seventeenth-century theologian Henry Dodwell). This stressed the importance of episcopal ministry as a necessary channel of sacramental grace. Without bishops in historical succession there could be no confidence that either baptism or the Eucharist would convey divine grace to those who received them. To quote Findon, Dodwell argued that just as

> There had been only one legitimate priesthood in Israel, whose sacrifices and ministrations could claim legal validity within the terms of the Old Covenant; likewise there was only one legitimate priesthood in the Church of Christ, whose ministrations had legal validity within the terms of the New Covenant. The only legitimate ministers, he claimed, were those episcopally ordained. The Christian believer could have no confidence that he would receive the benefits of sacramental grace outside the episcopal communion.[95]

2.6.9   These differences of opinion about the significance of episcopacy were never resolved within the Church of England. They became part of the Anglican tradition with the consequence that the existence of a range of views about episcopacy has been a feature of the Church of England ever since.

2.6.10   Five examples, two from the nineteenth century and three from more recent times will serve to illustrate this point.

2.6.11   In his commentary on Philippians to which we have already referred, Lightfoot makes two main points in regard to the Christian ministry.

2.6.12   First, Lightfoot argues that it does not have a 'sacerdotal' character. That is to say, the Christian minister is not a person who mediates between the believer and God:

> He does not interpose between God and man in such a way that direct communion with God is superseded on the one hand, or that his own mediation becomes indispensable on the other.[96]

2.6.13   This means, according to Lightfoot, that the role of the ordained minister (including, presumably, the episcopal role) is not indispensable in the Christian economy:

> It may be a general rule, it may be under ordinary circumstances a practically universal law, that the highest acts of congregational worship shall be performed through the principal officers of the congregation. But an emergency may arise when the spirit and not the letter must decide. The Christian ideal will then interpose and interpret our duty. The higher ordinances of the universal priesthood will overrule all special limitations. The layman will assume functions which are otherwise restricted to the ordained minister.[97]

2.6.14   Secondly, Lightfoot holds that the historical evidence indicates that 'the episcopate was created out of the presbytery'.[98] That is to say, as Lightfoot sees it, the terms presbyter and bishop were originally synonymous,[99] but gradually the term bishop became reserved for the person appointed as the chief presbyter of a particular church:

> If bishop was at first used as a synonym for presbyter and afterward came to designate the higher officer under whom the presbyters served, the episcopate properly so called would seem to have developed from the subordinate office. In other words, the episcopate was formed not out of the apostolic order by localization but out of the presbyteral by elevation: and the title, which originally was common to all, came at length to be appropriated to the chief among them.[100]

2.6.15   In *The Church and the Ministry* Charles Gore comes to very different conclusions from Lightfoot about the history and nature of the episcopate. On the historical issue Gore agrees with Lightfoot that presbyter and bishop were originally synonymous terms. However, he differs from him in seeing the emergence of episcopacy as a process of localization rather than one of elevation.

2.6.16   In his view it was not the case that some of the presbyters were elevated to the episcopate. Rather, the term 'bishop' came to be used to refer to those who were appointed in the local churches to exercise at the local level that authority over the Church which was originally exercised by apostles, prophets and teachers.[101] In Gore's words, the single bishops who became the norm from the second century onwards represent

> simply a localization in each community of the authority of apostles, prophets and teachers, which had been catholic or general, while the title 'bishop' was transferred from the lower to the higher grade of office.[102]

2.6.17   He goes on,

> the presbyters seem never to have held the powers later known as episcopal; but as church after church gained a local representative of apostolic authority, the title of bishop was very naturally confined in its use to distinguish this 'successor of the Apostles' among the local 'presbyters' with whom he was associated.[103]

2.6.18   These historical conclusions are theologically important to Gore because they enable him to make a clear distinction between the two orders of priests and bishops and to argue that the bishops are, as the second quotation indicates, the successors of the apostles.

2.6.19   Gore explains what he means by this latter point as follows:

> [The] Apostles must be supposed to have had a temporary function in their capacity as founders under Christ. In this capacity they held an office by its very nature not perpetual – the office of bearing witness to Christ's resurrection and making the original proclamation of the Gospel. But underlying this was another – a pastorate of souls, a stewardship of divine mysteries. This office, instituted in their persons, was intended to become perpetual, and that by being transmitted from its first depositaries. It was thus intended that there should be in each generation an authoritative stewardship of the grace and truth which came by Jesus Christ and a recognized

power to transmit it, derived from above by apostolic descent. The men who from time to time were to hold the various offices involved in the ministry would receive their authority to minister in whatever capacity, their qualifying consecration, in such sense that every ministerial act would be performed under the shelter of a commission, received by the transmission of the original pastoral authority which had been delegated by Christ Himself to His Apostles.[104]

2.6.20   The difference from Lightfoot is clear. For Lightfoot the starting point for ministry is the universal priesthood of the whole people of God which those who are ordained exercise in particular ways. For Gore the starting point is the ministerial commission given by Christ to the Apostles and thereafter transmitted by the bishops as their successors.

2.6.21   In the biblical material we see this development anticipated in the letters to Timothy and Titus where St Timothy and St Titus are seen as exercising apostolic authority given to them by St Paul. In Gore's words:

> In Timothy and Titus we are presented with apostolic delegates, exercising the apostolic supervision over the church of Ephesus and the churches of Crete respectively.[105]

2.6.22   The importance of bishops as successors of the Apostles was also stressed by Michael Ramsey in his classic study *The Gospel and the Catholic Church*, which was first published in 1936.

2.6.23   Unlike Lightfoot and Gore, Ramsey is not particularly interested in the precise historical origins of the episcopate. He dismisses this quest as an 'archaeological' approach to religion. For Ramsey what matters is the 'evangelical' significance of the episcopate as an expression of the message of the New Testament as a whole:

> To burrow in the New Testament for forms of ministry and imitate them is archaeological religion: to seek that form of ministry which the New Testament creates is the more evangelical way. And our view of the ministry had better be evangelical than archaeological.[106]

2.6.24   In this context he argues that bishops are to be seen as being in 'apostolic succession' and that this phrase has three meanings.

2.6.25 First, the continuous succession of bishops helps to secure the continuity of the apostolic faith in the Church:

> The succession of Bishop to Bishop in office secured a continuity of Christian teaching and tradition in every See. Each followed the teachings of his predecessor, and so the succession of Bishops was a guarantee that everywhere the Christians were taught the true Gospel of Jesus Christ in the flesh ... [W]hile the Church as a whole is the vessel into which the truth is poured, the Bishops are an important organ in its discharging of this task.[107]

2.6.26 Secondly, there is a continuity of apostolic function:

> The Bishops also succeeded the Apostles in the sense that they performed those functions, of preaching and ruling and ordaining, which the Apostles had performed ... The Bishop's place as celebrant in the Eucharist, interceding for his flock and family, sums up this whole relationship.[108]

2.6.27 Thirdly, there is a continuity in the transmission of grace:

> The phrase 'Apostolic succession' is also used to signify that grace is handed down from the Apostles through each generation of Bishops by the laying on of hands ... the succession of Bishops is not an isolated channel of grace, since from the first Christ bestows grace through every sacramental act of His body. But certain actions in this work of grace are confined to the bishops; and thereby the truth is taught that every local group or Church depends upon the one life of the one body, and that the Church of any generation shares in the one historic society which is not past and dead but alive in the present. Thus the Church's full and continuous life in grace does depend upon the succession of Bishops, whose work, however, is not isolated but bound up with the whole body.[109]

2.6.28 In conclusion Ramsey declares:

> We are led, therefore, to affirm that the Episcopate is of the *esse* of the universal Church; but we must beware of mis-stating the issue. All who are baptized into Christ are members of His Church, and Baptism is the first mark of churchmanship. Yet the growth of all Christians into the measure of the stature of the fullness of Christ means their growth with all the saints in the unity of the one body, and of this unity the Episcopate is the expression.[110]

2.6.29   A similar approach to Ramsey's is taken by H. W. Montefiore in his contribution to a collection of essays called *The Historic Episcopate* which was published in 1955 as a contribution to the debate that was then taking place in the Church of England about the recognition of the Church of South India. Unlike Ramsey, he does not want to say that episcopacy is of the *esse* or essence of the Church. He does want to say, however, that it belongs to the *plene esse* or 'fullness' of the Church:

> The historic episcopate is a matter not only of pastoral but also of direct theological importance. It provides the full embodiment of the Gospel in church order. It does this in two respects. Firstly, the historic episcopate provides the effectual sign of unity. It embodies in church order the biblical proclamation that Christ's Church is one. Secondly, it embodies in church order the principle of apostolicity. The episcopally ordained ministry is both 'sent' to represent Christ to His church and is representative of the church. It provides the guardianship of the Word and Sacraments, of the faith and the flock of Christ. The historic episcopate is thus an effectual sign of the relation of Christ to His church: for it manifests His authority within His church.

> The historic episcopate is therefore the outward means and pledge that Christ's church is one and apostolic. It proclaims that the real nature of the church is given by God, and serves to actualize what it proclaims. It is, not, however, a mere matter of the church's outward form. The church is sacramental, and its outward structure embodies grace and spirit. The historic episcopate will be a fully expressive and instrumental sign only in the future re-united church of Christendom. That does not mean that Anglicans can afford to undervalue it in the present, for those who possess the historic episcopate possess something here and now of the fullness of Christ which non-episcopal bodies lack.[111]

2.6.30   In his essay 'The Self-organizing Power of the Gospel of Christ: Episcopacy and Community Formation', which was published in 2001, John Webster agrees with Ramsey and Montefiore that there is a connection between episcopacy and the unity of the Church. However, his overall understanding of the place of the episcopate in the life of the Church is very different from that of the Catholic tradition represented by Montefiore, Ramsey and Gore.

2.6.31   Webster contends that the episcopal office neither constitutes nor symbolizes the unity of the Church. Its role is simply to testify to that unity given to the Church by Christ:

> Unity is evangelical; it is to that unity, established and formed by the gospel, that the ministry of oversight directs its own attention and the attention of the whole church. The office of bishop is not constitutive of the unity of the church; if it were, then the church would indeed be 'episcopocentric', and the sole headship of the Lord Jesus Christ to some degree compromised. Nor does the office of bishop symbolize the unity of the church, at least if by 'symbolize' we mean 'realize' or 'actualize'. Nor does the office of bishop represent the unity of the church. Rather, the office of bishop *indicates* the unity of the church, testifying in a public manner to the oneness of the people of God as it is set out in the gospel. Episcopal office is thus a focussed, public and institutional place through which attention can be turned to the given unity of the people of God through Spirit, baptism and confession. As such, episcopal office serves the unity of the church as it takes form in the congregation of the redeemed as one body with one Spirit, one hope, one Lord, one faith, one baptism, one God and Father of all (Ephesians 4.4-6).
>
> Episcopal office undertakes this in a variety of ways, but most centrally through teaching, through presiding at the sacraments and at the commissioning of ordered ministry, and through the exercise of discipline.[112]

2.6.32   He also advocates the first position noted by Findon, that the form of the episcopal office is not fixed in terms of the historic episcopate within a threefold order of ministry but may legitimately vary:

> there is a necessary distinction to be drawn between *episcope*, a ministry of oversight, and particular, contingent orderings of the episcopal office. I have suggested that oversight is a necessary implication of the gospel through which the church is brought into being and which it is commissioned to proclaim. But this is quite other than a defence of – for example – a threefold order of ministry headed by a regional episcopate, or of a 'historic episcopate', whether maintained by laying on of hands or by succession of the teaching office; nor, alternatively, does it necessarily entail a synodical or congregational episcopate. Such orderings are *adiaphora*.[113]

2.7 How the bishop's role is understood and exercised in the Church of England today

2.7.1   The examples we have given clearly demonstrate that a range of views about the episcopate has existed in the Church of England since the sixteenth century and continues to exist today. It therefore raises the issue of whether there is such a thing as a 'Church of England' view of episcopacy.

2.7.2   The existence of differing views about issues relating to episcopacy is not unique to the Church of England. For instance, the Roman Catholic representative on the working party, Dr Anthony Barratt, has drawn our attention to the continuing debate within the Roman Catholic Church in the wake of the Second Vatican Council about the relationship between the episcopate and the presbyterate and precisely where the difference between the two lies, a debate about the nature of episcopal order and its relationship to the presbyterate that, as we have seen, goes back through the Middle Ages into the patristic period.[114] As he explains in his paper 'The Sacrament of Order and the Second Vatican Council: The Presbyter-Bishop Relationship Revisited', in Roman Catholic theology there is one ordained priesthood within which there are two grades, the episcopate and the presbyterate, and the question is how these two grades relate to each other.[115]

2.7.3   However, the fact that other episcopally ordered churches also have their disagreements about matters to do with episcopacy does not solve the issue of the significance about such disagreements within the Church of England. Do they mean that no answer can be given to the question 'what does the Church of England believe about bishops?'

2.7.4   In fact an answer can be given to this question because in spite of the continuing debate about the nature of episcopacy to which we have drawn attention there is a body of material which provides an accepted Church of England position on the place of bishops in the life of the Church.

2.7.5   This material can be found in the Ordinal of 1662, the Ordinal contained in the *Alternative Service Book* (*ASB*), the Canons, legislation passed by General Synod and embodied in ecclesiastical measures, and the various ecumenical agreements which the Church of England has entered into and which have been noted above. In addition, attention also has to be paid to the various teaching documents on episcopacy issued by the House of Bishops, most notably *Apostolicity and Succession* and *Bishops in Communion*. Although these latter documents have not been formally endorsed by Synod as representing the teaching of the Church of England the fact that they represent the mind of the House of Bishops does give them a considerable degree of authority.

2.7.6   The 1990 report *Episcopal Ministry*,[116] produced by the Archbishops' Group on the Episcopate, contains a large amount of very useful material. However, because it was never officially endorsed by either the House of Bishops or General Synod as a whole it lacks the authoritative status of the other documents mentioned above.

2.7.7   It should be noted that what is said below applies to both diocesan and suffragan bishops. Both diocesan and suffragan bishops are ordained to the same basic ministry. The difference between them is that a suffragan bishop can only exercise those parts of the episcopal office that are delegated to him by his diocesan bishop. In the words of section 1 and 2 of Canon C 20:

> Every bishop suffragan shall endeavour himself faithfully to execute such things pertaining to the episcopal office as shall be delegated to him by the bishop of the diocese to whom he shall be suffragan.

> Every bishop suffragan shall use, or execute only such jurisdiction or episcopal power or authority in any diocese as shall be licensed or limited to him to use, have, or execute by the bishop of the same.

Continuity with the New Testament

2.7.8   If we look at the material which has just been mentioned, we find that a bishop's ministry is seen as a continuation of the pattern of ministry found in the New Testament. We have already noted the statement in the Preface to the 1662 Ordinal in this connection, but the same conviction is also expressed in a range of other places as well.

● Canon C1 declares that:

> The Church of England holds and teaches that from the Apostles' time there have been these orders in Christ's Church: bishops, priests, and deacons.

- The readings given in the services for the consecration of bishops in the 1662 Ordinal (1 Timothy 3.1-6, Acts 20.17-35, John 21.15-17, 20.19-22 and Matthew 28.18-20) and in the *ASB* (Numbers 27.15-20, 22-23, 2 Corinthians 4.1-10, John 21.15-17) point to the continuity between the role of the bishop in the Church today and the role of the apostles and bishops in New Testament times (and in the case of the *ASB* those who exercised authority over God's people in Old Testament times as well).

- Before the laying on of hands in the service for the consecration of a bishop in the 1662 Ordinal the archbishop recalls in his prayer that after Christ's ascension he

> poured down his gifts abundantly upon men, making some Apostles, some Prophets, some Evangelists, some Pastors and Doctors, to the edifying and making perfect his Church.

The clear implication of this reference to Ephesians 4.10-11 is that this gifting depicted in New Testament times is what is continuing in the Church today and is to be seen in the calling of people to the episcopal role.

Sign and instrument of apostolicity and catholicity

2.7.9 A bishop is called to be a sign and instrument of the apostolicity and catholicity of the local church in each diocese as part of the Church of England and the whole Catholic Church worldwide. *BEM* notes that:

> Under the particular historical circumstances of the growing Church in the early centuries, the succession of bishops became one of the ways, together with the transmission of the Gospel and the life of the community, in which the apostolic tradition of the Church was expressed. This succession was understood as serving, symbolizing and guarding the continuity of the apostolic faith and communion.

2.7.10 This carefully nuanced understanding of the meaning of the apostolic succession of bishops reflects a growing ecumenical consensus on the matter and is reflected in recent Church of England documents.

● Section IV of the *Porvoo Common Statement* declares:

> The whole Church is a sign of the Kingdom of God; the act of ordination is a sign of God's faithfulness to his Church, especially in relation to the oversight of its mission. To ordain a bishop in historic succession (that is, in intended continuity from the apostles themselves) is also a sign. In so doing the Church communicates its care for continuity in the whole of its life and mission, and reinforces its determination to manifest the permanent characteristics of the Church of the Apostles.[117]

● In similar fashion the 1994 House of Bishops' paper *Apostolicity and Succession* states:

> To ordain [a bishop] by prayer and the laying on of hands expresses the Church's trust in its Lord's promise to empower disciples and it expresses the Church's intention in response to be faithful in carrying out the apostolic ministry and mission. The participation of three bishops in the laying on of hands witnesses to the catholicity of the churches. The laying on of hands by bishops who have had hands laid on them in succession signifies continuity back to the Apostles. Both the act of consecration and the continuity of ministerial succession witnesses to the Church's fidelity to the teaching and mission of the Apostles. This continuity is integral to the continuity of the Church's life as a whole.[118]

Proclamation and defence of 'wholesome doctrine'

2.7.11 A bishop's ministry involves the proclamation and defence of the teaching contained in the Scriptures as this is understood by the Church of England. His authority as a teacher is not autonomous but is based on his fidelity to the apostolic witness contained in Holy Scripture.

● In the consecration service in the 1662 Ordinal, for example, the archbishop asks the candidate:

> Will you then faithfully exercise yourself in the same holy Scriptures, and call upon God by prayer, for the true understanding of the same; so as ye may be able by them to teach and exhort with wholesome doctrine, and to withstand and convince the gainsayers?

and

> Are you ready, with all faithful diligence, to banish and drive away all erroneous and strange doctrine contrary to God's Word; and both privately and openly to call upon and encourage others to do the same?

These questions do not explicitly identify 'wholesome doctrine' with the doctrine held by the Church of England, but this was always understood to be the case, with the bishop's commitment to the Church of England's doctrine being shown by subscription to the Thirty-Nine Articles.

- In the *ASB* consecration service, the bishop-elect uses the words of 'The Declaration of Assent' in Canon C 15 to declare his belief in 'the faith which is revealed in the holy Scriptures and set forth in the catholic creeds and to which the historic formularies of the Church of England bear witness'. The bishop-elect also states his belief in 'the doctrine of the Christian faith as the Church of England has received it' and promises to 'expound and teach it' in the course of his ministry.

- The doctrinal role of a bishop is also specified in Canon C 18(1) which states that

  > it appertains to his office to teach and uphold sound and wholesome doctrine, and to banish and drive away all erroneous and strange opinions.

2.7.12 The collective role of the bishops of the Church of England in teaching and safeguarding doctrine is also reflected in the Constitution of the General Synod. Under Article 7(1), any provision touching upon the doctrinal formulae of the Church of England has to be submitted for final approval in terms approved by the House of Bishops.

Sacramental ministry

2.7.13 A bishop's ministry involves the celebration of the sacraments. This is not an aspect of episcopal ministry that is mentioned in the 1662 Ordinal. However, it has always been a central part of episcopal ministry and it is clearly stated in the *ASB* Ordinand in which the archbishop declares that a bishop is called to 'baptize and confirm, preside at the Holy Communion, and to lead the offering of prayer and praise'.

2.7.14 As we have seen, in the early patristic period the bishop presided in person at baptism and chrismation and also at the celebration of the Eucharist, but as the Church grew in size this ceased to be possible and the sacraments came to be celebrated in services where the bishop was not present by priests (and in the case of baptism, deacons as well) acting on the bishop's behalf.

2.7.15 This is the pattern that has been retained in the Church of England with priests and deacons exercising a sacramental ministry as part of that ministry which they share with their bishop. However, the bishop's role as the chief sacramental minister continues to be reflected in the fact that confirmation (understood as completing the process of Christian initiation begun at baptism) is reserved to the bishop and in the fact that when a local bishop is present at a Eucharist it is the bishop who normally presides.

Pastoral oversight and the promotion of unity

2.7.16 A bishop is called to exercise pastoral oversight to the clergy and people of his diocese. In the words of Canon C 18(1), 'Every bishop is the chief pastor of all that are within his diocese, as well laity as clergy, and their father in God.' It is important to note in this quotation that the bishop is not just the 'superintendent of the pastors' on a Continental Lutheran model, but the 'chief pastor' of the laity as well as the clergy; he is the pastor of the people and not just the pastor of the pastors.

- The pastoral role of the bishop is reflected in the fact that John 21.15-17, containing the command of Christ to Peter to 'feed my sheep', is given as one of the Gospel readings at the consecration of a bishop in both the 1662 Ordinal and the *ASB*. The bishop is identified as a shepherd called to take care of Christ's flock.

2.7.17 This same view of a bishop's calling is also reflected elsewhere in the 1662 and *ASB* ordinals.

- For example, in the 1662 Ordinal, after the archbishop has presented a Bible to the new bishop, the archbishop declares:

  > Be to the flock of Christ a shepherd, not a wolf; feed them, devour them not. Hold up the weak, heal the sick, bind up the broken, bring again the out-casts, seek the lost. Be so merciful, that ye be not too remiss; so minister discipline, that you forget not mercy: that when the chief Shepherd shall appear ye may receive the never-fading crown of glory.

- In the ordination prayer in the *ASB* the archbishop likewise prays:

  > Through him increase your Church, renew its ministry, and unite its members in a holy fellowship of truth and love. Enable him as a true shepherd to feed and govern your flock.

2.7.18   The *ASB* also emphasizes the bishop's role in promoting unity in the archbishop's declaration concerning the bishop's calling which declares that:

> As a chief pastor he shares with his fellow bishops a special responsibility to maintain and further the unity of the Church.

2.7.19   In this quotation the unity of the Church is something that the bishop is called upon to promote. It is something that he has to seek to 'maintain and further'. This 'dynamic' view of the bishop's role in relation to unity could be seen as being in tension with the traditional view that a bishop is a 'focus of unity', a view that is expressed, for example, in the following extract from *Episcopal Ministry*:

> In the local church the bishop focuses and nurtures the unity of his people; in his sharing in the collegiality of bishops the local church is bound together with other local churches; and, through the succession of bishops the local community is related to the Church through the ages. Thus the bishop in his own person in the diocese; and in his collegial relations in the wider church; and through his place in the succession of bishops in their communities in faithfulness to the Gospel, is a sign and focus of the unity of the Church.[119]

2.7.20   This view has been criticized as suggesting the idea that a bishop unites the Church simply by virtue of being a bishop, and it has been argued that a more dynamic view of the bishop's role in relation to unity is to be preferred. However, it would be a mistake to see the two views of the bishop's role as being in opposition to each other. Instead, they are to be seen as complementary in that the office of bishop is a 'focus of unity' in the sense that it signifies the unity of the Church across space and time, but this unity is also something that a bishop is called upon to promote in the life of the Church through his episcopal activity.

2.7.21   An important contemporary aspect of a bishop's role in furthering unity is involvement in ecumenism. As part of his ministry of oversight the bishop has responsibility for overseeing the development of relations with other churches and the development of local ecumenical partnerships in particular.[120] In addition, the bishop is the natural person to establish personal relations with the leaders of the other Christian churches in the diocese and with other churches worldwide.

2.7.22   As *Bishops in Communion* notes:

> At the diocesan level, almost every diocese has some structure in
> place for bishops to share together in oversight and leadership with
> those who have been entrusted with *episkope* in other churches.
> In many places church leaders sign formal covenants which commit
> them to share together in witness. In Liverpool, Archbishop Derek
> Worlock, Bishop David Sheppard and latterly the Revd Dr John
> Newton showed what is possible in the sharing of oversight. Where
> local churches share together, especially in formally constituted
> Local Ecumenical Partnerships, Christians begin to look for a shared
> leadership which mirrors their local experience. Shared oversight is
> also focused in the office of the Ecumenical Moderator of Milton
> Keynes. Many of the diocesan responses to *Called To Be One* pleaded
> for a more prophetic ministry of shared oversight. As a result of the
> Porvoo Agreement English diocesan bishops are beginning to share
> oversight with their Nordic colleagues for Lutheran congregations
> in their dioceses. A similar arrangement is emerging in some of the
> Nordic countries for the chaplaincies of the Church of England
> Diocese in Europe.[121]

2.7.23   A point that is sometimes raised in response to Anglican
claims for the importance of episcopacy is that in the history of the
Church bishops have frequently been associated with disunity rather
than unity, and so Anglican claims for bishops as promoters of unity
ring somewhat hollow. T. W. Manson, for instance, responds as follows
to the claims for episcopacy made by a former Bishop of Oxford,
Kenneth Kirk:

> When the Bishop of Oxford says, for example, that 'whatever the
> schisms which have divided episcopal Christianity, they exhibit
> nothing remotely resembling the fissiparous fertility of non-episcopal
> Christendom' he lays himself open to the obvious retort that the
> major schisms in the Church, including the great schism of East and
> West, and the Reformation itself, took place when the Church was
> under universal and long-established episcopal government; that
> some of the major divisions in this country in the post-Reformation
> period have not been splits within the Free Churches but secessions
> or expulsions from the episcopal Church – the Presbyterians in
> 1662 and the Methodists at the close of the eighteenth century;
> that all the major heresies showed themselves when the Church
> was under episcopal control, and that many of them enjoyed
> episcopal patronage.[122]

2.7.24   All the points that Manson makes in this quotation about the history of schisms in the Church are valid. However, as he goes on to say:

> They do nothing except prove, what we already know, that any form of Church government in this world has to be in the hands of human beings, and that consequently error and sin cannot be excluded by any ecclesiastical constitution.[123]

2.7.25   The claim of the Church of England has never been that the existence of bishops in and of itself guarantees the unity of the Church. The point is rather that the office of bishop is a sign of the unity which is the gift and calling of God to his people and that bishops are called upon to promote this unity insofar as it lies within their power to do so.

2.7.26   A similar response can also be made to the further point that Manson makes about the relationship between bishops and heresy. What he says about the existence of heresy when the Church has been under episcopal government and about bishops having been patrons of heresy is true. However, the point that also needs to be made is that the ordination of bishops in historic succession is a sign of the desire of a church to be faithful to apostolic teaching and that if bishops do not proclaim and defend the apostolic faith it is because they are failing to live up to their calling.

Leadership in mission

2.7.27   As *An Anglican Methodist Covenant* notes, mission is first and foremost the activity of God, but it is one in which he calls the Church to participate:

> Mission is grounded in God: it is always God's mission. Its content and unsurpassable expression is Jesus Christ himself. God purposed in Christ to reconcile the world to himself and was incarnate in Christ to bring this about (Colossians 1.20, 2 Corinthians 5.18).

> By the power of the Holy Spirit God graciously enables us, as unworthy but forgiven sinners, to participate in the mission of God. Because God's mission is definitively expressed in Christ, our participation is located in the Body of Christ, the Church. The Church's task is to participate in God's mission ... In mission the Church seeks to reflect Jesus Christ in its life and worship and to proclaim him in word and deed.[124]

2.7.28   As the principal minister of the local church, a bishop is called to lead the Church in its participation in God's mission. As we have explained earlier in this chapter,[125] the missionary and evangelistic role of the bishop was a significant feature of the life of the Early Church in general and in the early history of the Church in England in particular. However, as England became a Christian country the missionary role of a bishop of the Church of England was refocused (although it became a significant feature in the growth of the Anglican Church worldwide).

2.7.29   The recovery of a sense of the missionary aspect of a bishop's ministry in the Church of England is reflected in the declaration in the *ASB* consecration service that a bishop is to 'promote' the Church's 'mission throughout the world'.

2.7.30   In 1998 the Section of the Lambeth Conference concerned with mission considered the missionary role of the bishop under the heading 'Being a Missionary Bishop in a Missionary Church'. The report of this section describes this role in the following terms:

> The bishop is a guardian of the faith received from earlier generations and which is now to be passed on gratefully and hopefully to the bishop's successors. Apostolic succession is not only a matter of formal historical continuity, but a responsibility to receive and transmit this gift. Thus, too, the bishop seeks to work from and with a community eager to share this news. As a public figure in many cultural and social contexts, the bishop has the opportunity of addressing large gatherings in the Church and in the wider community and of interacting with people in industry, commerce, government and education, with leaders of other religious communities and with those who form opinion in society. It is vital that these opportunities be seen in an apostolic light, as part of an intentional series of strategic actions flowing into the mission of God, not as signs of status. And in the Church, the bishop must foster the same sense of purpose and coherence, taking every opening to name the vision, articulate common goals and cultivate purposeful reflection about mission at every level in a diocese. The bishop will be at the heart of a team of pastors and servants – from archdeacons to intercessors to lay office-holders and administrators in the parish – holding this vision and purpose together, a corporate witness to the resurrection. In many contexts, though, the bishop's task is not to control but to recognize, affirm and give room for new initiatives coming from local communities, naming the gracious presence of Christ, who renews the Church in ways that are always unexpected.[126]

2.7.31   In the Church of England the role of the bishop in mission is exercised in a number of ways:

- In consultation and collaboration with the clergy and laity, bishops seek to foster and support the missionary vision and activity of their dioceses and to think strategically about how the missionary work of the dioceses can be carried out more effectively in the future.

- Bishops are involved in evangelistic and catechetical activity and support the mission of the Church worldwide by establishing and promoting links with Anglican dioceses in other parts of the world.

- Since the mission of God is not confined to the life of the Church, bishops promote engagement between the Church and wider society, particularly in connection with matters such as education, peace and justice and the promotion of good relationships between people of different faiths. As part of their engagement with interfaith issues, many bishops have entered into dialogue with leaders of other faith communities and have sought to work with them on issues of common concern.

- The presence of bishops in the House of Lords reflects the bishops' missionary role in that their presence enables them to express a Christian viewpoint in relation to political issues at a national level. The same is also true of the involvement of bishops with other levels of government such as the regional and county levels.

- Bishops also have opportunities for mission in civil society in numerous other ways as well. The involvement of bishops with civic and voluntary organizations such as groups working for the regeneration of the inner cities, or on behalf of homeless people or asylum seekers, and the way that they are called upon to play a mediatorial role at times of social division or unrest are examples of such opportunities.

Overall responsibility for the life of the diocese

2.7.32   As the principal minister of the local church the bishop has the overall responsibility for the life and worship of his diocese. As part of this he is responsible for ensuring that there are sufficient ministers within it and for ordaining new priests and deacons.

- This aspect of the bishop's role is set out in general terms in Canon C 18(4) which declares that:

  > Every bishop is, within his diocese, the principal minister, and to him belongs the right, save in places and over persons exempt by law and custom, of celebrating the rites of ordination and confirmation; of ordering, controlling and authorizing all services in churches, chapels, churchyards and consecrated burial grounds; of granting a faculty or licence for all alterations, additions, removals, or repairs to the walls, fabric, ornaments, or furniture of the same; of consecrating new churches, churchyards and burial grounds; of instituting to all vacant benefices, whether of his own collation or at the presentation of others; of admitting by licence to all other vacant ecclesiastical offices; of holding visitations at times limited by law or custom to the end that he may get some good knowledge of the state, sufficiency, and ability of the clergy and other persons whom he is to visit; of being president of the diocesan synod.

- It is also reflected in a variety of synodical measures such as the *Patronage and Benefice Measure*, the *Pastoral Measure* and the *Teams and Groups Measure*. Further information about the overall responsibility of bishops within their dioceses can be found in Appendix E, 'The Legal Role of Bishops', in the 2001 report *Resourcing Bishops*.[127]

- The role of the bishop in ensuring the provision of clergy is reflected in the question to the candidate in the 1662 consecration service: 'Will you be faithful in ordaining, sending, or laying hands upon others?' and in the declaration by the archbishop in the *ASB* service that a bishop: 'is to ordain and send new ministers, guiding those who serve with him and enabling them to fulfil their ministry'. It is also reflected in Canon C 18(6) which states that: 'Every bishop shall be faithful in admitting persons into holy orders ... and shall provide, as much as in him lies, that in every place within his diocese there shall be sufficient priests to minister the word and sacraments to the people that are therein.' As the reference to 'ministers' in the *ASB* indicates, bishops are not responsible solely for the provision of priests. Deacons come under the bishop's purview as well, as do lay ministers such as Church Army Officers, Readers and Lay Pastoral Assistants.

- The collective national responsibility of the bishops for the selection, training, deployment and conditions of service of the clergy is exercised through the work of the Bishops' Committee for Ministry.

The exercise of judicial authority

2.7.33   As another aspect of his ministry of oversight a bishop has a judicial role.

- In the consecration service in the 1662 Ordinal the archbishop asks:

   Will you maintain and set forward (as much as shall lie in you) quietness, peace and love among all men; and such as be unquiet, disobedient and criminous within your Diocese, correct and punish, according to such authority as you have by God's Word, and as to you shall be committed by the Ordinances of this Realm?

- Canon C 18(7) echoes the wording of this 1662 question virtually word for word. The *ASB* is much less forthright, but it too declares that a bishop is 'to minister discipline, but with mercy'.

- *Bishops in Communion* also notes that:

   Pastoral discipline is a proper and necessary use of authority in the Church. It is primarily the responsibility of bishops. They exercise this responsibility in the context of canon law which belongs to the ordering of all churches. In Anglicanism canon law is made through representative, synodical forms of church government and thus can be said to have the consent of the governed (the Anglican faithful). The jurisdiction of bishops carries the responsibility to apply and where necessary to enforce canon law.[128]

- In specific terms a bishop's judicial role in regard to the clergy is set out in both the current *Ecclesiastical Jurisdiction Measure* and the proposed *Clergy Discipline Measure*, both of which give the bishop a central role in the disciplinary process.

Personal, collegial and communal ministry

2.7.34   When looking at the role of the bishop in the patristic period we noted that although bishops exercise a particular ministry of their own they did not exercise that ministry in isolation. Rather they exercised their ministry of oversight together with their presbyters and with the assistance of their deacons, and each individual bishop was part of a wider episcopal college with whom he took counsel as the needs of the Church required.

2.7.35 This idea that a bishop is not meant to minister in isolation is expressed today by saying that a bishop is called to exercise ministry in personal, collegial and communal ways.

2.7.36 We noted at the beginning of this chapter that there is an ecumenical consensus expressed in *BEM* that the ministry of oversight needs to be exercised in personal, collegial and communal ways. As *BEM* explains:

> It should be *personal* because the presence of Christ among his people can most effectively be pointed to by the person ordained to proclaim the Gospel and to call the community to serve the Lord in unity of life and witness. It should also be *collegial*, for there is need for a college of ordained ministers sharing in the common task of representing the concerns of the community. Finally, the intimate relationship between the ordained ministry and the community should find expression in a *communal* dimension where the exercise of the ordained ministry is rooted in the life of the community and requires the community's effective participation in the discovery of God's will and the guidance of the Spirit.[129]

2.7.37 In the life of the Church of England bishops exercise their ministry of oversight in personal, collegial and communal ways.

2.7.38 As *Bishops in Communion* explains, although the ministry of a bishop is a 'personal' ministry in the sense that it is a ministry exercised by particular persons who are called to this role, this does not mean that it is an 'individual' ministry:

> Personal oversight is not an individual ministry. 'Persons' are not to be understood apart from their connection with the community. Bishops, like all Christians, are called to follow Christ the servant, who set his disciples an example by washing their feet (John 13.14-15). They are dependent upon the grace of God, through the power of the Holy Spirit bestowed in Christ Jesus. They receive the anointing of the same Spirit, who animates the life of all believers, and are inseparably bound to them. They should not be exalted above the community, but should point to the unique mediatorial role of Christ and not to themselves.[130]

2.7.39 It is also worth noting that the exercise of primacy, which takes place at a number of levels in the Church of England, is an extension of the idea of the personal ministry of the bishop.

2.7.40   Within an individual diocese the diocesan bishop exercises primacy as the chief pastor who has jurisdiction over the diocese as whole, jurisdiction which includes authority over any suffragan bishops in the diocese. Within the two provinces of Canterbury and York the Archbishops of Canterbury and York have primatial authority as the chief bishops of these provinces with rights of consecration, visitatorial powers and authority in appeals.[131] Finally, the Archbishop of Canterbury has a primatial role in relation to the Anglican Communion that is expressed in his convening the Lambeth Conference and meetings of other Anglican primates and a general pastoral ministry to Anglican bishops worldwide.

2.7.41   The idea of primacy focuses on the bishop's personal ministry. The concept of collegiality, on the other hand, focuses on the importance of the ministry that bishops share together. As *Bishops in Communion* explains, episcopal collegiality is based on

> the fact that all bishops have received the same ministry through their ordination as bishops. They are guardians of the same faith and overseers in the one Church.

2.7.42   Because they possess this common ministry, it is clearly right for bishops to take counsel together and this taking counsel together in order to seek the will of God for his Church is what the exercise of episcopal collegiality means.[132]

2.7.43   Within the Church of England there are various opportunities for bishops to take counsel together.

- In the dioceses the diocesan bishops meet together with their suffragan and assistant bishops.

- Diocesan and suffragan bishops meet together in regional bishops' groups.

- Those bishops who are members of the House of Bishops meet together as a House three times a year.

- Once a year all the diocesan and suffragan bishops meet together for a bishops' meeting.

- In all of these the Provincial Episcopal Visitors play a part and provide an additional dimension of consultation.

2.7.44 Although there is thus already a degree of collegiality between diocesan and suffragan bishops, a recent report on suffragan bishops produced by the North-West regional bishops' group has argued that this does not go far enough.

2.7.45 The report makes the point we have noted earlier, that although a suffragan bishop shares the same order of ministry as a diocesan bishop and is ordained to perform the same role within the Church, the exercise of episcopal authority is the prerogative of the diocesan bishop who is at liberty to choose which aspects of episcopal ministry he delegates to his suffragans.

2.7.46 *Episcopal Ministry* defends this view of the relation between diocesan and suffragan bishops on the grounds that a move towards a more collegial understanding of their relationship would 'mean a departure in principle from the norm of monepiscopacy'[133] by undermining the idea of the bishop as the personal focus of unity for the diocese. It argues that the suffragan bishop should be seen as the diocesan bishop's 'specifically episcopal representative' or 'vicar' who 'acts in the place of his diocesan when delegation or occasion requires'.[134]

2.7.47 The *Suffragan Bishops* report contends that this model of the relationship fails to do justice to the fact that a suffragan bishop is a bishop in his own right and is not merely the representative of his diocesan. It argues that what should be developed instead is a collaborative

> understanding of the ministry of several bishops in the diocese working as the one episcopate of that diocese under the primacy of the diocesan bishop.[135]

2.7.48 Taking this approach seriously means developing a collegial understanding of episcopacy in which *episcope* would be exercised in a collegial manner by the diocesan bishop together with his suffragan or area bishops and any assistant bishops within the diocese. In this context the diocesan bishop would be the *primus inter pares* (first among equals) with a specific role and specific rights of jurisdiction.

2.7.49 This kind of collaborative approach to episcopal ministry can be seen as being in line with the findings of recent New Testament research in two respects. First, this research has emphasized how St Paul and other apostles frequently associate themselves with 'co-workers' in significant contexts.[136] Secondly, this research has suggested that the term 'apostle' should be understood in a non-individualistic sense as referring to agency rather than agent. That is to say, what is important is the role of the apostle in pointing to Christ rather than the status of the individual doing the pointing.[137] However, the question that still needs to be considered is how a more collaborative approach relates to the traditional belief going back to the Early Church that there should be one person exercising a personal ministry of oversight in a particular diocese.

2.7.50   Two further points that need to be made about episcopal collegiality are that:

(a) The college of which Church of England bishops are a part is not confined to bishops of the Church of England. They are members of the college of bishops which consists of all the bishops of the Anglican Communion (a fact which finds expression in the coming together of these bishops to take counsel together at the Lambeth Conference every ten years). By virtue of ecumenical agreement, collegiality is also shared between the bishops of the Church of England and churches with which it is in communion such as the Old Catholic churches of the Union of Utrecht, the Mar Thoma Syrian Church of Malabar and the Nordic and Baltic churches covered by the Porvoo Agreement. Because of their consecration as bishops in the Church of God, bishops of the Church of England are also members of a college of bishops that embraces all bishops worldwide.

In the fragmented state of the worldwide Church there are limited opportunities for this last fact to find expression or even recognition. However, there is frequently informal recognition of universal ecclesial collegiality even when bishops are not formally in communion with each other.

The ecumenical sharing of oversight with the leaders of non-episcopal churches could also be seen as an extension of this same collegial principle to embrace those who exercise a ministry of *episcope* outside the historic episcopate.

(b) The collegial principle cannot be confined to relations between bishops. This is because, as the *Suffragan Bishops* report points out, the ministry of episcope is not the sole preserve of bishops. It is important to value highly the sharing of episcope between bishops and others, the most obvious examples being within the senior staff of a diocese, with rural/area deans, with specialist diocesan officers, and with clergy persons in their parochial ministry.[138]

The function of archdeacons and rural/area deans in sharing the bishop's ministry of oversight is an important one. They form a vital link between the bishop and the clergy and people of the diocese thus enabling a bishop to exercise his overall ministry of oversight in an effective manner.

Canon C 22 declares that every archdeacon

shall assist the bishop in his pastoral care and office, and particularly he shall see that all such as hold any ecclesiastical office within the same perform their duties with diligence and shall draw to the bishop's attention what calls for correction or merits praise.[139]

In similar fashion Canon C 23 declares that every rural dean

shall report to the bishop any matter in any parish within the deanery which it may be necessary or useful for the bishop to know, particularly any case of serious illness or other forms of distress amongst the clergy, the vacancy of any cure of souls and the measures taken by the sequestrators to secure the ministration of the word and sacraments and other rites of the Church during the said vacancy, and any case of a minister from another diocese officiating in any place otherwise than as provided for under Canon C 8.

2.7.51 If the collegial dimension of episcopal ministry is based on the existence of shared ministerial office, the communal dimension is based on the existence of a common baptism and mission. To quote *Bishops in Communion* again:

The communal (conciliar or synodal) life of the Church is grounded in the sacrament of baptism. All the baptized share a responsibility for the apostolic faith and witness of the Church. Conciliarity refers to the involvement of the whole body of the faithful – bishops, clergy and laity – in consultation, normally through representative and constitutional structures, for the sake of the well being of the Church and God's mission in the world. Conciliar life sustains all the baptized in a web of belonging of mutual accountability and support.[140]

2.7.52   The communal or conciliar principle finds its chief expression in the Church of England in its synodical system, which allows for episcopal, clerical and lay participation in the government of the Church. The bishops of the Church of England participate in this synodical system in four ways. At a diocesan level they take counsel with representatives of the clergy and laity at meetings of the Diocesan Synod and the Bishop's Council. At a national level they take counsel with representatives of the clergy and laity at meetings of the General Synod and the Archbishops' Council.

2.7.53   The relation between bishops and the synodical system is often described in terms of the Church of England being 'episcopally led and synodically governed'. This is misleading. Clergy and laity share with their bishops in the leadership of the Church and bishops play a central part in governing the Church.

Representative ministry

2.7.54   Underlying all that has been said so far about the ministry of a bishop in the Church of England is the idea that a bishop is someone who is a representative.

2.7.55   This idea is implicit in the statement in Article XXVI of the Thirty-Nine Articles that those who minister the word and the sacraments do so in Christ's name, and the declaration in the *ASB* service for the consecration of a bishop that it is the duty of a bishop to speak 'in the name of God'. This concept is more fully developed in *Bishops in Communion*.

2.7.56   *Bishops in Communion* argues that all the baptized have the calling to represent Christ:

> Through faith and baptism Christians are united with Christ. Their Christ-centred identity means that all Christians, when living out their calling represent Christ to others.[141]

2.7.57   This means, it says, that:

> Representativeness is thus a principle that applies to the whole Church. It transcends the distinction in calling between the lay and

the ordained, since all members of the apostolic community, the Church, are called to represent Christ, to be his ambassadors, to speak and act in his name. It is to the seventy-two as well as to the Twelve that Jesus says: 'He who welcomes/receives/listens to you welcomes/receives/listens to me and to him who sent me' (Matthew 10.1-40; Luke 10.1-16; cf John 13.20; cf Paul's apostolic ambassadorship: 2 Corinthians 5.20). Clergy and laity share a common fundamental calling, a partnership with one another in Christ (Hebrews 3.1-14).[142]

2.7.58   However, it goes on to say, those who are called to ordained ministry have a specific representative calling in that they are called to represent both Christ and the Christian community in whose name and on whose behalf they minister. It quotes the Anglican-Reformed dialogue *God's Reign and Our Unity* as expressing this point:

> The minister as leader has a representative character, to act 'as the one on behalf of the many', so that the whole Church is represented in his person as he carries on his heart the concerns of all his people. He does not act in his own name, but in the name of Christ, and in the name of the whole body of Christ, so that he is at once the mouthpiece of our Lord and the mouthpiece of his flock.[143]

2.7.59   Quoting the 1986 Board of Mission and Unity report *The Priesthood of the Ordained Ministry* it declares that the representative principle means that in an episcopal church such as the Church of England

> Bishops and presbyters represent both Christ and his people in their leadership of the Church and its mission, in the proclamation of the Gospel, in the articulation of the faith, and in the celebration of the sacraments.[144]

2.7.60   The representative character of the bishop's ministry is seen particularly clearly, it argues, in the bishop's role as the president at the Eucharist. The Eucharist is a sign of the unity of the local church with the universal Church across space and time and, as both the 'chief pastor of the local church' and a member of 'the universal college of pastors', the bishop in his presidential role is a further sign of this unity.[145]

2.7.61   *Bishops in Communion* also argues that the existence of a representative ministry entails a mutual responsibility:

Those who represent the community have a duty to listen to the community, to discern the mind of Christ in conversation with the local community, and in conversation with all local communities today and through the ages. They are called to seek always that which is in conformity with the normative witness of Holy Scripture. At the same time those who are represented are called to receive with attentiveness and respect the teaching of those set over them, with whom they stand in a relationship of critical solidarity. A representative ministry implies mutual responsibilities and mutual accountability in order that the whole Church may remain faithful to the gospel entrusted to it.[146]

An example of Godly living

2.7.62   Finally, it needs to be noted that a bishop is not only called upon to do certain things, but is also required to be a particular type of person living in a manner that bears witness to the gospel. This requirement is rooted in the teaching of the New Testament about the character required of bishops in 1 Timothy 3.1-7 and Titus 1.5-9 and is clearly expressed in the consecration services in both the 1662 and *ASB* ordinals.

2.7.63   In the 1662 Ordinal the archbishop asks the prospective bishop:

> Will you deny all ungodliness and worldly lusts, and live soberly, righteously and godly in this present world: that you may shew yourself in all things an example of good works unto others, that the adversary may be ashamed, having nothing to say against you?

and prays that the candidate 'may be to such as believe a wholesome example, in word, in conversation, in love, in faith, in chastity and in purity.'

2.7.64   In similar fashion in the *ASB* the archbishop asks the bishop-elect:

> Will you strive to fashion your own life and that of your household according to the way of Christ?

and prays,

> Defend him from all evil, that as a ruler over your household and an ambassador for Christ he may stand before you blameless.

2.8 **Summary and issues arising from this chapter**

2.8.1   In this chapter we have looked at the development of the episcopal office from the patristic period onwards and how the bishop's role is currently understood and exercised within the Church of England. We have noted that according to the Church of England:

- The ministry of a bishop is a continuation of the pattern of ministry found in the New Testament.

- It is a sign and instrument of apostolicity and catholicity.

- It involves the proclamation and defence of 'wholesome doctrine'.

- It involves the oversight of the celebration of the sacraments.

- It involves the exercise of pastoral oversight and the promotion of unity.

- It involves overall responsibility for the life of a diocese.

- It involves the exercise of judicial authority.

- It involves leadership in mission.

- It is exercised in personal, collegial and communal ways.

- It is a representative ministry.

- It involves living in a manner that bears witness to the gospel.

2.8.2   This outline of the role of a bishop in the Church of England raises three key issues in relation to the question whether the Church of England should consecrate women bishops.

2.8.3   The first of these issues is the issue of continuity. One of the things that is striking about the ministry of a bishop in the Church of England is that in general terms it remains the same ministry as that exercised by bishops in the patristic era.

- Like a bishop in patristic times a Church of England bishop is the principal minister of word and sacrament of the local church and has overall pastoral responsibility for his clergy and laity and he exercises his ministry together with his priests and deacons and as part of the wider episcopal college.

- Like a bishop in patristic times the role of a Church of England bishop is an instrument of unity.

- Like a bishop in patristic times a Church of England bishop is called to declare and uphold the apostolic faith which is revealed in Scripture and to which the tradition of the Church bears witness.

- Like a bishop in patristic times a Church of England bishop has the sole right to ordain priests and deacons.

- Like a bishop in patristic times a Church of England bishop is called to be a leader in mission.

2.8.4　　This convergence between the role of a Church of England bishop and that of a patristic bishop is not accidental. The Church of England has retained a traditional understanding of what the bishop's office involves in the same way that it has retained the office of bishop itself. The reason it has done so is the same in both cases, which is that it has wanted to maintain historical continuity with the Early Church both as a sign of its identity as part of the one holy catholic and apostolic Church and as a means of upholding that identity.

2.8.5　　However, alongside this continuity there has also been change. As we have explained, the office of bishop adapted to meet changing circumstances during the patristic period and it has continued to adapt ever since. What this means is that while the basic features of episcopal ministry today are the same as they were in the patristic era, the way that this ministry is exercised is different. A bishop today simply does not operate in the same way that a bishop operated in the second century or the sixth century.

2.8.6　　The relevance of this for the debate about the ordination of women bishops is that it raises the question of whether their ordination would simply be a further adaptation of the episcopal office to meet the circumstances of our time and our changed theological understanding of the relationship between men and women in the Church, or whether it would represent a fundamental break with the historic continuity of the episcopate which the Church of England has hitherto sought to maintain.

2.8.7   The second issue is whether a woman would be able to carry out the role of a bishop in the Church of England. This issue involves theological questions, such as whether it would be right for a woman bishop to exercise episcopal authority over men, and the practical question of whether a woman could effectively exercise an episcopal ministry in circumstances where there would be clergy and congregations whose theological position means that they would be unable to accept her ministry.

2.8.8   The third issue is whether any arrangements that might be made to meet the pastoral needs of those unable to accept the ministry of women bishops would be compatible with the accepted role of the bishop in the ecclesiology of the Church of England. For example, if a woman were to be made bishop, but there were clergy and parishes in her diocese that were under the oversight of another bishop because they were opposed to the ordination of women, this would call into question the principle that the diocesan bishop has pastoral oversight over all the clergy and people of the diocese.

2.8.9   We shall explore these issues in more detail in later chapters of this report, but in the next chapter we shall go on to look at how we should approach the basic question of whether it would be right in principle for a woman to be a bishop.

chapter 3

How should we approach the issue of whether women should be ordained as bishops?

3.1 Possible approaches to this issue

3.1.1   Having looked at the Church of England's present understanding of episcopacy we now have to turn to the question of whether in principle it would be right for a woman to be a bishop. The issue we need to decide is how we can gain a proper theological perspective on the matter. How can we decide in a manner that is in accord with God's will? In order to begin to explore this issue we shall first of all look at four popular approaches to the issue of whether women should be ordained as bishops.

The argument that it is self-evident that women should be bishops

3.1.2   The first approach is to say that it is simply self-evident that women should be ordained as bishops. This is the position adopted by a lot of people, especially younger people, today. They are so used to women exercising every kind of role in our society that they simply assume that this must be right and hence the idea that women should not be bishops would not even occur to them. Indeed, it sometimes comes as news to people that it is not already the case that women can be bishops in the Church of England.

3.1.3   However, the argument that it is simply self-evident that women should be ordained as bishops runs into two difficulties.

- First it has to reckon with the fact that this idea has not been self-evident to the majority of Christians down the centuries and does not appear to be self-evident to most Christians around the world today. Why should what seems to be self-evident to some Christians today be seen as being decisive in the matter when this involves a rejection of what has seemed self-evident to most other Christians, namely that it is inappropriate for women to be bishops?

- Secondly, and more importantly, in a fallen world in which the minds of human beings are darkened as a result of alienation from God (Romans 1.21) we cannot assume that what seems to be self-evident is in fact in accordance with the will of God.

3.1.4   Over the centuries many forms of behaviour such as polygamy, infanticide, slavery and the oppression of one race by another have seemed to be self-evidently justified, but the Christian Church has come to see that they are ways of behaving that are not in accordance with God's will. What is required is a more thorough exploration of what we know concerning the will of God in order to assess whether what seems to be self-evidently right is in fact a correct form of behaviour.

The argument from widespread support

3.1.5   The second approach is to say that we should consider ordaining women as bishops because there is widespread support for this idea within the Church of England. From a purely practical point of view it is obviously the case that it is because there is now considerable support for the idea of women bishops in the Church of England that the subject is being proposed for synodical discussion. If there were little or no support for the idea then it would not even get discussed.

3.1.6   However it is important not to confuse this practical issue with the deeper issue of what constitutes a proper basis for the discussion of whether we should have women bishops. At this deeper level the argument from widespread support does not provide an adequate starting point. Once again this is for two reasons.

- First, we have to take seriously the points made by the sixteenth-century Anglican theologian John Jewel who notes in his *Apology for the Church of England* that

> It hath been an old complaint, even from the first time of the patriarchs and prophets, and confirmed by the writings and testimonies of every age, that the truth wandereth here and there as a stranger in the world, and doth readily find enemies and slanderers amongst those who know her not.[1]

Jewel further notes that

> there was the greatest consent that might be amongst them that
> worshipped the golden calf, and among them which with one voice
> jointly cried against our Saviour Jesu Christ, 'Crucify him.'[2]

What these quotations from Jewel remind us in a memorable fashion
is that simply because a belief is unpopular does not mean that it is
untrue; and conversely the fact that there is unanimity of opinion
does not mean that that opinion is correct. There can be unanimity
in error as well as in truth.

- Secondly, we have to note that if taken to its logical conclusion the
argument that something should be considered true because it has
popular support also means conversely that if something does not
have popular support then this means that it should not be
considered true.

In the case of women's ministry this would mean that it only became
true that women should be ordained as priests once a majority in the
Church of England decided this was the case, and this is something
that few supporters of women's ordination would want to concede.
They would argue, perfectly reasonably, that even though the
argument for ordaining women initially attracted little support
it was nevertheless still correct even then. It did not become correct
at some later stage.

3.1.7 What all this points to is the fact that the question of
theological truth has to be separated out from the issue of popular
enthusiasm. There has to be some method of assessing whether popular
opinion is correct.

The argument from experience
3.1.8 The third approach is to appeal to the experience of women
ministers and those who have benefited from their ministry.

3.1.9 In the case of the experience of women ministers themselves
the appeal that is made is to their sense of vocation, their sense that
their call to the ministry is a call from God. The argument then goes
that this sense of vocation has to be seen as pointing us towards the
will of God in the matter.

3.1.10 In her 1986 ACCM paper *Towards a Theology of Vocation*

Mary Tanner writes as follows about the sense of vocation that she had encountered among women in ministry:

> What emerged from the stories was how, against all the odds of upbringing, existing role-models of male patterns of ministry, often in the face of being told to go away, think again, by the parish priest, certainly without any fostering of vocation by the bishop or the clergy, these women had become convinced of the call to minister to the Church, not always, and certainly never at first to a priestly ministry. And I was more and more struck by the fact that hardly ever was the feeling of call anything to do with a blinding flash, a Damascus road type of experience. Rather, it was a sense of awareness that grew slowly and painfully against all that was expected, wanted, hoped for. And even more striking is the fact that so many of the stories told of the coming of the call through others. These women were aware that the community was calling forth gifts that they themselves were often not aware they had to offer.[3]

3.1.11   In the face of this kind of testimony, it is asked, how can we deny that women have a genuine call from God to the ministry given that this is exactly the same sort of testimony that is accepted as evidence of a genuine vocation in the case of men?

3.1.12   In the case of the experience of women's ministry the argument that is put forward is that women should be ordained as bishops because people have had a very positive experience of women ministers. This is a point that has been made in a large number of the individual submissions presented to the Working Party. People have often written very movingly about how effective women have been as priests within the Church of England and how this has led them to believe that women should become bishops.

3.1.13   One letter sent to the Working Party declares, for instance:

> When our diocesan bishop recently asked each of the churches for their wishes for the future, our DCC spontaneously agreed that women bishops would be on our wish list. And this request was from a congregation of a catholic tradition previously non-supportive of women as priests.
>
> Of course congregations change and people alter their minds for many reasons. But I believe that our request for a woman bishop

was in no small way the result of the ministry of our NSM female curate. A working wife and mother without a Christian background she began her Christian journey after the birth of her first child – and now touches our lives with blessing. Proclaiming 'this is the Gospel of Christ' from the body of the church, presiding at the altar and exercising her pastoral care, she has brought a new dimension and richness to our Christian journey.

3.1.14   Another letter, reflecting on the contribution made by women priests in a particular diocese, states:

> One of the most impressive aspects of this for me has been the way in which women who took on the incumbency of some really quite depressed parishes have transformed them. In a number of cases women assumed incumbencies where there had been long interregna or previous incumbents who had really let parishes go downhill. The skill with which the women have rebuilt and inspired these parishes has been quite remarkable: in quite a number of cases pretty well all contact had been lost with the community, and especially with younger members and newcomers and a really noteworthy feature of the renewal of life has been the development of work with children, with schools and with people on the edge of the church's life. This has been achieved not only through hard work and commitment but through real insight, understanding and a range of talents and skills which do not seem to have been available in these situations before . . .

> All this has been extremely encouraging and inspiring. But if what has been achieved in this way is to have further potential then there must be the possibility of women in the most senior leadership roles in the Church. Without this the possibility of learning from their insights and skills is precluded.

3.1.15   The argument from the sense of vocation experienced by women in ministry is one that has to be taken seriously. A personal sense of being called by God is an important issue in deciding whether someone has a vocation to the ministry.

3.1.16   However, an argument for the ordination of women that is based on people's personal sense of vocation runs the risk of putting forward an excessively narrow understanding of how the Holy Spirit guides the Church. Traditionally the Church has always insisted that theological issues have to be decided not simply on the basis of the subjective convictions of individuals, which can be appealed to by both sides of the argument about the ordination of women, but on more objective and universally accessible criteria.

3.1.17   The same issue arises in connection with the argument that is also put forward that individuals have seen God at work calling women to ministry and then subsequently working powerfully through them. This is a powerful argument for the individuals concerned, but here again it is necessary to guard against undue subjectivity. The experience of individuals has to be tested against the more objective criteria of Scripture, tradition and reason which we shall look at later on in this chapter.

3.1.18   The argument from the Church's experience of women's ministry is an important tribute to the quality of the women priests within the Church of England, but it too has its limitations.

3.1.19   The basic problem is that it assumes that the question that is being asked is whether women have the necessary personal and professional skills and the necessary holiness to be effective as bishops. This is certainly something that one would rightly ask of any individual woman who was being considered as a possible bishop (in just the same way that one would want to ask the same questions of any male candidate).

3.1.20   However, the fundamental issue is not whether women have these qualities. This is something that almost nobody is now questioning, however much it may have been an issue in the past. Very few people would now seek to resurrect the old arguments that women are by nature unsuited to exercise authority in the Church because they are less rational than men, or emotionally and morally weaker than men, and therefore more likely to be led astray from the path of Christian truth.[4] As the 1976 papal encyclical *Inter Insigniores* notes, these are the kind of arguments against the ordination of women, 'that modern thought would have difficulty admitting or would even rightly reject'.[5] It is noteworthy that they have simply not occurred in the submissions made to the Working Party.

3.1.21   The issue today is whether, in the light of the order God has established for his human creatures through his creative and redemptive activity, it is right for women to exercise the gifts that they have as bishops or whether they should employ them in some other sphere of Christian service. This is an issue which cannot simply be decided by their own sense of vocation, or on the basis of other people's experience of their ministry – however positive that experience may have been.

The argument from justice

3.1.22   The fourth approach to this issue starts from the question of justice. The argument goes that God is a God of justice and expects his people to behave justly and that this means that women should be ordained as bishops.

3.1.23   This is because, it is argued, it is unjust to women, an infringement of their rights, if they are not allowed to be bishops, just as it would be an infringement of their rights if they were not allowed to be High Court judges, ministers of the Crown, or the chief executives of businesses.

3.1.24   This argument is very attractive in a society like ours in which the concept of the rights of the individual is widely accepted and any infringement of those rights is seen as an act of injustice for which a remedy is often sought through the legal system. It can appear to be highly unjust that the Church of England has an exemption from the *Sex Discrimination Act* that allows it to prevent women being appointed to certain offices within the Church.

3.1.25   The premise on which this argument is based is also one that all Christians would want to affirm. According to the biblical witness God is a God of justice. Thus the Psalmist declares concerning God: 'Righteousness and justice are the foundation of your throne' (Psalms 89.14) and the martyrs in the Book of Revelation cry out 'Just and true are your ways, King of the nations' (Revelation 15.3).

3.1.26   Furthermore, God does require justice from his people. Thus in Genesis God declares concerning Abraham: '. . . I have chosen him, that he may charge his children and his household after him to keep the way of the Lord by doing righteousness and justice' (Genesis 18.19) and the prophet Micah states: 'He has showed you, O mortal, what is good; and what does the Lord require of you but to do justice, and to love kindness, and to walk humbly with your God' (Micah 6.8).

3.1.27   However, the legitimacy of moving from the justice of God and the justice that he requires of his people to the need to ordain women as bishops can also be questioned from a Christian point of view inasmuch as this move tends to equate the biblical concept of justice with the contemporary understanding of the rights of the individual. It may not necessarily be correct always to identify the two.

3.1.28   According to the Christian faith, human beings have been created by God and given the gift of living life in a right relationship with him. This is what is described in the first two chapters of Genesis in which the narrative describes how the first human beings were placed in a garden where they had everything they needed for a fully satisfying life providing that they lived in obedience to God and did not seek to seize control of their own destiny by eating of the tree of the knowledge of good and evil.

3.1.29   The point of this narrative is vividly to demonstrate how human life was meant to be. Human beings are meant to find happiness by living within the structures that God has laid down. This, it says, is how human life was meant to be. The subsequent chapters of Genesis (3-11) go on to tell us about how human beings have rebelled against the pattern laid down by God with the consequence that they have become alienated from God and from each other and thus incapable of finding their true fulfilment.[6]

3.1.30   The rest of the biblical narrative from Genesis 12 onwards then goes on to tell us about how, beginning with Abraham, God began the long process of rectifying the consequences of human rebellion, a process which found its climax and fulfilment in the life, death and resurrection of his son Jesus Christ. Through Christ's obedience the disobedience of humanity was reversed, and a right relationship between God and humankind was restored (Romans 5.12-21), with the result that at the end of the biblical canon, in Revelation 21–22, we have a description of how all death, mourning, crying and pain have been done away with because human communion with God has been perfectly restored in a new heaven and earth in which there is perfect obedience to God's will.

3.1.31   The situation that is described in Revelation 21–22 is one that we do not yet see fully manifested, but the gift and calling of God to human beings is to live in obedience to God in the power of the Spirit in anticipation of that final fulfilment (Romans 8.12-27).

3.1.32 From this perspective the supreme right that any human being has is the right to live in obedience to the divine order given by God at creation and restored through the work of Jesus Christ. This in turn means that the Christian has to ask how any claim to rights made in our society relates to this supreme right.

3.1.33 We cannot simply assume that any claim to rights made by our society is correct. We have to ask the critical question as to whether the granting of this claim will lead to lives that are in accordance with the will of God because they respect the framework that he has laid down for his human creation. In the case of the particular issue with which this report is concerned, the question is whether ordaining women as bishops would help people to live lives in obedience to God by enabling to them to fulfil the roles which God laid down for men and women when he established human sexual differentiation as part of his good creation. As Nicholas Sagovsky writes:

> The understanding of equality that conforms to the Scriptural norm is one of gendered diversity and reciprocity, which gives each person, female and male, equal opportunity to fulfil their vocation in interaction with others. It is this that reflects the justice which is the will of God for the Church both in its internal ordering and in its worldly action. To put the point sharply, gender-blind 'equality' may be an ideal for human beings before the secular law, when it is the law that mediates Justice, but when Justice is mediated directly by Christ equality becomes a matter of equal freedom to fulfil the vocation given to women and men as women and men by God.[7]

3.1.34 What all this means is that there can be a justice-based argument for the ordination of women as bishops. The Church needs to be organized in a way that is in accord with the justice that God requires from his people. However, in order to be legitimate in Christian terms such an argument has to based on an overall understanding of God's purposes for his creation and the vocation of women and men within these purposes rather than on a simple appeal to the concept of justice as understood by contemporary British society.

3.1.35 If the approaches that have just been outlined are not appropriate places from which to begin to explore the question of whether women should be bishops in the Church of England, the question that has to be answered is, 'Where should we begin?'

3.2 The significance of the Bible

3.2.1   In order to answer this question we have to ask first of all where it is that we discover the order that God has established for his human creation. Where do we discover what it means to be truly and authentically human by living in the way that God intends?

3.2.2   As we have just noted when looking at the issue of human rights, the Christian faith declares that we find the answer to this question by paying attention to the story of how God, Father, Son and Spirit created us, redeemed us and enables us to begin to live as God intends.[8]

3.2.3   To use the currently popular terminology this is the Christian 'metanarrative', the overarching story that provides the Christian explanation of human existence, and in the context of which we understand our own individual life stories correctly.

3.2.4   This raises the question, however, as to the source of the Christian story. Whence do we learn of this God and of what he has done for humankind?

3.2.5   The consistent Christian answer has been that we learn of this story from the witness borne to it by the Bible. It is for this reason that Christians down the centuries, Christians of the Church of England included, have insisted on the authority of the biblical witness as the norm for all Christian theology and hence for the discussion of particular theological issues such as whether it is right for women to be bishops.

3.2.6   Two examples, one historical and one modern, will serve to illustrate this point.

3.2.7   The first example is Archbishop Thomas Cranmer's 1547 homily *A Fruitful Exhortation to the Reading and Knowledge of Holy Scripture*. As its title suggests, this homily was written by Archbishop Cranmer in order to encourage people to study the Bible, and the reason he gives why they should do so is as follows:

> In these books we shall find the Father from whom, the Son by whom, and the Holy Ghost in whom, all things have their being and keeping up; and these three persons to be but one God, and

one substance. In these books we may learn to know ourselves, how vile and miserable we be, and also to know God, how good he is of himself, and how he maketh us and all creatures partakers of his goodness. We may learn also in these books to know God's will and pleasure, as much as, for this present time, is convenient for us to know.[9]

3.2.8   What Cranmer is saying in this quotation is that we should study the Bible because it is through the biblical witness that we find out who God is, who we are, and what God has done for us, and receive all the guidance we need in order to live in obedience to God.

3.2.9   The second example is the 1958 Lambeth Conference report *The Holy Bible: its Authority and Message*. This report notes that the Bible should be seen as a 'drama disclosing the truth about God and man'. It then goes on to say that

> The great Christian doctrines are no more and no less than interpretations of the Biblical drama which the Church made under the guidance of the Holy Spirit. God the righteous and omnipotent creator; the utter dependence of all created existence upon him; the human race as possessing the divine likeness and yet torn from the divine fellowship by sinfulness; the impotence of the human race to fulfil itself without the divine rescue brought by Jesus Christ; the act of rescue in Christ's life, death and resurrection; his revelation of the Triune God, Father, Son and Holy Spirit; the Church as the community wherein by the dwelling of the Holy Spirit fellowship with God is found; the possession here and now of eternal life with him in the world to come the presence already of the reign of God within history and its final vindication yet to come. Such is the pattern of Christian belief. The Creeds summarize it. The Church expounds it in systematic form. But it is from the Bible that every right exposition of it derives.[10]

3.2.10   The argument in this quotation is not identical to that in the previous quotation from Cranmer, but it points us in the same direction. The biblical drama is the basis of Christian belief, and Christian doctrine is simply the coherent interpretation and exposition of it. The pattern of Christian belief is the pattern that the Bible provides.

3.2.11   If we ask why it is through these writings that we learn the story that tells us about God and our relationship with him, the answer that Christians have always given on the basis of texts such as 2 Timothy 3.16 and 2 Peter 1.21 is that it is because these writings were not simply the work of human authors but were inspired by the Spirit of God. That is to say, the Holy Spirit was at work in the biblical writers in such a way that what they wrote was capable of conveying to us the story of God and his activity. As the 1958 report puts it:

> inspiration means that the Spirit of God has been at work in
> a writer; and just as the Bible as a whole is the record of God's
> revelation of himself in Israel and in Jesus, so we believe that as
> a whole it is inspired by God. It is the whole of the Biblical drama
> and the whole of the Biblical literature which bears witness to
> God's revelation of himself in the story of Israel, with the
> shadows as well as the lights and the ups and downs of failure
> and recovery. Correlative with the divine revelation in the whole
> is the belief that his Spirit was at work in all the books which
> serve that revelation.[11]

3.2.12   Furthermore, it has also been the belief of the Church down the centuries not only that the Spirit inspired the writing of the Bible, but that through the biblical writings God continues to speak to his people through his Spirit today. Two contemporary examples will serve to illustrate this point.

3.2.13   The 1998 *Virginia Report* of the Inter-Anglican Theological and Doctrinal Commission states:

> Anglicans affirm the sovereign authority of the Holy Scriptures as
> the medium through which God by the Spirit communicates his word
> in the Church and thus enables people to respond with understanding
> and faith.[12]

3.2.14   Likewise the Second Vatican Council's Dogmatic Constitution on Divine Revelation *Dei Verbum* declares:

> in the sacred books, the Father who is in heaven meets His children
> with great love and speaks with them; and the force and power in the
> word of God is so great that it stands as the support
> and energy of the Church, the strength and faith for her sons, the
> food of the soul, the pure and everlasting source of spiritual life.
> Consequently these words are perfectly applicable to Sacred
> Scripture: 'For the word of God is living and active' (Heb. 4.12)
> and 'it has power to build you up and give you your heritage
> among all those who are sanctified' (Acts 20.32; see 1 Thess. 2.13).[13]

3.2.15   The way in which the Bible functions as the metanarrative through which we hear God speaking to us is helpfully described by Richard Bauckham in terms of our learning to find our true identity through reference to the biblical witness:

> The Bible's narrative does not simply require assent. Like all stories, it draws us into its world, engages us imaginatively, allows us at our own pace to grow accustomed to it. But to accept it as authoritative metanarrative means more than to indwell it, as we might a novel, imaginatively for the duration of our reading. Such an experience of a story may well affect our understanding and experience of the world. But to accept the Bible's metanarrative as authoritative is to privilege it above all other stories. It is to find our identity as characters in that story whose lives are an as yet untold part of the story. For the metanarrative is, of course, no more than a sketch. The Bible tells us that part of the plot that makes the general meaning of the whole clear and points us ahead to the way the plot must finally be resolved. But it leaves the way open to the inclusion of all other stories, including those we play some part in writing.[14]

3.2.16   In terms of the debate about women bishops this means learning to see how this debate fits into the overall biblical story about women, men, and the relationship between them, and then deciding whether in terms of that story ordaining women as bishops would be an act of obedience or disobedience by the Church. Would it be consonant with the overall biblical picture or would it not?

3.2.17   In our culture people can find the idea that the Bible possesses authority and requires our obedience a frightening one. This is due both to a general fear that any overall metanarrative is repressive because it restricts the range of human freedom and a specific fear of the way in which the Bible, like other religious texts, has been used to repress people in the past.

3.2.18   The Christian answer is that the authority of the Bible is the authority of grace met with the free obedience of love. To quote the American Old Testament scholar W. Bruegemann it is 'not coercive but generative, not repressive but emancipatory'.[15]

3.2.19   As Bauckham explains, this is because the authority of the Bible belongs in the first place to the story of God's gracious self-giving to us. In that context the authority of God's will for us expressed in commands is the authority of God's grace.

and,

Our response to grace is not the coerced submission of the slave, but the free obedience of love. Its paradigm is: 'I delight to do your will, O my God; your law is within my heart' (Ps 40.8). This is neither the autonomy that is contradicted by any authority nor the heteronomy that experiences authority as alien subjection to the will of another. It is the obedience to God of those who already glimpse the eschatological identity of their best desires with God's, who recognize God's will as the desire of their own hearts, whose experience of God's love makes love the freely chosen goal of their lives. Freedom is here not the rejection of all limits, but the free acceptance of those limits that enable loving relationships. Obedience is demanding but it is no more heteronomous than the athlete's acceptance of the demanding regime that she knows to be the way to the goals she has set herself.[16]

3.2.20 Of course, there are times when obedience to God is a baffling matter because we cannot see that what God is asking of us is an expression of his grace. The classic biblical examples of this problem are the story of God's call to Abraham to sacrifice Isaac in Genesis 22 and the story of Christ's wrestling with the prospect of his coming death in the Garden of Gethsemane (Luke 22.39-46). However, what both these biblical stories make clear is that the God whose purposes we cannot always understand is indeed the God of grace and that we can trust him to always bring good out of apparent evil. It is this conviction that makes Christian obedience possible.

3.3 Interpreting Scripture

3.3.1   If Christian obedience to God is thus rooted in the biblical witness it is clearly important that the Bible is read in a responsible fashion that enables us fully and properly to understand it.

3.3.2   There is sometimes a fear that an insistence on the importance of interpreting Scripture properly disenfranchises ordinary Christians by making the meaning of Scripture accessible only to an elite of trained biblical scholars. This concern needs to be taken seriously and it must always be remembered that God can and does speak through the Bible to Christians who are not biblical scholars as they study Scripture in their private devotions or hear it read and preached publicly in the context of the liturgy.

3.3.3   However, it must also be insisted that the fact that ordinary Christians can grasp the message of Scripture without formal training in biblical scholarship does not mean that such scholarship is unnecessary. There is always more to learn about the meaning of Scripture and when properly employed biblical scholarship can help all of God's people in this process of learning. It is worth remembering that those Reformers in the sixteenth century who were most insistent on the perspicuity of Scripture and the importance of its being available to the laity in vernacular translations were also insistent on the importance of using the best tools of humanist scholarship to understand the Scriptures better.

3.3.4   The first point that needs to be made in connection with learning to understand Scripture better is that a responsible reading of Scripture is one that takes seriously its dual character as both the 'word of God' and a compilation of human texts. This means addressing:

- 'Behind the text' issues to do with the background and context of the biblical writings. For example, what was the cultural and historical background to what St Paul says about women praying or prophesying in 1 Corinthians 11.2-16 and how do these verses fit into the overall structure of 1 Corinthians?

- 'In the text' issues to do with the how the particular words used by the biblical authors fit together to make up the texts of which they are a part. For example, what is the meaning of the word *kephale* (head) used by St Paul in 1 Corinthians 11.2-16 and how does this word contribute to the development of his argument in these verses?

- 'In front of the text' issues to do with how the texts fit into the canon as a whole, how they have spoken to Christians down the centuries and how they might address our own situation. For example, how does what St Paul says about the role of women in worship in 1 Corinthians 11.2-16 relate to what is said about this issue elsewhere in the Bible? How have these verses been understood and applied in the history of the Church? How should we understand them as God's word to us today given that our particular cultural and historical situation is different from that of first-century Corinth? [17]

3.3.5　　With regard to this last point it is helpful to bear in mind the observation made in the report *The Interpretation of the Bible in the Church* produced by the Pontifical Biblical Commission in 1994:

> The Word of God finds expression in the work of human authors. The thought and the words belong at one and the same time both to God and to human beings, in such a way that the whole Bible comes at once from God and from the inspired human author. This does not mean, however, that God has given the historical conditioning of the text a value that is absolute. It is open both to interpretation and to being brought up to date – which means being detached, to some extent, from its historical conditioning in the past and being translated into the historical conditioning of the present.[18]

3.3.6　　The question facing the interpreter is thus to discern how the text can be translated from its original context in such a way that it can address our historical context today without losing the status of the text as a 'control' in subsequent reformulations or interpretations of its meaning.

3.3.7　　To illustrate this point, Ian Henderson distinguishes between two types of interpretation. First, there is the interpretation of a code, in which the code is discarded once the interpretation has been made. Second, there is the interpretation of a masterpiece in which subsequent generations need to return again and again to the masterpiece itself.[19] The interpretation of the Bible needs to be seen in the terms of the interpretation of a masterpiece rather than in terms of the interpretation of a code.

3.3.8　　In the case of those biblical texts referring to the role of women in the Church, treating the biblical text as the control means, first of all, seeking to determine as precisely as possible the meaning of these texts in their original contexts in first-century Corinth or Ephesus. It then means asking how we translate what is said in them from this particular historical context to our historical situation in England today, a situation that was never envisaged by the human author when the texts were originally written.

3.3.9　　Secondly, a responsible reading of Scripture will also be one that seeks to make sense of the diversity of perspectives that the Bible contains on subjects such as the role of women.

3.3.10   Women feature in all sorts of contexts and roles within the biblical texts and if we are to make sense of these theologically we have to ask how these fit together as part of the overall biblical story. This means learning to read the Bible dynamically, seeing how the individual texts referring to women fit into the overall direction or trajectory of the biblical story. To quote Bauckham again:

> The Bible is a collection of very different types of writing written over a very long period by a large number of authors and editors. So in the nature of the case we cannot expect it to provide us with ready-made summaries of its own teaching in all its component parts.[20]

3.3.11   As a result, he says,

> For the most part, the task of discerning the general thrust and major components of the Bible's treatment of a topic is a difficult task of creative interpretation. It requires much more than the gathering of relevant information from all parts of Scripture. The appropriate categories may not be handed on a plate to the interpreter by Scripture itself; he or she may need to search for the most appropriate categories or to invent new ones. Without discounting any part of the scriptural witness, the interpreter will have to make judgments about what is central and what is peripheral, what is relative and what is absolute, or what is provisional and what is enduring.[21]

3.3.12   Furthermore,

> In some cases it will be important, not only to report the actual positions reached by particular biblical writings, but also to discover the direction in which biblical thinking is moving. For the bible contains the records of a dynamic, developing tradition of thought, and the aim of interpretation should be to let Scripture involve the reader in its own process of thought, so that the reader's thinking may continue in the direction it sets.[22]

3.3.13   As we shall see in Chapter 5, at the heart of the current debate about the ordination of women as bishops is precisely the question of how to correlate the relevant biblical material and discern its overall dynamic and direction.

3.3.14   Thirdly, reading Scripture responsibly means wrestling with the uncomfortable and difficult texts that it contains and not skating around them.

3.3.15 In the case of the biblical texts relating to women this means wrestling with what Phyllis Trible has called 'texts of terror'[23] – texts such as the rejection of Hagar (Genesis 16.1-16, 21.9-21) the rape of Tamar (2 Samuel 13.1-22), the sacrifice of Jephthah's daughter (Judges 11.29-40) and the betrayal, rape and murder of the Levite's concubine (Judges 19.1-30), which contain appalling acts of rejection and violence against women – and ask how they fit into the biblical picture.

3.3.16 If the biblical witness really is a witness to the grace of God, where do we find grace in texts such as these, and how should these texts challenge our behaviour today?

3.3.17 Fourthly, and finally, reading Scripture responsibly means asking whether applying the trajectory of the biblical narrative seriously leads us to go beyond the explicit teaching of the Bible itself in order to follow through that trajectory in our own historical situation.

3.3.18 This was an issue which was discussed in relation to the issue of ecclesiology by Richard Hooker in his debate with the radical Puritans in his *Laws of Ecclesiastical Polity*. Both Hooker and his opponents accepted that Scripture possessed normative authority. However while the radical Puritans argued that issues to do with worship and the government of the Church should be decided solely on the basis of what was taught in Scripture itself,[24] Hooker argued that this was too restrictive and that what needed to be asked was how to apply the basic principles of biblical teaching in situations which the Bible did not directly address or where the circumstances that had occasioned the biblical teaching had now changed.

3.3.19 It was also an issue which was discussed in relation to the issue of slavery in the eighteenth and nineteenth centuries. Those who defended slavery pointed to texts in the Old and New Testaments that permitted slavery and enjoined slaves to be obedient to their masters. Abolitionists, on the other hand, argued that these texts were related to particular historical circumstances. They saw the overall biblical teaching about the creation of all human beings in the image and likeness of God and the liberating work of God in Christ, together with the specific teaching of texts such as Galatians 3.28 and the letter to Philemon, as pointing inevitably towards the abolition of slavery.

3.3.20   In relation to the question of the ordination of women, reading Scripture in this way means asking, for instance, whether the overall dynamic of biblical teaching takes us beyond the restrictions on the activity of women that we appear to find in texts such as 1 Corinthians 11.2-16, 1 Corinthians 14.34-38 and 1 Timothy 2.11-15, and whether the fact that there do not appear to have been women elders in New Testament times means that women should not exercise ministerial office in churches today, or whether what the New Testament does say about the role of women in various forms of ministry would point towards this being permissible in our circumstances today?[25]

3.4 The use of tradition and reason

3.4.1   When seeking to understand the biblical texts in the way described above we also need to give attention to tradition and reason. This is not because Anglican theology is a 'three-legged stool' with Scripture, tradition and reason being equally fundamental. As we have already explained, the norm for Anglican theology is the revelation of God in Holy Scripture. However, the help of tradition and reason is required in order to understand Scripture properly and to live appropriately in the light of its teaching.

3.4.2   If we begin by considering tradition, the first point that needs to be made clear is the distinction that is now made between Tradition (with a capital T), tradition (with a lower case t) and traditions. The relationship between these three terms was explained as follows by the Fourth World Conference on Faith and Order held in Montreal in 1963:

> What is transmitted in the process of tradition is the Christian faith, not only as a sum of tenets, but as a living reality transmitted through the operation of the Holy Spirit. We can speak of the Christian Tradition (with a capital T), whose content is God's revelation and self-giving in Christ, present in the life of the Church.

> But this Tradition which is the work of the Holy Spirit is embodied in traditions (in the two senses of the word, both as referring to diversity in forms of expression and in the sense of separate communions). The traditions in Christian history are distinct from, and yet connected with, the Tradition. They are the expressions and manifestations in diverse historical forms of the one truth and reality which is Christ.[26]

3.4.3   In summary terms what this means is that tradition is the process by which the Christian faith (the 'Tradition') is handed on in

the Christian Church through a variety of different traditions. As
The Gift of Authority puts it, tradition is 'a dynamic process,
communicating to each generation what was delivered once for
all to the apostolic community'.[27]

3.4.4   Two key points concerning tradition are:

(a) Its *diverse* nature. The handing on of the Christian faith down the
    generations is something that takes place in a multitude of different
    ways. It is handed on, explicitly or implicitly, not just through the
    Church's formal theological teaching and exposition of Scripture,
    but also, as Roman Catholic and Orthodox theologians have rightly
    stressed, through the whole life of the Church, including its
    liturgies, hymnody and forms of ministry and church government.
    All of these in their different ways bear witness to the Church's
    understanding of the faith.

(b) Its *dynamic* nature. As *The Gift of Authority* says, tradition is
    a process in which the Church does not simply defend and pass
    on the heritage of the past but also adapts that heritage to new
    situations and thus passes it on in fresh ways to the next generation.
    In the words of Bauckham:

> the Christian tradition is by no means inevitably traditionalist.
> Its eschatological hope and its missionary orientation press it
> towards constantly changing contextualizations of the gospel, in
> which the resources of the past are brought into critical relationship
> with the present context with a view to the future.[28]

3.4.5   The point Bauckham makes here about having a view to the
future is a point that was also made by Metropolitan John Zizioulas
in his address to the 1988 Lambeth Conference:

> we are all gradually learning that the Omega is what gives
> meaning to the Alpha, and by having first a right vision of future
> things, of what God has prepared for his creation at the end of
> time, we can see what is demanded of us in the present.[29]

3.4.6   Because tradition is a process which involves a dynamic
engagement with the past, in the present, in the light of the future that
God has promised to us in Christ, it follows that Christian belief and

practice constantly develop, a point to which we shall return at the end of this chapter.

3.4.7   Since the earliest days of the Christian Church the importance of paying attention to the ways in which the Christian faith has found expression in the Church's traditions has been generally recognized.[30] However, there have been, and still are, those who are unconvinced of its value. They would ask why we cannot simply read the Bible and act directly on what it says.

3.4.8   In response to this question it can be said that there are three reasons why we need to take seriously the traditions of the Church:

- Taking these traditions seriously acknowledges the fact that God has made us historical beings and that this means that the only way that we can seek to make sense of the biblical message is in terms of the ways in which it has been transmitted to us by those Christians who have gone before us. We simply cannot avoid engagement with the traditions of the Christian community when reading the biblical text.[31]

- A belief in the communion of saints means taking seriously the beliefs and actions of those Christians who have gone before us just as we should take seriously the beliefs and actions of other Christians in our own day.

- Belief in the work of the Holy Spirit means taking seriously the fact that, in accordance with Christ's promise in John 16.12-15, God has been continuously at work through the Spirit guiding his Church in the direction he intends and that the traditions of the Church are thus the result of divine as well as human activity.

3.4.9   It is in the light of the last two points in particular that we should understand the Anglican insistence on the importance of the teaching and practice of the orthodox Fathers of the first five centuries.[32] God's people in both East and West, guided by God's Spirit, have accepted them as authoritative for a millennium and a half and therefore we should not lightly disregard what they have to teach us.

3.4.10   In terms of the debate about the ordination of women as bishops, taking tradition seriously means seeking to understand why it has been that for the best part of two thousand years the Christian

Church as whole has not had women bishops and being open to the possibility that this has not been simply the result of individual and cultural misogyny but, like other generally accepted Christian traditions, a result of obedience to the teaching of Scripture and the guidance of the Spirit.

3.4.11   On the other hand we also have to take seriously the point made earlier in this chapter[33] about the majority not always being right, the fact that past generations of Christians were just as subject to the effects of sin as we are, and the possibility that the Spirit may be saying something new to us in a new situation.

3.4.12   This means that we have constantly to ask whether the understanding of the Christian faith that is embodied in particular traditions is consonant with Scripture. As we have said, it is through the biblical witness that we learn the story concerning God and what he has done for us that forms the content of the Christian faith. Consequently, the Bible is the norm by which we must judge whether particular Christian traditions give legitimate expression to the faith.

3.4.13   For example, in earlier centuries the understanding of the Christian faith that was embodied in the reservation of the episcopate to men was that God created an ordered relationship between men and women in which men were to lead and women were to assist and to submit. This understanding has also often been supported by the belief, alluding to 1 Timothy 2.12-15 and 1 Peter 3.7, that women were spiritually and intellectually weaker than men (which was why Eve was deceived by the devil).[34] Such a view can, however, be held without recourse to such support.

3.4.14   Using the Bible as a norm means using the methods of biblical interpretation outlined earlier in the chapter and asking whether this understanding of the Christian faith is based on what the Bible actually says or on a misinterpretation of the biblical message.

3.4.15   Furthermore, because, under the guidance of the Spirit, the traditions of the Church have constantly to adapt to meet the demands of new situations, we have to ask whether we need to adapt the traditions concerning the role of women in order to meet the demands of our culture.

3.4.16 For example, over the centuries the Christian Church has consistently maintained that both women and men have equal value in the sight of God and both sides in the current debate about the ordination of women as bishops would want to uphold this principle. In our society the principles of equal value and equal opportunity are seen as belonging together. This means that we need to ask whether the message of equal value before God can continue to be embodied by a tradition which denies women the opportunity to be bishops, or whether the Spirit is now leading us to adapt this tradition in order to provide this opportunity.

3.4.17 Reason can be defined as the capacity for rational thought given to human beings by God by means of which they are able to understand the laws that govern both the natural order and the moral order. It is because human beings have this God-given capacity that they have been able to understand and control the natural world and have been able to engage in moral reflection about how human beings should behave and how society should be organized as a result.[35]

3.4.18 It is also because they have this capacity for rational thought that human beings are able to engage in theological reflection. In the words of Hooker:

> Theology, what is it but the science of things divine? What science can be attained unto without the help of natural discourse and reason? 'Judge you of that which I speak,' saith the Apostle [I Corinthians 10.15]. In vain it were to speak any thing of God, but that by reason men are able to judge of that they hear, and by discourse to discern how consonant it is to truth.[36]

3.4.19 Reason is thus vitally important. However, it has two limitations which are consequent upon its being part of the created order.

3.4.20 First, like all created things, it is contingent and therefore changeable, which is why what is seen as rational has changed and developed over the centuries in different cultures. That is why the *Virginia Report* is right to describe reason as the 'mind of a particular culture', with 'its characteristic ways of seeing things, asking about them and explaining them'.[37] The point being made here is that reason is not just a matter of the reason of the individual as in much post-Enlightenment thought. Nor is reason a means by which we can transcend time and attain to the eternal knowledge possessed by God.[38] When an individual exercises their God-given power of reason, the way that they think is inevitably shaped by the patterns of thought of the culture of which they are a part at a particular point in history. Taking reason seriously therefore means taking seriously those patterns of thought and asking how they relate to the Christian gospel.

3.4.21 Secondly, like the created order as a whole, reason is fallen and in need of redemption. As John Webster observes, this is not the way in which reason has typically been understood in Western thought since the Enlightenment:

> Modernity has characteristically regarded reason as a 'natural' faculty – a standard, unvarying and foundational feature of humankind, a basic human capacity or skill. As a natural faculty, reason is, crucially, not involved in the drama of God's saving work; it is not fallen, and so requires neither to be judged nor to be reconciled nor to be sanctified. Reason simply is; it is humankind in its intellectual nature.[39]

3.4.22 Nevertheless, as he goes on to say:

> Christian theology ... must beg to differ. It must beg to differ because the confession of the gospel by which theology governs its life requires it to say that humankind in its entirety, including reason, is enclosed within the history of sin and reconciliation. The history of sin and its overcoming by the grace of God concerns the remaking of humankind as a whole, not simply of what we identify restrictively as its 'spiritual' aspect. And so reason, no less than anything else, stands under the divine requirement that it be holy to the Lord its God.
>
> Christian theology is a particular instance of reason's holiness. Here, too – as in all truthful thinking – we are to trace what happens as reason is transformed by the judging, justifying and sanctifying work of the triune God. The sanctification of reason, moreover, involves a measure of difference: reason's transformation goes hand-in-hand with nonconformity. Holy reason is eschatological reason, reason submitting to the process of the renewal of all things as sin and falsehood are set aside, idolatry is reproved, and the new creation is confessed with repentance and delight.[40]

3.4.23 The issue of what it means to say that human reason is fallen is explored by Oliver O'Donovan in his book *Resurrection and Moral*

Order. He argues that even in our fallen state we remain human beings and as such our capacity to know remains. This means although in our fallen state our knowledge is confused and fragmentary it is, nonetheless, still knowledge.

3.4.24   If this is so, the question that then arises is what relationship exists between this knowledge and the understanding of the world that is given to us by means of divine revelation. According to O'Donovan the answer to this question is that the revelation given to us in Christ neither denies nor builds upon our existing human knowledge:

> ... revelation in Christ does not deny our fragmentary knowledge of the way things are, as though that knowledge were not there, or were of no significance; yet it does not build on it, as though it provided a perfectly acceptable foundation to which a further level of understanding can be added.[41]

3.4.25   What this means is that the Christian theologian has to take a middle path. On the one hand, he or she must not rule out the existence of genuine moral insight outside the Christian community. This would be to deny that those who do not have the Christian revelation are capable of knowledge. On the other hand, he or she must not affirm uncritically the moral insights of any particular culture, since in a fallen world these need to be challenged and renewed in the light of the gospel. To quote O'Donovan again:

> The Christian moral thinker ... has no need to proceed in a totalitarian way, denying the importance and relevance of all that he finds valued as moral conviction in the various cultures and traditions of the world (whether these be 'Christian', 'non-Christian' or 'post-Christian'). He has no need to prove that anything worthwhile in them has arisen historically from Christian influence. But neither can he simply embrace the perspectives of any such culture, not even – which is the most difficult to resist – the one in which he happens to belong and which therefore claims him as an active participant. He cannot set about building a theological ethic upon the moral *a priori* of a liberal culture, a revolutionary culture or any other kind of culture; for that is to make of theology an ideological justification for the cultural constructs of human misknowledge. He can only approach these phenomena critically, evaluating them and interpreting their significance from the place where true knowledge of moral order is given, under the authority of the gospel. From that position alone can be discerned what there

is to be found in these various moral traditions that may be of
interest or value.[42]

3.4.26   A further point that needs to be noted in connection with the
use of reason in theology is that we need to distinguish between the
rationalism that seeks to order data by 'mastery' and the cultivation
of wisdom by means of rational, interpersonal, listening and
discernment. The difference between the two is that seeking to order
data by mastery becomes an epistemology with the individual self at
the centre deploying merely 'calculative' or 'instrumental' reason,
whereas seeking wisdom is an exercise undertaken in a community
in which there is an attempt to discern truth for its own sake and
not merely as a means to an end.

3.4.27   In relation to the issue of the ordination of women as bishops
the points that we have just made about reason mean that:

- First, those engaged in the debate must be prepared to think
  rationally about the subject rather than approaching it simply on the
  basis of emotion, instinct or prejudice. Rational thought is a gift from
  God and we are called upon to use it. This means the arguments on
  both sides need to be assessed to see if they are rationally coherent.
  For example, does it follow that because the apostles were all men
  that women cannot be bishops today or, on the other side, does it
  follow that because women have equal spiritual value with men they
  must be free to exercise the same roles in the Church?

- Secondly, those engaged in the debate must be prepared to take into
  account the insights of our contemporary culture concerning the
  role of women and to ask whether these insights point us to ways
  of reading the biblical witness that we have previously overlooked.
  For example, the insight that it is wrong to see the role of women as
  being confined to that of housewife and mother might lead us to look
  again at the biblical material and ask about the significance of the fact
  that in the Bible women are not simply confined to a domestic role,
  but are also judges (Judges 4–5), prophetesses (2 Kings 22.11-20),
  and, arguably, leaders in the early Christian communities (Romans
  16.1-15, 1 Corinthians 1.11, Colossians 4.15, Philippians 4.2-3).[43]

- Thirdly, those engaged in the debate need to ask where the thinking
  of contemporary culture needs challenge and correction in the light

of the biblical witness. For example, it can be asked whether the current emphasis on equality between men and women does not run the risk of overlooking the equally important biblical principle that women and men were created by God not to be interchangeable, but to be distinctive and complementary (we can see this, for instance in biblical texts such as Genesis 2.18-25 and 1 Corinthians 11.2-16).

- Fourthly, those engaged in the debate need to be careful not to fall into the temptation of using the tools provided by reason simply to 'prove' their case over and against that of their opponents. Rather the debate needs to be an exercise in the cultivation of wisdom in which all involved seek together to discern the truth of what God wants for his people.

3.4.28   An important aspect of taking contemporary thought and the development of the Christian tradition seriously is paying attention to feminist readings of Scripture.

3.4.29   Ever since the pioneering work of Elizabeth Cady Stanton, whose *The Woman's Bible* was first published between 1895 and 1898, an increasing number of female scholars have attempted to develop a feminist reading of the Scriptures. As Deborah Sawyer explains, what is distinctive about this way of interpreting the Bible is that it offers

> an alternative assessment of the biblical evidence as seen through the eyes and experience of women readers and theologians.[44]

3.4.30   The point of this alternative assessment is to counterbalance and correct a perceived male bias in the interpretation of the Bible in the history of the Christian Church and the oppression of women that has resulted from this.

3.4.31   As Sawyer further explains, feminist theology has produced a variety of different approaches to interpreting the Scripture, but these can be classified under two main types:

> Attempts at solving the problems facing women as they approach the Bible form the bulk of the literature produced by feminist theologians. The varied types of solution offered show that feminist theology is a broad term encompassing many differing feminist theologies. The two main branches can be termed 'radical' and 'reformist'. In essence the former tends to reject the Bible and Christianity in favour of an

alternative, essentially feminine religious experience. The latter, while rejecting most Christian tradition about women, sees the Bible as the means of reconstructing a positive Christian theology for women.[45]

3.4.32   Examples of theologians taking the former approach would be Mary Daly in the United States[46] and Daphne Hampson in this country.[47] Examples of theologians taking the latter approach would be Phylis Trible, whose work was mentioned earlier in this chapter, and Elisabeth Schüssler Fiorenza.[48]

3.4.33   Because of the diversity of feminist theology it would be inappropriate to suggest a single response to feminist thought. Like the work of all theologians, the work of feminist theologians has to be understood and responded to on an individual case-by-case basis. However, this having been said, we would suggest that there are a number of issues which need to be borne in mind when engaging with feminist approaches to the Bible.

3.4.34   From the standpoint of Christian theology as the Church of England has traditionally understood it, it would be proper, in the context of the debate about women bishops, to

- Read the Bible in the light of feminist concerns as part of taking seriously reason and the development of tradition.

- Consider whether the traditional reading of Scripture has been biased by a dominant male perspective.

- Consider whether there are biblical texts referring to women or female biblical characters whose significance has been overlooked. Trible's 'texts of terror' would come in here.

3.4.35   However, it would be improper to

- Impose a feminist reading on the biblical text, in the same way that it would be improper to impose a traditional 'male' reading on the text.

- Privilege particular biblical texts (such as Galatians 3.28) in a way that distorts the overall biblical picture.

- Disregard texts (such as 1 Timothy 2.11-15) that are seen as oppressive to women.

- Develop an imaginative picture of early Christianity and the role of women within it that is unsupported by the available biblical evidence.

- Appeal to extra-canonical texts such as some of the Gnostic material as the basis for an alternative understanding of early Christianity.

3.4.36   The difference between these two sets of approaches is that the first remains within the framework of canonical authority while the second steps outside it. The fundamental question here is what is the norm, is it the biblical texts and the overall biblical metanarrative or is it feminist concerns? If the latter is the case then this is incompatible with the Anglican commitment to the Scriptures as the primary norm for theology.

3.5 Development

3.5.1   As Owen Chadwick explains in his work *From Bossuet to Newman*,[49] until the seventeenth century there was general acceptance of the belief that can be traced back to the debates with the Gnostics in the second and third centuries of the Christian era that innovation meant heresy. The argument by St Vincent of Lerins that Catholic orthodoxy was that which had been believed everywhere, always and by everyone (*quod ubique, quod semper, quod ab omnibus*)[50] was generally seen as axiomatic.

The deposit of Christian faith had been given by Christ to the apostles and orthodox Christianity had passed on this deposit unchanged from one generation to the next.[51]

3.5.2   From the seventeenth century onwards, however, this traditional belief became increasingly hard to sustain. Controversy between Catholics and Protestants over which side were the innovators and the rise of modern historical consciousness led both Catholic and Protestant scholars to accept that Christian doctrine had in fact varied and developed over time.

3.5.3   For example, it came to be accepted that the doctrine of the Trinity in its Nicene form was something that came into existence as a result of the fourth-century debates about the relationship between God the Father, God the Son and God the Holy Spirit. It was a development of Christian belief rather than something that had been part of the Christian faith from the beginning, even though it was a development that built on a biblical foundation and was anticipated by the orthodox Fathers of the pre-Nicene period.

3.5.4   The fact that Christian belief was not something that was unchanging had to be accounted for theologically and it eventually came to be accepted that there is a sense in which orthodox Christian doctrine can properly be said to change. This is because Christian belief is not something static but, as we have previously noted, something dynamic that necessarily moves forward as Christians continue to wrestle with Scripture in the light of reason and tradition.

3.5.5   The classic nineteenth-century exposition of the belief that doctrine is capable of legitimate change was J. H. Newman's *Essay on the Development of Christian Doctrine*, first published in 1845. The essay was written in response to the issue of how the Roman Catholic Church could be said to have maintained inviolate the true apostolic faith given that its beliefs had changed over the centuries. In it Newman argues that it is characteristic of all 'great ideas' that they grow and change over time:

> Its beginnings are no measure of its capabilities, nor of its scope. At first no one knows what it is or what it is worth. It remains perhaps for a time quiescent; it tries, as it were its limbs, and proves the ground under it, and feels its way. From time to time it makes essays which fail, and are in consequence abandoned. It seems in suspense which way to go; it wavers, and at length strikes out in a definite direction. In time it enters upon strange territory; points of controversy alter their bearing; parties rise and fall around it; dangers and hopes appear in new relations; and old principles reappear under new forms. It changes with them in order to remain the same. In a higher world it is otherwise, but here below to live is to change, and to be perfect is to have changed often.[52]

3.5.6   What is true of all other great ideas is also true of Christian doctrine, says Newman. It, too, is subject to change and development and this is something that was intended by God:

> From the necessity, then, of the case, from the history of all sects and parties in religion, and from the analogy and example of Scripture, we may fairly conclude that Christian doctrine admits of formal, legitimate and true developments, that is, of developments contemplated by its Divine Author.[53]

3.5.7   In the second part of his essay Newman outlines seven 'notes' which make it possible '. . . to discriminate healthy developments of an idea from its state of corruption and decay.'[54] In Chapter 5 these seven notes are listed as: 'preservation of type', 'continuity of principles', 'power of assimilation', 'logical sequence', 'anticipation of its future', 'conservative action upon its past' and 'chronic vigour'.[55]

3.5.8   The first six of these notes are variations on one basic theme, which is that a healthy development is one in which continuity is maintained in the midst of change. In his explanation of his first note Newman illustrates this idea by comparing healthy doctrinal development with the growth of a young animal into an adult. The animal changes, but it does not cease to be the same animal:

> the parts and proportions of the developed form, however, altered, correspond to those which belong to its rudiments. The adult animal has the same make, as it had on its birth; young birds do not grow into fishes, nor does the child degenerate into the brute, wild or domestic, of which he is by inheritance lord.[56]

3.5.9   The seventh note is the longevity of healthy development. According to Newman, doctrinal corruption does not last whilst healthy development does:

> Since the corruption of an idea, as far as the appearance goes, is a sort of accident or affection of its development, being the end of a course, and a transition-state leading to a crisis, it is, as has been observed above, a brief and rapid process. While ideas live in men's minds, they are ever emerging into fuller development: they will not be stationary in their corruption any more than before it; and dissolution is that further state towards which corruption tends. Corruption cannot, therefore, be of long standing; and thus *duration* is another test of a faithful development.[57]

3.5.10   Newman's basic point that there can be a valid development of Christian doctrine and practice has been widely accepted. However, there has been less widespread acceptance of his seven notes of true development. Many commentators have argued that these notes are too closely related to the particular issues facing Newman at the time the *Essay* was first written to have universal validity, and so alternative accounts of the development of doctrine have been put forward instead.

3.5.11   Looking at surveys of these accounts in works such as Aidan Nichols' *From Newman to Congar* or Peter Toon's *The Development of Doctrine in the Church*[58] it becomes clear that there are two basic differences between them.

3.5.12   First, there is a difference between those scholars who argue that Christian doctrine has developed in a progressive and evolutionary fashion with later developments building on those that preceded them and those scholars who argue that Christian doctrine has developed in a revolutionary fashion with later developments overthrowing earlier beliefs.[59]

3.5.13   This difference raises both historical and theological issues. Historically the issue is whether the evidence supports the first or second account (or a mixture of the two). Theologically the issue is whether the first account takes sufficiently seriously the fact that the effects of sin may cause Christian theologians to go drastically wrong and need drastic correction and whether the second account takes sufficiently seriously the action of God consistently maintaining the Church in truth.

3.5.14   Secondly, there is a difference between the criteria that scholars propose as means of assessing whether developments are legitimate or not.

3.5.15   For example, Nicholas Lash contends that a 'framework' for understanding the relationship between 'Scripture, history and the authority of today' is provided by the recollection of the saving acts of God at the Eucharist. He notes that

> in the life of the early church, as in the period of the New Testament, those events in the community's past in which it recognized the saving hand of God, or (which amounts to the same thing) which it interpreted as having revelatory significance, were recalled in the present in the conviction that they still spoke to the present (however different that present might be, and therefore however difficult it might be to apply the lessons of the past), and spoke to it of that future, that promise, held out to man in the past by God.[60]

And suggests that this indicates that

it is the church's task in every age to seek so to relate to its past (which means, above all, to its originating moment, definitively witnessed to in the New Testament), as to enable that past, interpreted in the present, effectively to function as a challenge: a challenge to look, and think, and trust, and act in the direction of that future which is promised to us in the New Testament.[61]

3.5.16 Maurice Wiles, on the other hand, suggests in his *The Making of Christian Doctrine* that

the only test of whether the development in question is a true one is for the Church to ask herself repeatedly whether she is expressing as fully as she is able the things to which her Scriptures, her worship and her experience of salvation bear witness.[62]

3.5.17 These two quotations not only illustrate the difference in criteria which was referred to above, but also illustrate a further issue, which is that all the criteria proposed tend to be general in nature and therefore not particularly useful in helping to decide a specific issue such as whether it would be doctrinally acceptable for women to be bishops.

3.5.18 Given the differences between eminent scholars that have just been outlined and the fact that no agreed criteria for assessing the development of doctrine have yet won general acceptance, it might seem rash to put forward another proposal in this area. However, building on the work that has been done on the development of doctrine, we would like to suggest the following.

3.5.19 First, a permissible development is one that is biblically based. Because the Bible forms the basis for Christian doctrine for the reasons discussed earlier in this chapter, any development that is not grounded in Scripture cannot be permissible. In the words of James Orr:

There may be disputes about the authority of Scripture, but there ought to be no dispute about this, that whatever has no place in Scripture, or cannot be legitimately deduced from it, is no part of the truth of revelation for which the Church is set as 'the ground and pillar'. [1 Timothy 3.15][63]

3.5.20 In terms of the debate about the ordination of women as bishops this means that the proposal to allow women to be bishops can only be permissible if it

- Has explicit or implicit support in specific biblical texts.

For example, it has been suggested that the place of women in leadership in the Church is given explicit support by the references to female leaders in texts such as Romans 16.1-16, 1 Corinthians 1.11, Colossians 4.15 and Philippians 4.2-3 and the role of St Mary Magdalene as 'apostle to the apostles' (Luke 24.10, John 20.11-18) and implicit support by what St Paul says about the abolition of the distinction between male and female in Galatians 3.27-28.

- Enables us to make coherent sense of the overall biblical picture of the role of women in the purposes of God.

Thus it has been argued that the story of the creation of Eve in Genesis 1.26-27 and 2.18-25 indicates that according to God's original intention women were not meant to be subordinate to men. Subordination was a result of the fall and has been overturned by Christ in whom women have been given back their equality with men. Having women bishops is appropriate because it reflects this restored equality.

- Takes the logic of the biblical material relating to women and applies it in a new cultural and historical context.

For instance, Kristen Aune maintains in her essay 'Evangelicals and Gender' that:

> The principle used by Jesus and the authors of the New Testament was to work within the societal structures of the time, primarily to aid evangelism, but transform them in the light of the gospel.[64]

Applying this principle today, she says, means accepting women in leadership roles within the Church:

> Given that Western societies enshrine gender equality in law, ministry needs to involve women alongside men at all levels. To forbid women leadership or preaching roles would be to violate Paul's principle and to hinder evangelism.[65]

As she sees it, many people today reject the Church because of what they see as its record of oppressing women and this 'immediately creates a barrier which prevents them from listening to any presentation of the gospel that Christians might give'.[66]

99

3.5.21   All these examples would be challenged by those opposed to the Church of England having women bishops, but what they illustrate is the kind of arguments that have been put forward in order to show that the ordination of women bishops can be seen as a biblically based and therefore theologically permissible development.

3.5.22   Secondly, a permissible development is one that takes tradition seriously. As we have explained, we cannot simply read the biblical text as if there had been no other Christians before us and as if God had not been at work through his Spirit maintaining his Church in truth. God has made us part of a historical community and we have to listen carefully to what God has to say to us through the other members of that community and act accordingly.

3.5.23   In terms of the debate about whether there should be women bishops this means that a permissible development is one that

- Shows awareness of what the traditions of the Church (as manifested in the totality of its life) have to tell us about the role of women in general and the role of women in ordained ministry in particular.

  It is important to note here that *all* the traditions of the Church need to be given due attention. As will be explained in Chapter 5, there is evidence that women were engaged in ordained ministry in the Early Church and that this is an aspect of the traditions of the Church that has subsequently been forgotten or ignored.

  On the other hand, it is also important that marginal traditions are not given disproportionate attention. It could be argued, for instance, that the fact that the ministry of ordained women did not remain part of the mainstream tradition of the Church shows that the Church as a whole was led to the conclusion that this was not an appropriate role for women to occupy.

- Shows that it has understood the reason(s) for the existence these traditions.

  It is not enough simply to note *what* the traditions of the Church have said. Critical reflection on the significance of these traditions also demands an awareness of *why* they said it. For example, if it could be shown that the tradition of having a male-only episcopate was based on a faulty exegesis of the Bible, or on a mistaken belief in female intellectual weakness, or was a response to a specific cultural context which no longer exists, the case that it is a tradition that should be upheld would be weaker than if it could be shown that it was a tradition based on accurate biblical interpretation, a proper estimate of female psychology and a set of theological principles that apply regardless of cultural context.

- Builds on the Church's existing traditions rather than simply rejecting them.

Newman's insistence that in a healthy development of Christian doctrine there has to be continuity in the midst is something that we need to take seriously. If the main theological reason for attending to tradition is a conviction that the Holy Spirit has been at work down the centuries maintaining the Church in truth, it follows that an approach that simply rejects the traditions of the past is theologically questionable. What is required is an approach that is genuinely a *development* of what has gone before.

Orr expresses the matter helpfully:

> I am very far from disputing that there is still room for fresh developments in theology. Existing systems are not final; as works of human understanding they are necessarily imperfect; there is none which is not in some degree affected by the nature of the intellectual environment, and the factors the mind had, at the time of its formation, to work with. I do not question, therefore, that there are still aspects of divine truth to which full justice has not yet been accorded; improvements that can be made in our conception and formulation of all the doctrines, and in their correlation with each other. All I am contending for is, that such a development shall be a development within Christianity and not away from it; that it shall recognize its connection with the past, and unite itself organically with it; and that it shall not spurn the past development, as if nothing of value had been accomplished by it.[67]

In terms of the debate about the ordination of women as bishops, what this means is that it would need to be shown that such a move by the Church of England did have the character of an organic development, that it built on existing traditions in such a way as to be an evolutionary rather than a revolutionary change.

3.5.24 Thirdly, a permissible development is one that takes reason seriously. This means that

- It can be shown in a rational and coherent fashion that such a development is rooted in Scripture and tradition in the ways outlined above.

- Such a development will enable the Church to respond creatively and persuasively to the issues raised by contemporary culture and contemporary Christian experience.

In the case of the debate about the ordination of women bishops, this means that such a development will be one that both builds on Scripture and tradition, and also addresses the belief in our society that equal opportunities for women are a moral good, the conviction of women within the Church of England that they have a vocation to the ordained ministry, and the positive experience of the ministry of women priests in the Church of England over the last decade.

- Such a development will be rooted in an exercise in the corporate seeking of wisdom in which the will of God is discerned by the Church as a whole and will not simply be the result of the victory of one side of the debate in a synodical discussion.

Reception

3.6.1 The last bullet point in the previous section brings us on to the issue of reception, since reception is the name given to the process by which the corporate discernment of the will of God is finally brought to completion. In looking further at the concept of reception the first thing that needs to be noted is that in theological discussion the term 'reception' is used in four ways.

3.6.2 First, it is used to describe the process of assimilation by means of which a development becomes part of the life of the Church.

3.6.3 The term reception was originally used in legal studies to describe the way in which Roman law came to be assimilated into European, and specifically German, law at the end of the Middle Ages.

3.6.4 It then came to be used in the 1970s by Roman Catholic theologians such as Alois Grillmeier and Yves Congar to describe the way in which new developments in the life of the Church, such as the decisions of Ecumenical Councils, the definition of the canon of Scripture, new forms of liturgy, and new forms of law and discipline came to be accepted into the life of the Church and continued to be developed and re-appropriated in the life of the Church thereafter. Grillmeier looked, for example, at the way in which the Christological definition produced by the Council of Chalcedon in 451 came to be accepted as authoritative in the Church and has continued be the basis for further exploration of the mystery of the Incarnation to the present day.[68]

3.6.5   Congar broadened the concept of reception as outlined by Grillmeier.[69] While recognizing with Grillmeier that any act of reception presupposes a certain giving and receiving, Congar stressed that local churches were not autonomous entities but exist in spiritual communion. However, what both Grillmeier and Congar were agreed about was that the old scholastic model of the acceptance of doctrinal and liturgical developments in which a local church simply passively accepted a decision made by a higher authority as an act of obedience was inadequate. Rather, reception was to be seen as an act of active spiritual discernment in which a local church came to perceive on the basis of its own spiritual insight that what was proposed was a legitimate development of the Catholic faith.

3.6.6   In an article published in 1972 Congar describes this way of understanding reception as follows:

> By reception we mean the process by which a church tradition appropriates a truth which has not arisen out of that tradition, but which it yet recognizes and adopts as a formulation of the faith. In the process of reception we understand something other than that which the Scholastics meant by obedience. For them, this was the act whereby a subordinate regulated his will and his conduct according to the legitimate precepts of a superior, out of respect for his/her authority. Reception is not merely the expression of the relationship *secundum et supra*; it includes the active giving of assent, even the exercise of judgement, where the life of a body which draws upon its original spiritual resources is expressed.[70]

3.6.7   The second use of the concept of reception is to describe the acceptance of ecumenical agreements. This use developed because it came to be realized that the understanding of reception that had developed in Roman Catholic theology could be applied to the way in which ecumenical agreements came to be accepted into the life of the churches involved. Thus the American Lutheran William Rusch writes in his 1988 study *Reception: An Ecumenical Opportunity* that ecumenical reception includes

> all phases and aspects of an ongoing process by which a church under the guidance of God's spirit makes the results of a bilateral or a multilateral conversation a part of its faith and life because the results are seen to be in conformity with the teachings of Christ and of the apostolic community, that is, the gospel as witnessed to in Scripture.[71]

3.6.8   The third use of the concept of reception is in biblical studies. A feature of biblical studies in recent years has been a growing interest in what is called 'reception history'. This area of study has built on the theoretical work on the reading of texts undertaken by scholars such as Hans Gadamer[72] and H. R. Jauss[73] and has attempted to supplement the older critical concentration on the original meaning of biblical texts by looking at how they have subsequently been read in the Church and the impact they have had in theology, liturgy, ethics, art and life.[74]

3.6.9   The fourth use of the term, which is a development of the first two we have mentioned, is its use in recent Anglican discussion of the ordination of women. As the quotation from Rusch in 3.6.7 illustrates, in the ecumenical discussion of reception, as in the Roman Catholic discussion which preceded it, the emphasis is still on a process by which a development comes to be accepted. In recent Anglican discussion, however, a slightly different use of the concept has emerged.

3.6.10   In this use of the concept what has come to be called an 'open process of reception' is used to describe a process of discernment by which the rightness or otherwise of a development is considered by the universal Church. Whereas previous uses of reception had described the way in which a development was received, the Anglican use described the process of discernment by which a development could be either accepted or rejected. This use of the term can be seen in the reports of the Eames Commission on the issue of the ordination of women bishops in the Anglican Communion.

3.6.11   The First Report of the Commission declares that:

Once a synodical decision has been made then that necessarily must be respected on all sides as a considered judgement of that particular representative gathering. However, it has always been recognized that councils not only may, but have, erred. Conciliar and synodical decisions would still have to be received and owned by the whole people of God as consonant with the faith of the Church throughout the ages professed and lived today.

In the continuing and dynamic process of reception, freedom and space must be available until a consensus of opinion one way or the other has been achieved.[75]

3.6.12   In similar fashion the Commission's Fourth Report quotes from the *Grindrod Report*, produced by a working party of the Primates of the Anglican Communion, explains:

Whenever a matter is tested by the Church there is necessarily an openness about the question. The continuing communion of Christians with one another in faith and worship maintains the underlying unity of the Church while the reception process is at work. The openness needs to be recognized and accepted by those on both sides of the debate. There needs to be openness to the possibility of the new thing being accepted by the Church or rejected by the Church. It also entails a willingness to live with diversity throughout the 'reception' process.[76]

3.6.13   When the Church of England decided to proceed with ordination of women to the priesthood it did so on the understanding that this decision would be subject to an 'open process of reception' in the sense described by the Eames Commission.

3.6.14   Thus, the second report by the House of Bishops on the ordination of women to the priesthood, published in 1988, states that

many of us have come to recognize the significance of the place of reception in the matter of the ordination of women. They believe that the continuing fellowship of Anglicans with one another in faith and sacramental fellowship by the grace of God will protect the underlying unity of our Communion while the reception process is at work. If, as a result of these debates, the Church of England decides to proceed with the ordination of women, its decision will not be contrary to the guidance of the bishops of the entire Communion as set forth in the resolutions of the 1978 Lambeth Conference.

That decision will still have to be tested in the dioceses of the Church of England. In the course of such testing, sensitivity to those who remain opposed is essential. And care needs to be expressed through detailed safeguards to ensure that people are not forced to accept the ministration of a women against their conscience.

Even if the reception process is completed by the Church of England, the decision still has to be accepted by the entire Anglican Communion and indeed by the universal Church before it can be deemed to be the will of God.[77]

3.6.15   Likewise, the 1993 House of Bishops report *Bonds of Peace* states:

The Church of England made its decision to ordain women to the priestly ministry of the Church of God as one part of the Universal Church using its own decision-making structures, in consultation with the wider Anglican Communion and in knowledge of the different practices of its ecumenical partners. Discernment of the matter is now to be seen within a much broader and longer process of discernment within the whole Church under the Spirit's guidance.

We now enter a process in which it is desirable that both those in favour and those opposed should be recognized as holding legitimate positions while the whole Church seeks to come to a common mind. The Church of England needs to understand itself as a communion in dialogue, committed to remaining together in the ongoing process of the discernment of truth within the wider fellowship of the Christian Church.[78]

3.6.16   What these last two quotations make clear is both that the issue of whether or not the 1992 decision to ordain women priests was the right decision is one that is subject to a continuing process of discussion and discernment, and also that this process will continue until not just the Church of England but the 'whole Church' comes to a common mind about the matter.

3.6.17   The concept of reception as it has been developed in the context of the debates about the ordination of women in the Anglican Communion has been strongly criticized by Peter Toon in his leaflet *Reforming Forwards? – The Doctrine of Reception and the Consecration of Women as Bishops*. Toon argues that in the history of the Church those seeking to justify a theological position or a course of action have traditionally appealed to antiquity. They have appealed to the scriptural witness and to the Church's ancient and unbroken traditions. Reception has meant the process of testing this appeal to antiquity:

> When a council issued its decrees, the people of the Church in their various local jurisdictions were expected to confirm or deny that the members of the council had remained consistent with the received doctrine and practice of the Church. If they confirmed a council, they 'received' it, in the sense that they recognized the council as not having departed from the faith once delivered. This perspective, of course, was based, once again, on the use of the past in evaluating and confirming the present.[79]

3.6.18   However, says Toon, the current Anglican concept of reception is based not on an appeal to sureties of the past, but on an appeal to what might be in the future:

> In its present form, Anglican 'reception' is not an appeal to the sureties of the past, or even to what has been. Instead, it is an appeal to what might be someday, with the associated permission to test or experiment with the proposed possibilities of the future. This kind of 'reception' is, thus, a novelty in itself. It is no longer a 'reformation' (an effort to achieve the original, pristine form). Rather it is a 'reformation forward,' so that the true form of the Church may not have been seen or achieved yet. That is not, however, an eschatological consideration, according to which we are not completely sure of what Christ will make of us. Rather, it is an inversion, an experiment to determine what we will discover of Christ and his Body, the Church.

> In the end, one is faced with this question: Is there justification provided in the Scriptures for a principle of experimentation? No previous effort at reformation or renewal has looked to the future, rather than to the settled past. It may even be said that the reformation forward is contrary to every basic principle of church polity. For the experiment to proceed, it must be permitted by human authority. But until the experiment succeeds, it cannot be known if the human authorities granting permission have the divinely given authority to allow the experiment.[80]

3.6.19   Toon is right to claim that in Christian theology appeal has traditionally been made to the authority of antiquity. In what we have said about Scripture and tradition we have affirmed the importance of this appeal to the past. However, it is not clear that Toon is right to claim that the modern Anglican concept of reception involves an appeal to the future rather than to the past.

3.6.20   Those in the Church of England who have supported the ordination of women have generally argued that their ordination is consistent with the witness of Scripture and tradition. Thus, in his speech opening the General Synod debate on the ordination of women to the priesthood in November 1992, the Bishop of Guildford, Michael Adie, declared: 'the ordination of women is a reasoned development, consonant with Scripture, required by tradition'.[81]

3.6.21   Toon is therefore mistaken when he contends that what is being suggested is that 'whatever is proposed to be received may contradict, overrule, and supplant that which previously has been received'.[82] Rather, what is being suggested is that a particular church which has introduced a development that it believes to be consistent with that which has previously been received should then submit that development to the judgement of the universal Church, with the development being regarded as provisional so that a consensus on the matter may be reached.

3.6.22   Theologically, this form of reception is justified by three factors:

(a) The conviction that a particular church has the right, limited by what has been commanded or forbidden by God, to determine its own polity. This is a conviction that is reflected in Article XXXIV and which is defended by John Jewel in his *Apology for the Church of England.*[83]

(b) An awareness that particular churches can make decisions that are in error (a point made in Article XIX of the Thirty-Nine Articles) even when they think that what they are doing is justified by Scripture, tradition and reason. This awareness then leads to the belief that such decisions need wider examination so that the wisdom of the whole people of God can be brought into play in making a judgement on the matter.

(c) The fact that in our present context of division, in which there is no one body that can speak for the universal Church, the judgement of the whole people of God can only be expressed by means of ecumenical consensus.

3.6.23 Biblically, a parallel with what is proposed in the current Anglican doctrine of reception is provided by the record of the admission of Gentiles to the Church in chapters 10-15 of Acts. In these chapters we find first St Peter and then other Christians preaching the faith to the Gentiles and admitting them to the Church without their needing to become Jews (10.1 – 14.28). This development is then challenged by conservative Jewish Christians from Judea (15.1-5) and the matter is decided by the judgement of a council which is held in Jerusalem but which is seen as representing the Church as a whole (15.6-35).

3.6.24 A further point which needs to be considered in connection with the concept of reception is what it does and does not say about the orders of women priests in the Church of England. As Paul Avis explains, it is

> clearly implied in the open process of the reception of the decision of the Church of England to provide for the ordination of women that the decision could be reappraised. In other words, it is hypothetically reversible. If the General Synod were so minded, it could change its canons to the *status quo ante* 1993, with the result that no more women would be ordained priest after that point.[84]

3.6.25 However, it also needs to be noted that this does not mean that the orders of individual women priests currently ordained in the Church of England are open to question. As Avis goes on to say:

> It is not the ordinations (orders) of individual women clergy that is subject to the process of open reception. They are duly and canonically ordained and are on a par with their male counterparts.[85]

3.6.26 It may sound paradoxical, if not contradictory, to say that the decision to ordain women priests is open to question, but the orders of those women who have been ordained are not. However, this apparent paradox is simply the result of the fact that the Church of England has to act on what it believes to be right at any given time, while at the same time remaining open to the possibility that its decision might in the end be judged unacceptable by the universal Church.

3.6.27 From that perspective it necessarily holds, in line with Canon A 4, that its women priests hold valid orders and can therefore rightly perform those functions in the Church appropriate to their order.[86]

Nevertheless, the Church of England is also aware of its own fallibility, and of only being part of the wider Catholic Church, and is therefore open to having its decisions corrected.

3.6.28   The idea of the provisionality of Church decisions which the Anglican understanding of reception involves is one that many people find difficult. However, what needs to be realized is that it is not a new idea. It is one that is a normal part of the life of churches across the world. Two examples will serve to illustrate this point.

3.6.29   First, in the Orthodox tradition the decisions of a council of the Church cannot be said to have been received until they are ratified by a subsequent council. Until that happens these decisions are, strictly speaking, provisional. However, this does not mean that these decisions are seen as having no value. Rather they are acted upon unless or until a later council decides that they were mistaken.

3.6.30   Secondly, and more familiar to Anglicans, our interpretation of a biblical text may develop or other people may lead us to read the text differently. Anthony Thiselton argues that Christian faith means trusting that God is at work in this process of interpretation, leading us to an understanding of his will for our lives that he will ratify at the last judgement. In his words:

> I entrust my daily life to the consequences and commitments entailed in acts of promise, commission, appointment, address, directive and pledge of love spoken in the name of God or God in Christ in Scripture, even though the definitive corroboration of these linguistic acts awaits final confirmation at the last judgment. Just as sanctification entails a process of transformation into the image of Christ, although through justification I am already 'in Christ', clothed in his righteousness, even so interpretation and understanding of Scripture entails a process of grasping more fully the implications, entailments, nuances, and perhaps further commitments and promises that develop what has been appropriated in faith.[87]

3.6.31   In this context, says Thiselton,

> we need not regard conflicts of interpretation with dismay. For they belong to a broad process of testing, correcting, and initiating readiness for fresh advance, even if from time to time they also enter

blind alleys. But such is the nature of appropriating the gifts and grace of God which is both fallible and bold, touched by sin, yet empowered and directed by the Holy Spirit.[88]

3.6.32   What these examples show us is that it is possible to live with provisionality, and so the provisionality involved in the Anglican understanding of reception does not present us with an insoluble difficulty. Provisionality is simply a necessary result of the fact that the Church is *in via*, a pilgrim people who will one day receive perfect knowledge but who have not received it yet. Provisionality is also a stimulus to humility and trust, humility because it reminds us of our limitations, and trust because it means we have to trust that God will preserve the Church from irreparable error even if it makes mistakes along the way.

3.6.33   No time limit has been set for the process of the reception of the decision to ordain women priests to be concluded, because the fact that reception is a dynamic and open-ended process means that it cannot be arbitrarily halted on a given date. What is clear, however, is that while there is still substantial opposition to or hesitation about the ordination of women both within the Church of England and ecumenically the process of reception is not complete.

3.6.34   It has been suggested by many people that a decision by the Church of England to ordain women bishops would bring an end to the process of reception. The point that they make is that once a decision is made to ordain women bishops the issue of whether it is right to ordain women will be a closed one so far as the Church of England is concerned. This is because the ecclesiology of the Church of England requires that the orders of its bishops are not in doubt and were a process of reception to continue the orders of at least some of its bishops would be in doubt.

3.6.35   Others would disagree with this argument. They would point out that the idea of an open process of reception was developed by the Eames Commission and the *Grindrod Report* precisely in the context of the debate about the ordination of women bishops, and that Resolution III.2 of the 1998 Lambeth Conference called on the churches of the Anglican Communion to uphold the principle of open reception, both in respect of the ordination of women to the priesthood and in respect of the ordination of women to the episcopate.[89]

3.6.36   As they see it, the ordination of women to the episcopate would mark an important step in the reception of the ordination of women within the Church of England. However, the process of reception would not be at an end. Theological consistency would demand that if the decision to ordain women as priests required a process of reception by the universal Church so also would a decision to ordain them as bishops. Just as with the ordination of women to the priesthood, the orders of its women bishops would not be in doubt so far as the Church of England was concerned. Nevertheless, it would still remain open to the possibility that its decision to ordain women bishops might in the end be judged unacceptable by the Church as whole.

3.6.37   The concept of reception raises three issues in respect of the debate about the ordination of women bishops.

(1) Is it right for a particular church to act on its own? Would it not be better for a church to wait for an ecumenical consensus to exist before introducing a development rather than making the development and then seeing whether the development is eventually received?

(2) Would it be right to proceed with the ordination of women as bishops while the process of reception of the decision to ordain women as priests was still continuing?

(3) Would a decision to ordain women as bishops in the Church of England mean the end of the process of reception of the ordination of women, or would theological consistency, as well as adherence to the resolution of the 1998 Lambeth Conference, mean that the process of reception would still need to continue?

In the case of the decision to ordain women priests, the recognition that the Church of England was entering into a process of reception about the matter led to provision being made for those unable to accept the decision on the grounds that their position was still accepted as a legitimate one within the Church and that the process of reception involved living with diversity. The question that will need to be considered in the debate about the ordination of women as bishops is whether, in the event of the Church of England deciding to ordain women bishops, similar provision should not also be made for those unable to accept this decision and, if so, what form this provision should take.

3.6.38   In the final four chapters of this report we shall be looking at the current debate about the ordination of women as bishops in the light of these issues and the other issues considered in this chapter. However, in the next chapter we shall first of all explore the context for the current debate by looking at the development of the ministry of women in the Church of England.

chapter 4

The development of women's ministry in the Church of England

4.1 The place of women in the history of the Church

4.1.1   To anyone who has become sensitized to questions of sexual equality a striking feature of the standard histories of the Church of England is not only the fact that they have been written by men, but also the fact that in them women are largely invisible.

4.1.2   In the index to Stephen Neill's *Anglicanism*, for example, only four women are listed – Elizabeth I, Mary I, Mary II and Queen Victoria[1] – and they are only mentioned because of their roles as reigning monarchs. With these exceptions it looks as though women played no part in the history of the Church.

4.1.3   The index to J. R. H. Moorman's *A History of the Church in England* does better. It has 25 women listed. However, this represents a tiny minority of the several hundred names listed and seven of those listed were queens. The overall picture of the under-representation of women remains the same.[2]

4.1.4   In seeking to explain why women are largely invisible in these histories it would be possible to follow the argument put forward by Gillian Cloke in her book *This Female Man of God: Women and Spiritual Power in the Patristic Age AD 350–450*[3] that the fact that Church history has largely been written by men means that it reflects a male perspective. Looked at in this light the reason why Neill and Moorman do not mention women more frequently is because as male historians they were simply unaware of the role women have played in the history of the English Church.

4.1.5   This would, however, be too simplistic an explanation. Stephen Neill, for example, was a fine historian who was, in fact, well aware of the presence of women in the life of the Church of England down the centuries, and in the Epilogue to his work he notes with cautious approval the early moves towards the ordination of women in the

Anglican Communion.[4] The reason he does not mention women more frequently is that *Anglicanism*, like most other traditional histories of the Church of England and the Anglican Communion, focuses on the activities of the bishops, statesmen and theologians who have shaped the development of the Anglican tradition and these have almost without exception been men.

4.1.6 The fact that women have not exercised positions of leadership throughout most of the history of the Church of England does not mean, however, that they did not play their own part in the life of the Church of England and the development of its history. As recent works such as Sean Gill's *Women and the Church of England*[5] are beginning to remind us, women have played a central role in the life of the Church. It is simply that their role has for the most part been separate and distinct from the role played by men and has been overlooked in the Church of England's written history.

4.1.7 If we ask what role women have sought to play in the history of the Church of England the first answer is that to a large extent they have sought to be faithful daughters, wives and mothers. Throughout the centuries women have prayed, read their bibles, attended church, looked after their families (often working outside the home as well to make ends meet) and sought to raise their children in the love and fear of the Lord. This form of domestic discipleship is one that is not as characteristic of women's lives as it used to be, but since it is rooted in the creation narratives in Genesis 1–3 and firmly endorsed elsewhere in Scripture (see for example Proverbs 31.10-31, Ephesians 5.21-33, 1 Peter 3.1-7) it is one that ought not to be overlooked or disparaged.

4.1.8 The second answer is that women have sought to fulfil their vocation in the context of a variety of other roles as well. For example, women have been religious benefactors to churches and other religious institutions, mystics, hymn writers, martyrs, evangelists, missionaries, tract writers, catalysts for social reform such as Florence Nightingale and Josephine Butler, and, as reigning monarchs, supreme governors. They have also had a vital role as the faithful mainstay of many congregations, enabling the daily life of worship to be maintained while men have been at work.

4.1.9 All the women who exercised these various roles played their part in the history of the Church of England and that part was vitally important. As Cecilia Ady notes:

> From the earliest times women have taken their share of Church
> work; much of it indeed has been traditionally women's work.
> Women in every age have been primarily responsible for the care
> of the sick and the poor and the training of children in the Christian
> faith. Without their co-operation there is hardly a parish in the
> Church of England of which the work could at any time have been
> carried on.[6]

4.1.10   However, until the latter part of the nineteenth century the
only roles for women that were officially recognized by the Church
of England were the domestic role, the calling of midwives to baptize
babies who were in danger of imminent death, membership of a
religious community, or the role of supreme governor. With the
exception of female monarchs, women had no role in the
government of the Church and they were not permitted to
be part of the ordained ministry.

4.2 The development of the ordained ministry of women in the Church of England

4.2.1   The development that led to this situation changing can be seen
to have begun with the revival of religious communities for women in
the Church of England in the 1840s. These communities, the first of
which was founded at Park Village West in London in 1845, had a dual
focus. They were intended to provide women both with the opportunity
for a dedicated life of prayer and with the opportunity to undertake
organized charitable activity among the poor and needy.

4.2.2   As Gill argues, the significance of the existence of these
Anglican female religious communities, or 'sisterhoods' as they were
known, was that they provided an alternative model of vocation for
women that challenged the inevitability of the domestic role:

> even though their numbers were small, both for the women who
> dedicated themselves to the religious life and for the example that
> they gave to their society, the sisterhoods had a significance out of
> all proportion to their numbers. At the time of their creation, so
> powerful was the Victorian ideology of married domesticity and
> compulsory motherhood for middle- and upper-class women, that
> those who either chose not to marry or who increasingly were unable
> to do so for demographic reasons could be labelled as 'redundant',
> and suggestions made that such women might be shipped like surplus
> merchandise to the colonies. By contrast, sisterhoods upheld the

ideal of voluntarily chosen celibacy as worthwhile for women, and offered an example of a life lived in community in which the highest ideals of holiness were combined with a practical outreach of Christian love and charity that encouraged women to do meaningful and significant work.[7]

4.2.3   The need to provide an organized context for women to exercise a religious vocation and to engage in charitable work also led to the establishment of the order of deaconess in the Church of England from the 1860s onwards.

4.2.4   This began in 1861 with the foundation of the Deaconess Community of St Andrew by Elizabeth Ferard with the support of the then Bishop of London, Archibald Tait. As Brian Heeny notes, although the creation of a female diaconate in the Church of England can be seen to have been influenced by the Lutheran order of deaconesses which had been founded at Kaiserwerth in Germany 1836, it was also seen as a revival of an order of ministry that had existed in the Early Church:

> It was seen as a re-establishment of an ancient order, a revival under contemporary conditions and discipline of the function apparently once held by Phoebe in the Apostolic Church and confirmed later on in the Church both East and West, although subsequently dropped in medieval times.[8]

Deaconesses worked in the parishes under the authority of the parish clergy and were an officially recognized part of the Church's ministry, although the question of whether they were in Holy Orders was left unclear.[9]

4.2.5   Alongside the order of deaconesses there had also developed by the end of the nineteenth century other forms of lay women's ministry recognized by the Church such as the work of parochial women missioners and Church Army Sisters.[10]

4.2.6   By the beginning of the twentieth century there were therefore several hundred women who were officially employed as full-time church workers and in addition thousands of women were engaged in various forms of church work on a voluntary basis.

4.2.7   Women were not permitted to be ordained as bishops, priests or deacons and in 1897 the Convocations had voted to bar women from serving on the new Parochial Church Councils, a decision that was not reversed until 1914.[11] Nevertheless, the fact that women were working for the Church in this country and also serving as missionaries overseas,[12] together with the general change in social attitudes to the role of women within wider society, inevitably raised the question of whether women ought not to be admitted to the Church's traditional threefold order of ministry.

4.2.8   As the twentieth century progressed, women came to enjoy ever greater opportunities in the spheres of education and employment and, after a long campaign by the suffragette movement, women over thirty were given the vote in 1918 and all women were given the vote in 1928.[13] These social changes were the result of developments in the place of women in society that had begun to take place from the mid-Victorian period onwards as a result of the so called 'first wave' of feminism challenging the ideology of domesticity and compulsory motherhood mentioned above. However, as Elaine Storkey notes in her study *Created or Constructed – The Great Gender Debate*, they accelerated after World War I, partly in response to the fact that so many young men had been killed.

> Thousands of women lost their husbands, fiancés and sweethearts and were never to marry again. It is no coincidence that the 1920s in Britain saw an upsurge in spiritualist interest among women as they tried to contact the dead. But, more usefully, it also saw the burgeoning of new openings for women in the professions. Certainly, women were now educated for these roles, but there was also the necessity of ordering a society in a way that did not require equal numbers of marriageable men and women in the population. Consequently, the growth in women's education, the opening up of the professions and the acceptance that a single woman no longer had to be economically dependent on her male relatives all brought an excess of women into areas of work which had previously been the sole preserve of men.[14]

In the face of these changes the question of why women could not be admitted to the ministry in the same way as they had been admitted to the universities, the professions and parliament was one that could not be avoided.

4.2.9   Campaigning groups such as the League of the Church Militant and the Anglican Group for the Ordination of Women (AGOW), led by women such as Maude Royden,[15] Betty Ridley and Lady Stansgate, started to raise this issue in the years between the wars with the assistance of sympathetic male clergy such as Canon Charles Raven and the Dean of St Paul's, W. R. Matthews.

4.2.10   However, in spite of their efforts, a series of reports from the Church of England and resolutions from Lambeth Conferences continued to rule out the possibility of women being ordained into the traditional threefold Order.

4.2.11   In 1917 the Archbishop of Canterbury appointed a committee (which had only one woman member!) to consider 'the sanctions and restrictions which govern the ministrations of women in the life of the Church and status and work of deaconesses'. This committee reported in 1919 and presented an exhaustive historical survey of the evidence relating to the ministry of women in the New Testament and the subsequent history of the Church.

4.2.12   While the report did not specifically rule out the ordination of women as priests it argued that there was a lack of biblical and historical precedent for this move.

4.2.13   With regard to the New Testament evidence the report concluded:

> The historic Ministry of the Church of Christ has been transmitted through the male sex from the days of the Apostles. The restriction of the priesthood may have been due to the fact that in those times women would not have been entrusted with official posts of public administration; it may have been due to the influence of Jewish usage in the Temple and Synagogue; it may have been due to the recognition of fundamental differences in function and calling inherent in the natural variety of sex. It is not our province to discuss these questions. We simply record the fact that the restriction of the Ministry of the priesthood to men originated in a generation which was guided by the special gifts of the Holy Spirit. The evidence of the New Testament is the evidence of that generation.[16]

4.2.14   With regard to the evidence from Church history the report declared:

> We find no evidence for the admission of women to the priesthood. Save among heretical or obscure sects, there have been no Christian priestesses.[17]

4.2.15   However, the report also went on to say:

> this is not to say that women have never been admitted to any form of Holy Orders, still less that they have not been allowed to take part in the formal liturgical services of the Church, or that they have had no power in things ecclesiastical. The deaconess, the abbess, and the churches of women religious, whether nuns or canonesses, afford irrefutable evidence to the contrary.[18]

4.2.16   The report noted the development of women's ministries in the Church of England mentioned earlier in this chapter, and although it offered no definite conclusions it seemed to see these as offering the way forward for ministry by women in the Church.

4.2.17   In 1920 Resolution 48 of the Lambeth Conference declared that

> The order of deaconesses is for women the one and only order of the ministry which has the stamp of apostolic approval, and is for women the only order of the ministry which we can recommend that our branch of the Catholic Church should recognize and use.[19]

4.2.18   In 1930 the Lambeth Conference was asked for an enquiry into the reasons why it was said to be impossible for women to be ordained as priests. The Conference recognized the need for further theological work on the matter, but reiterated the argument that the ordination of women as priests was simply not possible.

4.2.19   The Conference report notes that a majority of the sub-committee set up to consider the issue

> believes that that there are theological principles which constitute an insuperable obstacle to the admission of women to the Priesthood, apart from all considerations of expediency. Others who do not agree with them on the matter of principle see grave difficulties of a practical nature in the way of such admission.[20]

4.2.20   Like the previous Lambeth Conference, the Conference of 1930 saw the development of the Order of Deaconesses, 'distinct from and complementary to the historic Orders of the Church',[21] as the way forward for the ministry of women in the Anglican Communion.

4.2.21 In 1935 an Archbishops' Commission of the Church of England was set up to look in more detail at the question of the ministry of women. Its conclusions were both positive and negative.

4.2.22 Positively it concluded that deaconesses were in Holy Orders, and should be recognized as members of the clergy:

> We are ... convinced that for all religious and ecclesiastical purposes she ought to be regarded and described as a person who is in Holy Orders, even though there may be situations (as, for instance, when the relation of the deaconesses to the civil law is involved) in which the use of the phrase will create difficulties. Though the Order of Deaconesses is not in our opinion precisely parallel to any of the three orders open to men, we nevertheless think that it is among the clergy and not among the laity that the deaconess ought to be ranked.[22]

It argued that deaconesses should have an appropriate liturgical role, including baptizing and preaching, and it expressed the hope that deaconesses and women lay workers would receive greater acceptance in the Church:

> The Commission hope that clergy and laity will unite in welcoming women to more definite status in the Church and so enable their work to attain its full and natural development.[23]

4.2.23 Negatively, with W. R. Matthews as the one significant dissenting voice, the Commission concluded that the Order of Deaconesses was the only existing Holy Order for women, and that it was not right for women to be ordained to the orders of bishop, priest or deacon:

> While the Commission as a whole would not give their positive assent to the view that a woman is inherently incapable of receiving the grace of Order, and consequently of admission to any of the three Orders, we believe that the general mind of the Church is still in accord with the continuous tradition of a male priesthood. It is our conviction that this consensus of tradition and opinion is based on the will of God and is, for the Church of today, a sufficient witness to the guidance of the Holy Spirit. We are therefore of the opinion

that the case for a change in the Church's rule has not been made out. The theological justification offered in support of such a change does not appear to us to be convincing, nor do we believe that the objections to the admission of women to the traditional Orders are mere prejudices based on outworn notions of the relations of men and women to one another.[24]

4.2.24   For over fifty years after the 1935 Commission the position in the Church remained the same. There was scope for women to exercise ministry in the Church as deaconesses, lay workers, Church Army Sisters and, from 1969, Readers. They could also take part in the national government of the Church as members of the Church Assembly. What was not possible was for women to be ordained as bishops, priests or deacons.[25]

4.2.25   The continuing ambivalence of the Church about the status of deaconesses is clearly shown by the Canons which, in spite of the conclusion of the 1935 Commission that deaconesses should be seen as clergy rather than laity, had one section dealing with those in 'holy orders' and a separate section which dealt with deaconesses. As the 1966 Church of England report *Women and Holy Orders* put the matter:

> A deaconess is 'ordained'. She receives 'character'. She is dedicated to a 'life long service'. She is a member of an ordained ministry. She is in 'a Holy Order'. But she is not in 'Holy Orders'.[26]

4.2.26   However, the fact that nothing officially happened did not mean that nothing changed. During this fifty years the roles exercised by women in wider society continued to grow as the social changes noted in 4.2.8 continued.

4.2.27   In the years immediately after World War II there was a return to traditional attitudes about the roles of women and men. To quote Storkey again:

> Being allowed to be homemakers, and continue as homemakers long after children had left home, was experienced as liberation for those [women] who had been required to go out to work during the war. The emphasis on the male breadwinner was reinforced by the media, by schools, and by public policies. Education programmes made some nod towards the need to equip women for dual careers of motherhood and work, but by and large, work was seen along

strong lines of gender demarcation. Gender history was put on hold, and those who were Christianly inclined saw those roles as laid down by God.[27]

However, as Storkey goes on to say:

> the status quo would not hold for long. The assumption that there was an unbroken line of fixed sex and gender roles from the garden of Eden to the middle of the twentieth century was soon going to be shattered.[28]

4.2.28 As Adrian Hastings notes in his *A History of English Christianity 1920–1985*, the 1960s were marked by

> a crisis of the relevance (or capacity for sheer survival) of long-standing patterns of thought and institution of all sorts in a time of intense, and rather self-conscious, modernization.[29]

4.2.29 Among those things that were questioned were the traditional attitudes about the roles of men and women outlined by Storkey. Just as the 'first wave' of feminists in the Victorian period had challenged the prevalent thinking about the role of women in their day, so also the 'second wave' of feminists in the 1960s, including such seminal figures as Betty Friedan and Germaine Greer, challenged the idea of women as primarily housewives and mothers that was prevalent in the 1950s. The feminist movement of the 1960s was a diverse movement that embraced people with many different ideas, but a key emphasis of the movement was its stress on the essential similarity of men and women in spite of the biological differences between them. In Storkey's words, the feminist argument was that:

> Biology did not provide any framework for understanding what was essential in human relationships. In fact, if anything was seen to be essential in the relation between male and female, it was a common humanity, and that highlighted the need for mutual justice and equality.

> The new perspective moved away from biological reductionism, and once old assumptions about the primacy of biology were discarded, all kinds of new possibilities were opened up. Instead of being hung up on their differences, we could look at *similiarities* between women and men. For men and women are really quite alike. They reflect one another in all kinds of characteristics, capabilities,

intellect or stamina. Men organize, women organize; women teach, men teach; men heal the sick, women heal the sick. It was simply that women in the past had not been given the chance to develop their assets as fully and freely as they could. But once they did, and women were given equality in law, education and training, they would have access to roles normally occupied by men. Then we would see the gender-segregated structure of society begin to collapse.[30]

4.2.30   The idea that women should be given equal rights and opportunities alongside men was reflected in the *Equal Pay Act* of 1970 which required that women and men should be given equal pay for equal work and the *Sex Discrimination Act* of 1975 which outlawed discrimination on the basis of sex or marital status in employment, education and other areas of life. The latter act also established the Equal Opportunities Commission with the remit of working towards the elimination of discrimination and the promotion of opportunity between men and women.

4.2.31   Today, some thirty years after the passing of this legislation, there is still debate as to how far the goal of equality of rights and opportunity between men and women has been achieved. There are those who would maintain that the way in which society is structured still poses specific problems for women and prevents them from achieving their full potential. There are also those who would argue that the attempt to produce equality between women and men has in itself caused social harm. What is clear, however, is that the idea of equal rights and opportunities for women is now one that has become very widely accepted. This has in turn meant that the Church of England's restrictions on women occupying ministerial office have increasingly put it at odds with the prevailing ethos of our society.

4.2.32   These social changes affected those in the Church of England alongside everyone else, and inside the Church of England the ministry of women became evermore widespread and accepted. In addition, women were ordained in other churches[31] and in other parts of the Anglican Communion.[32] In the light of all these factors the pressure for the negative verdict of 1935 to be reconsidered continued to grow.

4.2.33   The result was a succession of Church of England reports on women and ministry:

CA 1617   *Women and Holy Orders* (1966)

GS 104   *The Ordination of Women to the Priesthood* (1972)

GS Misc 88   *The Ordination of Women* (1978)

GS Misc 198   *The Ordination of Women to the Priesthood: Further Report* (1984)

None of these reports ruled out the ordination of women but they were all cautious about whether the time was right for the Church of England to move in this direction.

4.2.34   For example, the 1966 report from which we have already quoted focused on the question of whether it would be right for the Church of England to ordain women as priests. It deliberately refrained from taking a position and instead set out the case for the ordination of women to the priesthood, the case against, and the case for what it calls a 'third view', that while it was not impossible for women to be ordained as priests there were good reasons for the Church of England not doing so at that particular time.

4.2.35   There was also a succession of debates in Church Assembly and General Synod. However the role of women in the Church remained the same.

4.2.36   In 1975 General Synod passed the motion: 'That this Synod considers that there are no fundamental objections to the ordination of women to the priesthood', but it did not pass a second motion asking for the legal barriers to women's ordination to be removed and legislation to permit their ordination to be brought forward.

4.2.37   In 1978 the motion:

> That this Synod asks the Standing Committee to prepare and bring forward legislation to remove the barriers to the ordination of women to the priesthood and their consecration to the episcopate

was passed by the House of Bishops and the House of Laity, but was lost in the House of Clergy by 94 votes to 149.

4.2.38   From 1984 onwards, however, things began to change. In November of that year General Synod debated the motion:

> That this Synod asks the Standing Committee of General Synod to
> bring forward legislation to permit the ordination of women to the
> Priesthood in the Provinces of Canterbury and York.

4.2.39   This time there was a majority in all three Houses in favour
of the motion and the work of preparing the necessary legislation
began. As part of this process two reports were published. GS 764
*The Ordination of Women to the Priesthood: A Report by the House
of Bishops* was published in 1987 and GS 829 *The Ordination of
Women to the Priesthood: A Second Report by the House of Bishops*,
which contained further reflection on the theological issues involved,
was published the following year.

4.2.40   While the legislation for the ordination of women as priests
was being prepared, General Synod voted in July 1986 to permit
women to be ordained as deacons. For the first time women were
permitted to be part of one of the historic threefold orders of ministry
in the Church of England and the first women deacons were duly
ordained the following year.

4.2.41   In July 1988 General Synod gave general approval to draft
legislation to enable women to be ordained as priests in the Church of
England and after further discussion in the dioceses (where 38 out of 44
Diocesan Synods voted in favour) in General Synod and in Convocation
the measure to permit women to be ordained as priests was debated by
General Synod on 11 November 1992.

4.2.42   After an extensive debate the measure received the necessary
two thirds majority in all three Houses.[33] Synod also approved a
measure providing for financial provision for clergy who resigned
their offices over the issue of women's ordination.

4.2.43   In January 1993 the House of Bishops issued a statement
following its meeting in Manchester (the 'Manchester Statement').
This statement reaffirmed the theology of open reception which we
looked at in the last chapter:

> We all recognize that the vote of the General Synod must be seen
> as part of a wider process within the Church of England, within the
> Anglican Communion and within the universal Church in which the
> question of women's ordination to the priesthood is being tested.

> ... The Synod's decision expresses the mind of the majority of the Church of England insofar as this can be ascertained, and (if it is confirmed by Parliament) will determine our canonical position as a Church in which women are ordained to the priesthood. We recognize, however, that there are those who doubt the theological and/or ecclesiological basis of the decision, and we accept that these are views which will continue to be held within the Church of England, and that those who hold them remain valued and loyal members of the Anglican family. At the same time as we affirm that differing views about the ordination of women to the priesthood can continue to be held with integrity within the Church of England, we encourage a willingness on the part of all to listen with respect to the views of those from whom they differ, and to afford a recognition of the value and integrity of each other's position within the Church.[34]

On this basis it committed itself to 'accommodating a diversity of convictions, particularly in matters relating to the Church's sacramental life', while also maintaining the unity of the Church.[35] The House built upon the principles set out in the Manchester Statement in the report *Bonds of Peace* in June 1993 in which it set out pastoral arrangements for those who could not accept the ministry of women priests in a draft Act of Synod.

4.2.44   In the light of these pastoral arrangements proposed by the House, the Ecclesiastical Committee of the Houses of Parliament found the measure expedient and it subsequently received Parliamentary approval in both Houses. The measure received Royal Assent on 5 November 1993.[36]

4.2.45   *The Episcopal Ministry Act of Synod*[37] was approved by the General Synod on 11 November 1993 by a decisive margin in all three Houses.[38] It was duly proclaimed an Act of Synod by the General Synod on 22 February 1994, the same day that the Canon formally allowing the ordination of women priests was promulged.

4.2.46   Under the measure permitting the ordination of women priests parishes were allowed to vote for resolutions A or B declaring that they would not accept either a woman priest celebrating Holy Communion or pronouncing absolution or a woman as their incumbent, and similar provision was made for cathedrals.[39]

4.2.47   The Act of Synod went further. It was based on three principles:

(i)   discernment in the wider Church of the rightness or otherwise of the Church of England's decision to ordain women to the priesthood should be as open a process as possible;

(ii)   the highest possible degree of communion should be maintained within each diocese; and

(iii)   the integrity of differing beliefs and positions concerning the ordination of women to the priesthood should be mutually recognized and respected.[40]

In order to reflect these principles the Act did three things:

- It laid down that there should be no discrimination against candidates, 'either for ordination or for appointment to senior office in the Church of England' on the grounds of 'their views or positions about the ordination of women to the priesthood'.[41]

- Whilst maintaining the canonical position that the diocesan bishop has jurisdiction within his diocese,[42] it allowed parishes opposed to the ordination of women priests to apply to their diocesan bishop for extended episcopal care by a bishop of their persuasion whom their diocesan would invite to function within his diocese.

- It made provision for the ordination, licensing and institution of women priests in dioceses where the diocesan bishop was opposed to the ordination of women priests.

4.2.48   The Provincial Episcopal Visitors or PEVs (popularly known as 'flying bishops') were established by the Act of Synod as one way in which extended episcopal care might be provided, the other two ways being through the establishment of a regional scheme or through arrangements made internally within a diocese.

4.2.49   As we shall see in more detail in Chapter 6, in a series of letters from 1975–86 Pope Paul VI, Pope John Paul II and Cardinal Willebrands warned Archbishop Donald Coggan and Archbishop Robert Runcie that a decision by the Church of England to ordain women as priests would have a seriously harmful effect on the development of

Anglican–Roman Catholic relations.[43] Despite these warnings, and the known opposition of the Orthodox and Oriental Orthodox churches to the ordination of women,[44] in the end it was felt that Roman Catholic and Orthodox opposition should not be seen as a sufficient reason for the Church of England not to take this decision.

4.3 The situation today

4.3.1   All the necessary legislation having been passed, the first women priests in the Church of England were ordained at Bristol Cathedral on 12 March 1994.[45] Research indicates that ten years later the decision to ordain women priests has the support of the majority of people within the Church. For example, in his recent study *Women and the Priesthood in the Church of England ten years on*, Ian Jones writes:

> a clear majority of clergy and lay respondents in the current survey agree with the Church of England's decision of 1992 to ordain women as priests. In the case studies considered here, agreement/strong agreement with women's ordination as priests currently runs above seventy per cent of clergy (and in some deaneries clergy support is virtually unanimous). If surveys of the case study congregations are at all representative, levels of agreement among Anglican laity are very often even higher.[46]

4.3.2   Since 1994 there has also been a steady increase in the number of women ordained in the Church of England. The latest available figures (for 2002) tell us that there are now 1262 stipendiary women clergy serving in dioceses in the Church of England.[47] In addition over 700 women have been ordained as NSM or OLM clergy since 1994.[48] Of those now entering training for the priesthood about half are women.

4.3.3   Some of the ordained women in the Church of England are deacons (either transitional or permanent) but most are priests. Of those who are priests many are now in charge of parishes or churches within team ministries. A number of these are now rural or area deans, four are currently archdeacons and two are deans. In addition a substantial number of women have diocesan responsibilities or serve in various forms of sector ministry.

4.3.4   The ordination of women as deacons and priests has brought the Church of England into line with other Anglican provinces who have women deacons and priests and other churches which ordain women ministers. However, it means it now differs from other Anglican provinces who have not ordained women and from those churches, most notably the Orthodox and Roman Catholic churches, who continue to regard the ordination of women as theologically unacceptable.

4.3.5 Although the long campaign for the ordination of women as priests in the Church of England might thus seem to have reached a successful conclusion, there are many in the Church, led by groups such as Women and the Church (WATCH) and the Group for the Rescinding of the Act of Synod (GRAS), who feel that there is further to go before the ministry of women is fully accepted and established in the Church of England. They highlight two issues in particular which they feel need to be addressed.

4.3.6 The first issue is the continuing existence of the Act of Synod. GRAS and those who think like them argue that it ought to be abolished. They point out what they see as the following problems:

- It is theologically anomalous and inconsistent with Canon A 4 to allow the ministrations of some Anglican priests and bishops not to be accepted by other members of the Church of England.

- It both discriminates against women by creating 'no-go areas' for women priests and serves to marginalize those opposed to the ordination of women. In both these ways it is destructive of the communion between Christians which should be at the heart of the Church's life.

- By entrenching division between women and men it hinders the Church from addressing the wider issue of how to create new forms of relationship between them that makes full use of the distinctive gifts that both sexes have to offer.

- It perpetuates a situation in which people may continue to foster opposition within the Church to women's ordination.[49]

4.3.7 All of these criticisms really apply to the 1993 measure and not simply to the Act of Synod. It was the measure that allowed members of the Church of England not to accept the ministrations of some Anglican priests, and created the possibility of 'no-go' areas for women priests. What the Act of Synod did was to develop the fundamental principles set out in the measure. It should also be noted that the Act of Synod prevented entire dioceses becoming 'no-go areas' for women priests by making provision for them in dioceses where the diocesan bishop was unwilling to ordain, license or institute them.

4.3.8 Nevertheless, the fact remains that GRAS and others see the present situation in the Church of England as unsatisfactory for the reasons listed above and the issue of whether their criticisms should be directed at the measure as well as the Act of Synod is to this extent beside the point. Their problems remain, regardless of where they originated.

4.3.9 The second issue is the fact that although women can be deacons or priests they still cannot be bishops in the Church of England. The 1993 measure which permitted women to be ordained as priests states explicitly:

> Nothing in this Measure shall make it lawful for a woman to be consecrated to the office of bishop.[50]

4.3.10 Although it can be argued that this limitation was a contributory factor to the measure being passed by General Synod, for a large number of people in the Church of England it is nevertheless unacceptable. As they see it the agenda the Church ought to be pursuing is the one set out in the failed 1978 Synod motion which called for women to be ordained both to the priesthood and the episcopate. As we shall see in more detail in Chapter 5 of this report, the main reasons they give in support of this position are the following:

- The theological logic that made it right for women to be ordained as priests also makes it right for them to be ordained as bishops.

- Women priests have exercised a valuable ministry in the life of the Church and there are now senior and experienced women who ought to be allowed to exercise their undoubted gifts as bishops.

- As long as women cannot be bishops women priests will inevitably be seen as somehow 'second class'.

- In our society the existence of a 'glass ceiling' that discriminates against women undermines the credibility of the Church and its message.

- The fact that the Church of England does not have women bishops means that it differs from the Anglican provinces (Canada, New Zealand and the United States) who have them, two of the Lutheran churches of the Porvoo agreement (Sweden and Norway) who likewise have them, and other ecumenical partners such as the Methodist Church for whom the equal openness of all ministries to both women and men is a non-negotiable principle.

4.3.11 It also needs to be borne in mind, however, that, as the voting figures in November 1992 made clear, the decision to ordain women as priests was by no means unanimous. A substantial minority within the Church felt that either this was not the right decision to make, or that it was not the right time at which to make it, or that the General Synod of the Church of England did not have the theological authority to make it in isolation from other churches with which the historic ministry is shared.

4.3.12 Furthermore, since the ordination of women as priests this opposition has not died away. To quote Jones again:

> if those who were uncertain of their position in 1992 have generally tended to move towards strong agreement with the decision, a significant minority (perhaps fifteen to twenty per cent in some cases) continue to remain firmly unconvinced that the right step was taken.[51]

The continuing opposition to women priests is reflected in the fact that 810 parishes have passed resolution A, 980 have passed resolution B (6.3 per cent and 7.6 per cent of Church of England parishes respectively) and 315 parishes (2.4 per cent of Church of England parishes) have been granted some form of extended episcopal care.[52] We need also to recognize that a number of clergy and lay people have left the Church of England over this issue.

4.3.13 The picture is of course more complex than these figures indicate, since there are individuals within these parishes who do not support the parochial decision and would be happy with a women priest, while on the other hand there may be individuals outside such parishes who remain opposed to women priests but whose parishes do not take the same view.[53]

4.3.14 There is also a continuing flow of ordinands from both the Catholic and the Evangelical traditions who are opposed to the ordination of women, and a number of women who feel that it is more appropriate to exercise ministry within the Church as permanent deacons or in some form of lay ministry.[54]

4.3.15   As the 2001 House of Bishops report on working of the Act of Synod explains, the provision of extended episcopal care has been made in a number of different ways, although the majority of dioceses have put in place provincial arrangements involving the use of the Provincial Episcopal Visitors:

> judging by the responses to diocesan questionnaires ... the majority of diocesan bishops – twenty five – have made wholly provincial arrangements. Eleven have made arrangements either wholly or partly within the diocese, though of these five are shared with regional or provincial arrangements, leaving Blackburn, London, Newcastle, Winchester and York as the only dioceses where provision is made wholly from within the diocese. (It should be noted that in the Diocese of Oxford where the PEV is an Assistant Bishop, this is interpreted as a 'Diocesan arrangement'.) Regional arrangements are functioning in seven dioceses, though in two cases these are shared with provincial cover. The remaining schemes are the reciprocal ones between the dioceses of Carlisle and Sodor and Man, and that between the Dioceses of Chichester and Guildford, and the regional cover provided by the Bishop of Fulham in the Dioceses of Rochester and Southwark.[55]

It should be noted that the 2001 report reflects the situation when it was written. The precise way in which extended episcopal care is provided is subject to change as bishops move and retire and new bishops are appointed.

4.3.16   Just as WATCH and GRAS campaign on behalf of those who support the ordination of women to the priesthood and wish them to be ordained to the episcopate as well, so also there are groups who campaign on behalf of those who take the opposite point of view. The two most prominent of these are Forward in Faith on the Anglo-Catholic side and Reform on the Evangelical side. These two groups continue to argue that the Church of England made the wrong decision in 1992 and that ordaining women as bishops would only compound the problem.

4.3.17   As we shall see in more detail in the next chapter, those who take this position bring forward, amongst other arguments, the following:

- The theological logic that made it inappropriate for women to be ordained as priests would make it even more inappropriate for them to be ordained as bishops.

- When women were ordained as priests it was agreed that there should be a period of 'reception' in which the rightness or otherwise of that decision could be discerned by the Church. This period of reception is still taking place and therefore it would be inappropriate to take the further step of ordaining women as bishops.

- The place of bishops within Anglican ecclesiology means that if women were ordained as bishops it would be difficult to see how those opposed to women's ordination could continue to exist within the Church of England.

- Ordaining women as bishops would be missiologically damaging as it would contribute to an increasingly feminized Church that would be even less able to attract men, particularly young men, than at present.

- Individual provinces of the Church do not have the authority to change the Catholic orders of the universal Church without the ecumenical agreement which is currently lacking.

- Ordaining women as bishops would lead the Church of England to differ from those provinces within the Anglican Communion who do not have women bishops and would further damage ecumenical relationships with those churches, such as the Orthodox and Roman Catholic churches, in which, as we have noted, the ordination of women is not accepted.

4.3.18   Those opposed to the ordination of women as priests (and others who are sympathetic to the situation in which they find themselves) argue that the existence of resolutions A and B and the provision of extended episcopal care have been valuable in allowing them to retain a place within the life of the Church of England. They are therefore keen to ensure that they remain in place and oppose any calls for their abolition.

4.3.19   It has also been argued, however, that if women were to be ordained as bishops the existing arrangements would no longer give effective provision to those opposed to the ordination of women, and that therefore some alternative arrangements would need to be put in place in order to meet their needs. The creation of a Third Province with its own bishops and parochial structure has been widely canvassed in this connection, but as we shall see in Chapter 7, there are a number of other possibilities that might also be considered.

4.3.20   A further issue which has also been raised is whether the ordination of women as bishops would have the effect of obscuring the need for a wider debate about the proper relationship between men and women in the Church. The argument goes that if women were ordained as bishops the tendency would be to think that the question of the place of women in the Church had been 'solved' while ignoring the fact that women would still be operating within paradigms for ministry constructed by and for men which prevent the full flourishing of both women and men in the Church. We shall look at this in more detail in the next chapter.

chapter 5

Can it be right in principle for women to be consecrated as bishops in the Church of England?

5.1 Introduction

5.1.1   In this chapter we shall first of all look at the arguments that have been put forward for retaining the current stance of the Church of England. We shall then look at the arguments that have been put forward for ordaining women as bishops in the Church of England.

5.1.2   It should be noted that the order of sections 2 and 3 of this chapter does not indicate a preference either for or against the ordination of women as bishops. In the nature of the case one of these sections had to come first, and the choice of the present order is a matter of chronology. The current position of the Church of England is not to ordain women as bishops and so it seems fair to begin with the arguments of those who want to maintain this position before then going on to look at the arguments of those who want to change it.

5.1.3   Those who are in favour of the ordination of women as bishops may find it frustrating to have to work through the arguments of those on the other side of the debate before reaching the arguments for their own side. What needs to be borne in mind, however, is that if there is to be an informed debate about the ordination of women as bishops in the Church of England then both sides need to listen to, and think carefully about, the arguments of those with whom they disagree. In order to help this process of careful reflection part four of this chapter sets out the critical questions raised by the arguments in the previous two sections.

5.1.4   What also needs to be borne in mind is that the inclusion of an argument in this chapter does not mean that it is endorsed by the Working Party. Arguments are included in this chapter on the basis that they are those that are currently being used in the debate about women and the episcopate.

5.2 Arguments for retaining the current stance of the Church of England

5.2.1   Looking at the arguments that have been put forward in favour of the present position in the Church of England, it is clear that there are two sets of arguments. The first set is largely supported by people who are in the Catholic Anglican tradition and the second is largely supported by people who are in the Conservative Evangelical tradition.

5.2.2   This does not mean that everyone who is in favour of retaining the status quo is necessarily either a Catholic Anglican or a Conservative Evangelical. Nor does it mean that all Catholic Anglicans or Conservative Evangelicals support the present position. It simply means that the arguments that we have encountered as a Working Party can be seen to reflect these two traditions.

5.2.3   There is a good deal of common ground between the two sets of arguments, and it would be possible to try to present a synthesis of the two positions, arranged by topics, that looked in turn at:

- arguments that revolve around the authority of Scripture

- arguments that revolve around tradition

- arguments that revolve around ecumenical relations, and

- arguments that revolve around culture, society and mission.

5.2.4   However, such a synthesis would fail to do justice to the particular nature of the arguments put forward by the representatives of each of the two traditions. It therefore seems better to look at each set of arguments in turn so that the distinctive character of each is reflected more accurately.

A. Arguments from a Catholic Anglican perspective

Mission
5.2.5   The first argument is that it would be wrong to change the Church's tradition simply in order to respond to the beliefs of contemporary society. This is a point that is strongly made, for example, by Geoffrey Kirk in his comments on a meeting between the Working Party and representatives of Forward in Faith.

5.2.6   In response to the question as to whether the ordination of women as bishops might not be necessary for the Church to engage evangelistically with secular feminism in today's society, he writes as follows:

> There is ... a question whether changing a consistent teaching or practice of the church over millennia in order to accommodate a particular social grouping can ever properly be called evangelization. Evangelization involves the call to *metanoia* and to a new life in fellowship with the Christian community. To change the teachings and practices of the faith over millennia in order to accommodate a particular social grouping or attitude might well be thought, by those within the Church and outside it, to be mere compromise.[1]

Scripture and tradition

5.2.7   A second argument is historical: that there is no evidence that either Jesus or St Paul were interested in the sort of arguments for the equality between the sexes that only emerged at the Enlightenment. As the Forward in Faith submission *By Their Fruits* puts it:

> Without currently prevailing contemporary assumptions about equality and human rights (both of which are products of the Enlightenment in the modern West) the ordination of women to the priesthood and the episcopate would be literally unthinkable. None of the immediate and pressing concerns of modern campaigners would have been intelligible to the original audience of the letters of Paul or the four Gospels. There was, for example, no demand for the cultic parity of women and men in first century Judaism. There is no attempt, in the parables or sayings of Jesus, to establish parity between women and men; rather the opposite. In this the attitude of Jesus to women seems not to differ significantly from that of other Rabbis of the time.[2]

5.2.8   A third argument, which follows on from the second, is that the introduction of women bishops is not consonant with scriptural passages such as 1 Corinthians 11.12-16, 14.34-38, 1 Timothy 2.11-15, Ephesians 5.21 and Galatians 3.27-28, and is unsupported by tradition. For example, David Lickess writes in his submission to the Working Party that the ordination of women as priests or bishops

> is clearly un-Scriptural and against the whole of Church tradition – surely weighty points. Obviously from the beginning women played a large part in spreading the Christian Gospel and

ministering pastorally to others. But there are clear NT markers that women are not to have authority in the Church to exercise headship (1 Tim 2.12), & there's no record of any women doing so in the Early Church, or of one having a sacramental or episcopal ministry.[3]

5.2.9   In similar fashion, the submission made by the vicar, churchwardens and PCC of Holy Trinity, Reading, declares that the ordination of women to the priesthood and therefore to the episcopate:

> ... is unproven in Scripture.

Whilst it is true to say that the New Testament does not provide us with an entirely unambiguous or settled understanding of ministry in the early church, the overwhelming weight of the evidence points towards the restriction of ordained ministry to males:

- Our Lord chose only men among the Twelve, despite His willingness to associate with women, indeed to have women counted among his closest friends and followers, in a way which entirely disregarded the social *mores* of the day;

- women play key roles in the central events of the Paschal mystery of the Lord's death and resurrection, without being counted as Apostles; the most obvious example of this being S Mary Magdalen, the first to encounter the Risen Christ;

- there is a consistent body of teaching in the Pauline and Pastoral Epistles attesting to the leadership of men within the community of faith (a leadership which, S Paul makes clear, is not to be confused with the baptismal covenant, in which all – male and female, slave and free, Jew and Greek – are to be counted equal in Christ).

> ... is absent from the tradition.

The ordination of women as presbyters/priests or bishops is found nowhere in the Tradition of Christendom in early Apostolic, patristic, medieval or modern times, whether in the undivided Church of the first eleven centuries, or within Orthodoxy or (western) Catholicism since 1054. All attempts to show the (purported) existence of female priests at any point in the history of the church have been entirely conjectural and unconvincing. We believe that this unbroken tradition is not trivial or accidental but rather an expression of the church's beliefs about the role and function of the ordained priest, especially at the celebration of the Eucharist. In modern times, protestant and independent denominations which have accepted female ministers and pastors have, precisely, rejected any concept of the ministerial priesthood, that is, any understanding that, in presiding at the celebration of the Lord's Supper or Mass, the priest, acting in persona Christi, sacramentally re-enacts the saving sacrifice of Calvary. It is thus only by overturning the Eucharistic doctrine of East and West that one of the most powerful arguments from Tradition against the ordination of women can itself be overturned. At the altar, the priest represents Christ the bridegroom, and this sacramental sign is lost entirely when the celebrant is female. Without overwhelming evidence to the contrary, and without the consent of the whole Church, we believe that the Church of England should not (indeed, cannot) overturn this unbroken and universal tradition of the male priesthood and episcopate.[4]

5.2.10   A fourth argument, already included in the previous quotation from Holy Trinity, Reading, is that the claim that there is evidence for the presence of women in the leadership of the Early Church is historically unconvincing. To quote the Forward in Faith submission *By Their Fruits* again:

> Upon the slenderest of epigraphical evidence, and in some cases no evidence at all, the impression has been given that the earliest Christians were ardent sexual egalitarians. A female 'apostle' has been conjured out of the margins of the Letter to the Romans, and the Roman catacombs have been peopled with women concelebrants. The extreme paucity of evidence for any of this is explained in terms of a 'male conspiracy' in later ages to obliterate the truth.[5]

The givenness of human sexual differentiation

5.2.11   A fifth argument is that the use of male and female language in the Bible, in the Christian tradition and in human cultures worldwide point us to the fact that human sexual differentiation and the patriarchal ordering of society are part of the givenness of the human situation as created by God. This argument is supported by an appeal to the point made by Steven Goldberg in his book *The Inevitability of Patriarchy*[6] about the way in which male authority has been a feature of all known societies across human history. For example, Kirk declares:

> 'Sex' is the great divide of humanity (its root 'se-' means to cut, as in secateurs, section, etc.). Sexual imagery is remarkable because it is both experienced and learned; and differently by both sexes. We both

know our sexuality experientially and we learn its expression in the rich patterns of our culture, of whose art it is the primary subject. The great themes of the canon of Western literature, from Homer, through Shakespeare to Proust, Beckett and Joyce are sex and death. The two are closely related, as they are in the image patterns of many religions, of which Christianity is only one. Though by no means the greatest of Shakespeare's plays, the one most easily transposed into a wide variety of cultures is *Romeo and Juliet*. 'West Side Story' is not alone. I have seen adaptations into Japanese Noh and Peking Opera.

There is, moreover, a remarkable degree of agreement across cultures about appropriate social expressions of sexual differentiation. For example, all known societies have been patriarchal.[7]

5.2.12   Seen in this light, there is nothing odd about the existence of sexual differentiation in the life of the Church or the patriarchal way in which it has traditionally been ordered. These things simply reflect something that has been a characteristic of all forms of human existence and culture.

The maleness of Christ
5.2.13   A sixth argument concerns the significance of Christ's assumption of male humanity.

5.2.14   In an article entitled 'The Ordination of Women and the "Maleness" of Christ' the American Anglican theologian R. A. Norris drew attention to the point made by Gregory of Nazianzen against Apollinarius that in order to save us Christ had to take upon himself human nature in all its fullness because 'what is not assumed is not healed'. As Norris saw the matter, the significance of Gregory's argument in relation to the ordination of women was that in order to save both women and men Christ had to take upon himself a human nature that was inclusive of both female and male humanity. It therefore followed that Christ could, and indeed should, be represented by women as well as by men.[8]

5.2.15   This line of argument is challenged in two ways in Forward in Faith's 2001 submission to the Working Party.

● First, it is noted that the Christian tradition has seen the maleness of Christ's humanity as theologically significant:

The problem is that the Fathers and the Schoolmen were unanimously agreed ... that the maleness of Christ *is* Christologically significant. They affirmed that he was the Messiah, the Son of David; and that he was the Son of the Father. They rightly understood those categories to be male and to be located in the Jewishness of the chosen culture of our redemption [John 4.22; Romans 11.11-12]. They affirmed the saving particularity of the divine revelation and of the incarnation.[9]

- Secondly it is further noted that the idea that Christ took upon himself a sexually undifferentiated human nature undercuts the very point that Gregory of Nazianzen was making:

> Gregory was countering the assertion of Apollinarius that the humanity assumed at the incarnation was in some sense special or tailor-made. Had Gregory maintained, with Norris, that Jesus' humanity in some sense 'included' femaleness as well as maleness, in a way which the humanity of some other men (for example, male priests) does not, he would obviously have conceded the very point he was striving to defend.[10]

5.2.16   The argument that follows from these two points is the one put forward in the submission from Holy Trinity, Reading. If a priest or bishop has an iconographic function as a representative of the incarnate Christ, particularly at the celebration of the Eucharist, then he has to be male for the representation to be appropriate. Just as the historical particularity of the Last Supper can only be properly represented by the use of bread and wine, so the historical particularity of the incarnation can only be properly represented by someone who is male.

5.2.17   A similar issue about the significance of Christ's male humanity is raised by a submission made to the working party by the Master and Guardians of the Shrine at Walsingham. They write as follows:

> We would ask, therefore, whether the case against an all-male episcopate raises questions similar to those raised by some theologians about how women may be expected to relate to the Christian gospel of a male redeemer. We recognise the possibility of seeing in both genders the capacity for one to represent additionally the other. In contrast, and not in parallel, to the image of Jesus as the new Adam who represents all mankind we would cite Mary portrayed as a personification of the Church (the dual identity of mother and Church is alluded to by the use of Revelation 11.19–12.6 as one of

the readings at the Eucharist provided in the *Common Worship* lectionary for the feast of Mary on 15 August). What is less clear is the use of a duality that functions independently, as male and female, to represent a unity – the source and origin, under Christ, of sacramental life. The temptation may be to abandon the gender distinction, on the basis of Galatians 3.28. But the representational image does not work that way; in relation to humanity, Jesus is clearly male, Mary female.[11]

5.2.18   We may note in passing that the argument that it is necessary for Jesus to be represented by a male priesthood (and by extension a male episcopate) has continued to be very important in Roman Catholic theology. It was maintained strongly, for instance, by Hans Urs Von Balthasar. In his study of this aspect of Von Balthasar's thought Robert Pesarchick summarizes it as follows:

> The ordered hierarchical priesthood is related analogously to the 'commissioned representational' aspect of Christ's priesthood. In and through the ministerial priesthood, ordained to act *in persona Christi*, Christ the Head/Bridegroom acts and makes himself present to the Church his Body/Bride. The ministerial priesthood is commissioned to represent (*repräsentieren*) Christ as Christ is commissioned to represent the Father. Just as the maleness of Jesus is intrinsic to this aspect of his mission/priesthood, so maleness is intrinsic to the ordained priesthood's task of commissioned representation. The natural symbolism of the male gender is necessary for the sacramental signification of the male Christ by the ministerial priesthood.[12]

The ecumenical objection

5.2.19   A seventh argument is that there is insufficient ecumenical agreement to proceed with the ordination of women as bishops. Thus Lickess writes:

> If they come it will break a 2000 year tradition and must inevitably force a further breach not only between Anglicans, but also between our Church & those with whom we claim to share the historic episcopate and threefold ministry dating back to the time of the undivided Church, namely Rome and the Orthodox. The idea that the Anglican Communion or the C/E can act on its own in matters such as having women bishops questions the whole claim of our Church to be part of the One Holy Catholic and Apostolic Church, when the greater part of Catholic Christendom does not yet agree with this move. Catholic Anglicans have always believed that the

Apostolic Ministry is of the *esse* of the Church, not just the *bene esse*, and that Churches which have or do reject it are deficient – a point recently made by the Vatican CDF statement. A major part of my opposition to women bishops is that this would be done by the C/E on its own, without agreement to do so with the other Churches that possess the historic ministry, or even the whole Anglican Communion, where a number of provinces still don't accept women priests let alone women bishops!

Surely the unity of Christ's Church here on earth is ultimately more important than our forms of valid ministry – see Jesus's Prayer in John chap.17? If we do something that will cause greater division – within the C/E, as well as between us and the RC & Orthodox Churches – we shall severely harm Christian fellowship and hopes for closer union.[13]

5.2.20   The same point is also made by Forward in Faith. Having noted the warnings by the Roman Catholic Church that the ordination of women would create a further impediment in the way of its recognition of Anglican orders, they go on to say:

Tragically the further impairment of communion occasioned by women bishops would not be confined to relations with the Roman church. It would extend to other churches of the Anglican Communion and to ecclesial bodies both Eastern and Western. From the Missouri Synod of the Lutheran Church (now active in Eastern Europe) to the Syrians, Armenians and Copts, the adoption of a female episcopate in the Church of England would finally signal the reception of an irreconcilable ministry and ecclesiology.[14]

The problem of sacramental assurance

5.2.21   An eighth argument concerns the issue of sacramental assurance. This is a point that is raised in the Forward in Faith paper *By Their Fruits* referred to earlier in this chapter. The section of the paper headed 'Sacramental Assurance' declares that:

Holy Orders are 'a principal instrument given by God for the maintenance of true communion' not only because by their mutual equivalence and interchangeability they both express and effect that communion between dioceses and provinces, but also because, by their continuity 'from the Apostles' time', they offer assurance of the authenticity of the sacraments they mediate. This assurance is more than a mere passive continuance over time. Rather it is the expression of an active will to do what the Lord has commanded, and so gratefully to receive and appropriate the grace he promises.

It is an assurance, moreover, which the Church exists to give. Without that self-conscious assurance of the authenticity of its sacraments and the apostolicity of its doctrine, an ecclesial structure of whatever kind has no *raison d'être*.[15]

5.2.22   Having made this point, the section goes on to argue that:

The statements made by Anglicans (for example in the reports of the Grindrod Commission and subsequently the Eames Commission) and by the proposer of the motion in the General Synod of the Church of England (all subsequently endorsed by the General Synod of the Church of England in the Episcopal Ministry Act of Synod 1993) can reasonably be interpreted as putting an end to any intention on the part of the Church of England, of guarding such sacramental assurance.[16]

5.2.23   This is argued on the grounds that when the ordination of women as priests was agreed by the Church of England it was also agreed that members of the Church of England might legitimately refuse to accept their sacramental ministry. A situation then existed when not all ministries and sacraments in the Church of England were accepted by all its members, a situation which contradicted the very purposes for which Holy Orders exist:

The purpose of orders is not to authorize discrete groups to celebrate discrepant sacraments in an impairment of communion which embraces them all, but so to order the life of the whole church that the sacraments of all are open and acceptable to each. Validity and universality are necessarily related concepts.[17]

5.2.24   From the perspective of Forward in Faith and those sympathetic to their position the ordination of women as bishops could only make matters worse. At the moment it is only the orders of female priests that are in question. If women were ordained as bishops episcopal orders would also be in question, as would the priestly or diaconal orders of anyone (male or female) ordained by a woman bishop.

5.2.25   This latter point is emphasized by David Houlding in a submission to the working party made on behalf of the Catholic Group on General Synod. His submission is entitled *Reception and*

Communion and in it he contends that the concept of reception, which we looked at in Chapter 3, cannot properly be employed when the matter in question is the validity of orders:

> There is further the question of whether 'reception' can apply to changes in *order*. Once an opinion has been incarnated in the persons of an order reception is no longer applicable. If dubiety exists in the priesthood, then the certainty of the sacraments, which are so celebrated, is also called into question. You cannot – which is what the Catholic Church is saying – and so what the Church of England has also previously said – 'try out' sacraments. They are not experimental! It is of their very nature that they are trustworthy and authoritative. They are to be guaranteed signs of Christ's presence and activity in the world. If they are not that, then they are of little worth.

> Bishop Kenneth Kirk enunciated the principle in a paper for the Church Assembly in 1947 which stated that 'where sacraments are concerned the church is always obliged to take the least doubtful course.' Through the ordination of women as bishops the level of confusion is increased by the possibility that the orders conferred on men as well as women would also now be in doubt. That in turn, as time goes on, would be a situation that could only increase and not be lessened. 'Communion' 'Koinonia' is impossible – division will be inevitable at all levels of the Church's life.[18]

The inability of a woman bishop to be a focus of unity

5.2.26   Houlding's final point about the division that will result from the appointment of women bishops brings us to a ninth and final argument on the Catholic side, which is that if women were appointed as bishops the episcopate would no longer be able to fulfil its central function of being a focus or sign of unity within the Church.

5.2.27   This is a point that is emphasized, for example, both by Houlding and by the Master and Guardians of Walsingham.

5.2.28   Houlding makes two points in this connection.

- First, a woman bishop could not be a focus of unity because there would be parishes who would not accept her ministry:

> Since apostolic times the bishop has always been the *focus of unity* for the local church. He relates the local to the universal and the

146

universal to the local; it is difficult to understand how a woman ordained can be such for the Church of England in the present situation. If the period of reception for women in the priesthood has not been terminated and presumably if alone for conscience sake cannot be for the foreseeable future, it is impossible for the church to proceed with the admission of women as bishops without stifling 'conscience' and imposing its doctrine. In this position, although a woman bishop may hold juridical and ecclesiastical authority, if any of the parishes within the diocese (or the episcopal area over which she exercises her episcopate) do not receive her ministry, she cannot be said to be the focus of sacramental unity. Therefore, down the line, the bishop may exercise a ministry of pastoral administration but no longer can she be able to exemplify the *plene bene esse* (the fullness of life) of the church.[19]

[handwritten marginal note: doesn't Act of Synod do this to present Bishops?]

- Secondly, a woman bishop could not be a focus of unity because the introduction of women bishops would lead to the rupturing of communion within the episcopate and thus destroy that very unity of the Church which bishops are meant to focus.

> *'Where the bishop is there is the Church.'* When bishops are no longer in communion with one another, where is the Church? Can the Church exist when its episcopal orders are no longer interchangeable? It will no longer be a question of impaired communion, but communion will be ruptured at its source. It will simply no longer be possible to talk about the bishops as the focus of unity, for that very unity itself will no longer exist. The bishop will *de facto* become something else from what he is at present.[20]

5.2.29   The Walsingham submission makes two similar points:

- First, it declares that:

> The difficulties that we perceive in the ordination of women to the episcopate cluster around the bishop's role as a sign of unity; thus our difficulties are for the most part different from those that we have concerning the ordination of women to the presbyterate. The bishop is a source (under Christ and within the Church) of sacramental life in a sense that the presbyter is not. The bishop does not merely celebrate sacraments, but empowers others to do so. Those who have chosen to remain within the Church of England and commit themselves to positive use of the provisions for those unable to accept the ordination of women to the presbyterate would therefore find

themselves facing new and deeper difficulties in the introduction of further division, already experienced in the exercise of presbyteral ministry, but then to be experienced at the source of sacramental life and unity.[21]

- Secondly it argues that the proposal to ordain women bishops threatens an essential element of Anglican ecclesial identity by calling into question the ability of the episcopate to act as a focus for unity and a source of holy order within the Church:

> In our view, the issue, legitimately raised, of the ordination of women to the episcopate calls into question the way in which the episcopate has functioned in the Church of England from its inception (beyond Augustine), that is, as an expression of unity and source of holy order. Our misgivings lead us to ask what kind of Church this development would create and whether it is a development consistent with its own self-understanding.[22]

B. Arguments from a Conservative Evangelical perspective

The argument about women's ordination was not decided in 1992

5.2.30   A first argument from this perspective is that it cannot be said that the theological issue of the ordination of women as such was decided once for all by the vote to ordain women as priests/presbyters in November 1992, because doctrinal issues cannot properly be decided by a majority vote.

5.2.31   As David Banting puts it in his submission to the Working Party on behalf of Reform:

> We are not therefore able to approach the question of the consecration of women to the episcopate on the basis of the affirmative vote which, after several negative votes, the General Synod gave to the ordination of women as presbyters nine years ago. We do not believe that doctrinal questions can be decided by majority voting, and we continue to be convinced that this affirmative vote was a mistaken decision, in which the General Synod departed from the Church of England's commitment to the authority of Scripture (Articles VI and XX), and which the Church will sooner or later have to reverse, as has happened in some other Churches elsewhere (notably the Lutheran Church of Latvia and the Presbyterian Church of Australia).[23]

The principle of 'functional subordination'

5.2.32 A second argument is that just as there is an order within the life of the Holy Trinity in which God the Son submits to the authority of God the Father although they are equal as God, so also, although men and women are equal as human beings, there is a proper order of human relations ('headship') in which women are to submit to the authority of men. To quote Gerald Bray:

> Father and Son need each other in order to be themselves, and this mutuality is worked out in the submissiveness of the Son just as much as it is in the 'authority' of the Father who raises him from the dead and thereby validates his sacrifice. Similarly, male and female need each other in order to be themselves, and their interrelationship is also expressed in terms of submission and sacrifice. The link between the divine and the human is provided by the incarnate Son, who is at once both priest and victim, judge and sacrifice. The whole pattern of our salvation is worked out in this complex structure of 'order', which the Church is called to proclaim and reflect in its public worship.[24]

5.2.33 A third argument is that this order is set out in the creation narrative in Genesis 1-2 and is presupposed by the rest of Scripture. In Genesis 2 there is 'functional subordination' as shown by the naming of Eve by Adam.[25] This 'subordination' is rooted in and reflects above all the filial relationship between the Father and the Son, from which we learn both of their equality of being and the filial subordination of Son to the Father. This is the argument we have seen made in the previous quotation from Bray and in its defence reference is made to patristic statements such as the account of the Trinity given by Hilary of Poitiers.[26] It is this 'functional subordination' to which St Paul refers in his discussion of headship in 1 Corinthians 11.12-16 and which is reflected in the teaching about the relationship of husbands and wives in texts such as Colossians 3.18, Ephesians 5.21-33 and 1 Peter 3.1-7.[27]

5.2.34 In his article 'The Economy of Salvation and Ecclesiastical Tyranny', Mike Ovey writes:

> Genesis 2 does envisage headship between husband and wife, Adam and Eve. This shows Adam's actions in Genesis 3 to be a refusal to accept responsibility and headship, but instead an adoption of submission to one who should have been submitting to him. Hence the criticism of Genesis 3.17.

One can thus see Genesis 3 as an inversion of the appropriate orders of creation. The serpent suborns Eve, who overrules her head, who defies his God. Athanasius accordingly rightly depicts the Fall as an undoing of creation. In this context Genesis 3.16, far from being a further punishment on the woman, is a preservation of the original creation order – a sign that marriage authentically continues in a fallen world (as Genesis 2.24 envisages), albeit under the shadow of masculine failures.

What this means is that a restored humanity in terms of its husband/wife relationships, would be marked not by *soi-disant* egalitarianism or 'mutual submission'. Rather a re-created marriage would be marked by the original creational marriage contours, namely complementarity and obedience within a loving relationship. It would be precisely the ordinal relationship of headship that marks marriage in the redeemed community before Christ's return.[28]

5.2.35   In similar fashion Carrie Sandom declares in a presentation to the Working Party from Reform:

The Biblical principle of male headship and female submission needs to be upheld as a way of ordering relationships within marriage and the church. I believe that Jesus Himself serves as an example of both – in His humble submission to His Father's will in the garden of Gethsemane and His sacrificial leadership of the church as He gave up His life for her at Calvary. This pattern of sacrificial leadership and humble submission needs to be modelled within marriage and the church. The feminist agenda tells us that equality of being necessitates the removal of all gender distinctions and insists on identical roles for men and women. God's word demands a complementarity of roles that has its roots in the Godhead itself.[29]

5.2.36   A fourth argument is that it is this principle of female submission to male authority that underlies the restriction on women's ministry in 1 Corinthians 14.34-36 and 1 Timothy 2.12-15. Attempts to re-interpret these passages and to argue that they only refer to specific historical circumstances that no longer apply do not do justice to the accepted principles of biblical scholarship.

5.2.37   For example, the statement from the Latimer Trust's Ministry Work Group on the ministry of women in the Church today comments on both the passages that have just been mentioned.

- On 1 Corinthians 14.34-36 the statement notes that there is a degree of uncertainty about precisely what activity St Paul is prohibiting women from undertaking, but then states:

> Whatever the precise nature of the activity, it was regarded by the apostle as a denial of biblical teaching. When he says 'it is shameful for a woman to speak in church', he has in mind behaviour which is inconsistent with the subordinate or submissive role required of them in 'the law' (14.34). The reference is apparently to the creation narratives in Genesis, on which the apostle more obviously bases his argument in 1 Corinthians 11.2-16. So Paul is concerned about behaviour in church that undermines appropriate relationships between husbands and wives in the Lord.[30]

- On 1 Timothy 2.11-15 the statement declares:

> Debate continues about the precise meaning and significance of 2.14-15. But whatever we conclude about the details, it is clear that there are profound theological reasons behind the prohibition of 2.11-12. Paul is not simply using Old Testament texts and perspectives in an *ad hominem* way. Neither is he simply giving instructions for a particular church in the first century AD. The next chapter goes on to declare that Paul's instructions in this letter are designed to show 'how one ought to behave in the household of God' (3.15). Prior to this, he has outlined the requirements for 'overseers' in the church, focussing on spiritual maturity, aptness to teach and the ability of a man to 'manage his own household well' (3.1-7). There is a link between family leadership and a godly pattern of leadership by males in the Christian congregation. And 'the household of God' is a term that clearly applies beyond the confines of the Ephesian church.
>
> Congregational life should therefore reflect and support the pattern of family life outlined in the New Testament. 1 Timothy 2.11-12 implies that women who teach in the congregation in a way that exercises authority over men, challenge the pattern of relationship required by God in Christian marriage. This is not to deny complementarity but to express the teaching found elsewhere about the husband being the 'head' of the wife. Whether women are married or not, their exercise of this authoritative teaching role cuts across the model of congregational leadership that the apostle goes on to outline in 1 Timothy 3.1-7.[31]

151

Galatians 3.28 is not a general statement about equality

5.2.38   A fifth argument is that Galatians 3.28, a text which is often appealed to as a general statement of the equality of women and men, is in fact about the specific issue of the inheritance of the blessing of Abraham.

5.2.39   To quote Ovey again:

> Paul asserts there is neither Jew nor Greek, bond nor free, male nor female in the context of who inherits the blessing of Abraham and on what grounds.

> This means that one violates the principle of Galatians 3.28 if one asserts a difference between human groups which impliedly undercuts the adequacy and necessity of Christ's work in making us heirs of Abraham. It is very far from obvious that this is the case in the question of consecrating women to the episcopate.[32]

A woman bishop could not be an icon of God the Father

5.2.40   A sixth argument is that a woman bishop could not function as an icon of God the Father as suggested by St Ignatius of Antioch because the Fatherhood of God is something that is paternal rather than maternal in nature. In the words of Ovey:

> [Ignatius of Antioch] suggests that the bishop is a type or icon of the Father. While one might dissent from this judgement, one must also recognize its influence. It is to some extent problematic to see a female bishop as an icon of the Father. Symbolically she would tend to convey maternal rather than paternal associations. Yet the patristic thought with regard to the First person of the Trinity is that he is essentially Father (by virtue of his eternal relationship with the Son). Maternal associations might well be thought to obscure this and to depart both from the economic revelation of Fatherhood/Sonship as well as the tradition of the church.[33]

The inappropriateness of a woman exercising episcopal authority

5.2.41   A seventh argument is that the principle of headship that makes it inappropriate for a woman to exercise authority over men as a presbyter makes it equally if not more inappropriate for her to exercise the additional authority involved in the episcopal office.

5.2.42   As Roger Beckwith puts it in a submission to the Working Party on behalf of the Third Province Movement:

According to the testimony of St Paul in First Corinthians 11 and 14 and First Timothy 2, headship in the congregation, as in the home, should be exercised by a member or members of the male sex. He declares male headship to be [a] creation ordinance, which was reinforced at the fall, and still obtains after the coming of Christ. The offices of presbyter and bishop are offices of headship, as their very titles, meaning 'senior man' and 'overseer', indicate. The title of deacon, on the other hand, meaning 'servant or 'assistant', is not a title of headship and does not indicate an office of headship. It is an honourable title and office, for service, in the Christian understanding, is an honourable task. So, if women are admitted to this office, there would appear to be nothing inappropriate about it, since it really makes them assistants to the presbyters and bishops. In the New Testament and the Apostolic Fathers, deacons are regularly mentioned in association with bishops or presbyters, but they are always mentioned second, as their assistants. And yet, as is so often noted, to be their assistants is an honourable role.

It inevitably follows from this that the ordination of women as presbyters was an inappropriate step for the Church of England to take, at variance with its historic commitment to Scripture and antiquity, and that the consecration of women as bishops would be no less inappropriate than their ordination as presbyters. On the contrary, it would be more so.[34]

5.2.43   In similar fashion Banting states in his submission to the Working Party:

it is clear that the objections that prevent us from recognising women presbyters would even more emphatically prevent us from recognising women bishops. It would be a still more flagrant repudiation of the teaching of the apostle on male headship.[35]

The lack of consensus about ordaining women bishops

5.2.44   An eighth argument is that there is no consensus about female episcopal consecration. In his contribution to the Reform presentation to the Working Party Nigel Atkinson argues, for example, that it would be rash to proceed with the ordination of women as bishops when 'it has not yet been proved that female presbyteral ordination has been fully accepted not only in the Church of England but across the whole Communion'.

5.2.45 Furthermore, he says,

> not only has female episcopal consecration not achieved consensus
> in the present; it is unable to achieve this consensus with the Church
> of the past. This is an obvious but significant point. True Catholicity
> can be recognized by the presence of a doctrine, not in any one
> particular age or in any one particular regional or national Church
> but across the ages. Otherwise it is very easy to absolutize
> permanently the partial or imperfect insights of any Church or age.
> However in defending an all male Episcopate and priesthood the
> orthodox can not only call upon the witness of the whole Church
> but also the witness of the Apostolic age.[36]

5.2.46 A ninth argument is that the lack of current consensus means
that a woman bishop could not be a focus of unity and order since there
would be those in the Church who would simply be unable to accept
her ministry and submit to her authority.

5.2.47 As Banting puts the matter in the Reform presentation to the
Working Party:

> women bishops will be a focus of *disunity* – a Bishop can only be
> a focus of unity if the unity is grounded in the gospel. There is already
> *dismay* among ordinands, some of whom are already withdrawing
> from training, and among those who labour in evangelism among
> men. There will be extensive *disruption* – early surveys suggest that
> up to 90% of mainstream evangelicals (Peter Brierley's demarcation)
> would have difficulties with an oath of allegiance to a female bishop,
> while others would find their beliefs coerced and their ministry
> marginalized, for no movement of their own. *Disobedience* would
> be inevitable, if secure provision or alternative oversight continues
> to be denied. In a word, *dis*-order – we say again, this is a serious
> issue of order and authority.[37]

5.2.48 In his article 'Bishops, Presbyters and Women' quoted above,
Bray develops the argument about unity with specific reference to the
fact that the Church of England has recognized that people can hold
different positions with integrity over the matter of the ordination of
women:

> Those who favour women bishops are not opposed to having men,
> but those who do not will not accept women, which means that if the
> two integrities are to be held together, only men can be appointed as
> bishops. To appoint a woman bishop would be to split the church by

denying the legitimacy of one of the integrities. The principle that this should be avoided has a precedent in the New Testament, in the circumcision of Timothy (Acts 16.3). This was imposed on him by the Apostle Paul, in spite of the latter's well-known and frequently articulated opposition to circumcision as a theological necessity, in order to make Timothy more acceptable to Jewish Christians, who were the other integrity of their day. Timothy had to be acceptable without question by everyone, which was enough to mandate a practice which the apostle would never have justified on theological grounds.[38]

Ordaining women bishops would be contrary to the principle of reception

5.2.49 A tenth argument is that the concept of reception raises difficulties for the idea that women should be ordained as bishops in the Church of England. This is the argument put forward, for example, by Peter Toon in his Latimer Trust booklet *Reforming Forwards?* to which we referred in Chapter 3. He argues that the Church of England is still in a process of reception with regard to the decision to ordain women as priests and it would be wrong to disrupt this process by ordaining women as bishops:

> the Church of England began in its own form of testing and discernment ten years ago and ... this ongoing process should not be interrupted by what would be a very major change in the life of the National Church. There are in place now the structures and the guidelines, not to mention the experience, for allowing the process of reception to proceed in a reasonable, convivial and mature way and thus for true discernment and testing to take place. Whatever would be the individual holiness and charm of a woman bishop, her presence as a female *episcopos* would seriously disturb the present fragile means of maintaining a basic level of communion, respect and integrity, and would make extremely difficult the continuation of the open process of reception. The calls for a Third Province would intensify and the Church of England would probably enter into a legalized form of internal schism.[39]

5.2.50 As Toon sees it,

> While there is a vocal, well-informed and theologically literate minority (Evangelicals, Anglo-Catholics and others) who oppose the ordination of women to the presbyterate and episcopate either on biblical/theological or ecumenical principles, it cannot be said that the process of reception is completed. In fact, it must be admitted that it is still ongoing and the testing and discernment must surely

continue. Further, this is also the case in the vast majority of the 38 provinces of the Anglican Communion, and the right understanding of the doctrine of reception includes the taking into account what is happening in the whole Anglican family.

Therefore, rather than pressing for the consecration of women as *episcopoi* what the House of Bishops and General Synod ought to be doing is making clear to all the proper context of fellowship and mutuality where people of different opinions can live together in reasonable harmony as they patiently engage in testing and discernment of this innovation. In other words, the House of Bishops should recall its own teaching of 1993 and of 2000 in published documents and seek to lead the Church to accept it and to follow it. It should remind its flocks of the fact that 'the process of reception in the Church can be difficult and time-consuming; there is no predetermined result'.[40]

The danger of the 'feminization' of the Church of England

5.2.51   An eleventh argument is that the Church of England needs to retain a male leadership if it is to avoid feminization and reach out successfully to men. For instance, Sandom argues:

> Men will be driven out of the church if women are too prominent within it and won't be drawn into it if men are too scarce. The growing feminization of the church has been a problem, many would argue, since the end of the first-world war. If the church is going to be at all credible in the 21st century it needs to have more men at the heart of its leadership – men who value the unique role of women, and seek to uphold it, while at them same time recognising their own unique role as men.[41]

5.2.52   A final argument is that instead of moving further down the road begun with the ordination of women to the priesthood, the Church ought instead to be encouraging appropriate forms of ministry for women that make use of their talents and abilities in ways that are consonant with Scripture and honour the order of male-female relationships which God has established. This argument is developed in detail in Sandom's booklet *Fellow Workers in Christ*.

5.3 Arguments for introducing women bishops in the Church of England

5.3.1   The arguments in favour of the ordination of women bishops come from all theological positions, including the Catholic and

Evangelical, and cannot be divided along the lines of Church traditions in the same way as the arguments against their ordination. The arguments will therefore be presented in one block.

A new way of looking at the biblical material

5.3.2   The first argument is that experience of women's ministry in the Church of England and other churches has created a new context in which to look again at the biblical material in the same way that the Church was led to reconsider the biblical material relating to gentiles and slaves.

5.3.3   As David Gillett notes in his paper for the Working Party, *A Fresh Hermeneutical Lens on the Ordination of Women to the Episcopate*, this new context has led many people in the Church to view the task of biblical interpretation (what he calls the 'hermeneutical task') in a new light:

> The hermeneutical task includes new elements and fresh evidence: hermeneutics has a different shape to it for many members of the Church of England. The positive experience of the ministry of women priests is a new factor in the hermeneutical task which now faces us in relation to the question of the ordination of women to the episcopate. We possess some significantly new and compelling evidence as part of the present context which informs the way in which we ask questions of the scriptural texts. This is not to claim that the recent experience of women's ordination is an independent counterbalancing authority but rather that such experience is a hermeneutical lens in our reading of scripture.[42]

5.3.4   This in turn means, he says, that the question that many people are now asking has changed from:

> Is there a case to be made for the ordination of women, or are the hesitations expressed by St Paul in relation to some of the earliest church communities binding on us now, as most have considered them to be throughout the history of the Church until this point?

to:

> Given that the Biblical material so strongly supports the ordination of both women and men, which inclusivity has become a given within our understanding and experience of the Church, when do we proceed to express the full weight of the Biblical testimony and ordain women to the episcopate?[43]

The overall trajectory of Scripture

5.3.5   A second argument is that the reason the biblical material can be said strongly to support the ordination of both women and men is that:

> The main teaching of Scripture is the essential dignity, equality and complementarity of the whole of humanity before God.[44]

5.3.6   More precisely, the argument is that in the biblical material there is an overall trajectory in which the equality between women and men established by God at creation is disrupted by the Fall, but is then fully restored in the New Testament as a result of the work of Christ and the gift of the Holy Spirit.

5.3.7   The trajectory begins in the creation narratives of Genesis 1 and 2 which clearly teach the equality and complementarity between men and women. In the words of David Atkinson in his commentary on Genesis 1 – 11:

> Genesis 1 and 2 make the equality of men and women, as the image of God, unmistakably clear. The removal of a piece of the man in order to create the woman implies that from now on neither is complete without the other. The man needs the woman for his wholeness, and the woman needs the man for hers. Each is equal in relation to the other. Nothing could make clearer the complementarity and equality of the sexes.[45]

5.3.8   It is only in Genesis 3 that inequality emerges as result of the Fall. In the words of Mary Hayter in her book *The New Eve in Christ*:

> in Genesis 3 female subordination is shown to be a consequence of sexual polarization and a result of sin. It is Genesis 2, not 3.16, which represents the Creator's intention. God designed male and female to be suitable partners, peers, for each other; that woman was often the subject of man's arbitrary dominance is here ascribed to human interference with a higher design (cf Matt. 19.8).[46]

5.3.9   In the Old Testament the role given to women reflects the patriarchal nature of society after the Fall, but this is not the whole picture. To quote Mary Evans:

> In the Old Testament as a whole, woman, after the fall, is seen as secondary. Even though Deuteronomy 29.9-18 makes it clear that she is a full member of the covenant community who must assume

full responsibility for playing her part in it, nevertheless she is placed low down the order of those who are described as entering the covenant. She is seen as relative to a man, whether her husband or her father, and generally subject to him. However, when we consider all that the Old Testament has to say about women, it is clear that the androcentricity is not total, that patriarchy cannot accurately be described as having 'God on its side' and that just because androcentricity is recognized as existing, it cannot from the Old Testament be defended as a 'God-ordained and inevitable concept.' Women were full members of the covenant community. They had a significant role to play in the life of the nation, not only in their role as mothers and in the home, but also as individuals, and they were not barred from leadership when the circumstances required it.[47]

5.3.10   Moving on to the New Testament, it is argued that Jesus radically challenged the prevailing belief in the inferiority of women in the way in which he included women in his life and ministry even though he observed the cultural constraints of his day in not choosing a woman as one of the Twelve.

5.3.11   Gillett, for example, contends that what we see in the New Testament from Pentecost (Acts 2.16-18) onwards is the fulfilment of the promise made through the prophet Joel (Joel 2.28-29) that in the last days the Holy Spirit would be poured out equally on both sexes, thus restoring the original equality between them lost at the Fall. As he sees it,

> Jesus foreshadows this regaining of the fullness of God's gift in the way he included women in his life and ministry. The New Testament was clearly written in a first century culture in which Jesus immersed himself. The fact that he did not choose any woman as part of the twelve *is* a theological statement, but *not* that no women could ever be allowed such a position within the kingdom of God. Rather it says that the incarnation of God's Son was real and historical – he became fully part of the first century world and lived and spoke through that particular culture. As the incarnate Son of God he entered fully into the human experience there and then. In doing so he made quite clear the kingdom principles that would challenge his culture and ours in the coming years.

> As Rabbinic tradition developed women were regarded as minors all their lives. She could be divorced only at the will of her husband. She had an inferior legal position. She was not taught the Torah with her

brothers. She could not go through the gentile porch in Herod's temple. A man could not be alone with a woman unless they were married. Jesus challenged radically such attitudes to women, more by his surprising actions than by his direct teaching.

Jesus appears to be a unique and sometimes radical reformer of the views of women and their roles that were commonly held among his people.[48]

5.3.12 Following the example of Jesus and as an outworking of the gift of the Spirit at Pentecost what we see in Acts and the epistles is women working alongside men in the life and ministry of the early Church (Acts 9.36-42, 16.14-15, 18.18-24, Romans 16.1-16, 1 Corinthians 11.5, Philippians 4.2-3, and 2 Timothy 4.19). In the words of Evans:

> The impression is gained from both acts and the epistles that the leaders and in particular the senior leaders in the churches were far more often male than female. However, women, in some cases, clearly did play a major role in leadership. There is no indication that leadership, when it was exercised by women, was in any sense different from that exercised by men. Just as with the part played by men and women in worship, the only differences in the task carried out are those intangible ones that result from the men worshipping and leading as men, and the women as women.[49]

5.3.13 The point made here by Evans is reinforced by the work of Campbell. Drawing on the evidence of Acts and the letters of St Paul he notes that

> women feature prominently in the Pauline mission. ... There is no need to rehearse the evidence from women among Paul's fellow workers: Priscilla, Mary, Tryphaena and Tryphosa, Euodia and Syntyche. Women are found enabling the mission of the church by opening their homes, like Lydia at Philippi and Nympha at Colossae, and Phoebe is commended as a *diakonos* of the church at Cenchrae and as someone who had given Paul significant help and protection. There is no reason to doubt that such women were able to 'contribute significantly to the spread of Christianity in the early years of its expansion', or that Paul's approach in this matter was deliberate, unusual, and 'resulted in the elevation of women to a place in religious work for which we have little contemporary parallel.'[50]

5.3.14   Campbell also argues that although it is doubtful whether it was normal for women to preside at a mixed meeting of a household church, nevertheless,

> where women were already heads of their households, as a result of being widowed or divorced, this probably provided women leaders in the churches, at least in the early days.[51]

5.3.15   What is also seen as significant is the fact that a woman called Junia is described as an 'apostle' in Romans 16.7[52] and that ancient tradition describes Mary Magdalene as the 'apostle to the apostles' on the basis of John 20.11-18.[53] The reason this is seen as significant is that the office of bishop has traditionally been seen as a representing the continuation of the ministry of the apostles in the later life of the Church. Hooker, for instance, sees the apostles as the first to exercise episcopal oversight in the Church and bishops as their successors in this regard:

> The Apostles ... were the first which had such authority, and all others who have it after them in orderly sort are their lawful successors, whether they succeed in any particular church, where before them some Apostle hath been seated, as Simon succeeded James in Jerusalem; or else be otherwise endued with the same kind of bishoply power, although it be not where any Apostle before hath been. For to succeed them, is after them to have that episcopal kind of power which was first given to them. 'All bishops are' saith Jerome, 'the Apostles' successors'.[54]

This being the case, evidence that women exercised some kind of apostolic function in the Early Church would point towards the appropriateness of women being permitted to exercise an episcopal role in the Church today.

5.3.16   Galatians 3.28 is viewed as the foundational text which makes clear the equality of women and men in Christ, and thus sums up the trajectory of the Bible as a whole. To quote Hayter:

> What Galatians 3.27f affirms ... is that all the baptized are one in Christ. 'In Christ', racial, social and sexual distinctions are transcended and transformed. What is good and God-given in them is retained, but those aspects which have become distorted or perverted – including male dominance – are to be removed, in theory and practice, from the Christian community.

Moreover, as several commentators point out, it is probable that these verses represent a pre-Pauline liturgical (baptismal) formula. The text does not simply preserve a theological 'breakthrough' achieved by Paul; rather it provided insight into the theological understanding of the early Christian community. The early Christians understood themselves as freed by the Holy Spirit to a new life of egalitarian discipleship. Over against the patriarchal patterns of 'the world', over against the commonly accepted ratification of sexual discrimination in Judaism and Hellenism, they set the equality and freedom of the children of God.[55]

The problems with the argument from 'headship'

5.3.17   A third argument is that the argument from male headship, which, as we have seen, has been central to Conservative Evangelical objections to the ordination of women, misinterprets the biblical material.

- First, it is argued that there is no foundation in the creation narratives in Genesis 1–2 for a theory of male headship. As we have just indicated, these chapters are seen as teaching the essential equality of men and women as created by God.

- Secondly, it is argued that the two New Testament texts (1 Corinthians 11.3 and Ephesians 5.22-23) which use the language of headship are not in fact relevant to the issue of the role of women in the life of the Church. This second point is emphasized, for example, by Paula Gooder in her essay 'Headship: A Consideration of the Concept in the Writings of Paul'.

5.3.18   Gooder declares that with regard to Ephesians 5.22-23:

> it is clear that the words refer to the relationship between husband and wife, as the Greek reads literally 'the women to their own men as to the Lord' (the verb 'subject yourself' is to be understood from the previous verse). Consequently, the Ephesians passage is about internal domestic relationships not about Church order.[56]

5.3.19   Gooder then notes the continuing debate and uncertainty about the precise meaning of the term 'head' in 1 Corinthians 11.3 and asks how in the light of this we should understand the meaning of the verse:

> It may help to consider the whole passage of 1 Corinthians 11.2-16. The context of the passage is a general discussion of worship and of

clothing most appropriate to worship for men and women. It is very striking that later on in this passage Paul specifically establishes the clothing in which it is appropriate for women to pray and prophesy ('but any woman who prays or prophesies with her head unveiled disgraces her head', 1 Corinthians 11.5). Women are not forbidden from engaging fully in the public profession of worship but are encouraged to do so in appropriate clothing. The point seems not to be subordination of one to the other but gender differentiation.[57]

5.3.20   Gooder's conclusion is that

> The issue of 'headship,' therefore, does not really help in a discussion of the role of women in the church. The Ephesians passage refers to internal domestic order and also includes the proper attitude of slaves to their masters. It is concerned not with what happens in church but what happens in the home. The Corinthians passage that is concerned with worship is primarily focused on how this worship should take place in such a way as to avoid bringing shame on the Church. Paul's comments here are aimed at men as much as at women – they should all dress appropriately in worship because they are all related through Christ to God. The language he uses to describe this relationship is metaphorical; to limit his metaphor to a single meaning is to impoverish the richness of the image he offers here.[58]

In his commentary on 1 Corinthians, which preceded Gooder's work, Anthony Thiselton takes a similar view of the interpretation of the Corinthians passage. He also holds that the concept of headship should be seen as having multiple meanings. In his words, it is a 'polymorphous' concept.[59] Like Gooder, he too sees the issue of shame as being central to what the passage is about:

> at Corinth women as well as men tended to place 'knowledge' and 'freedom' as part of the gospel new creation before love in the Christian sense. Paul does not permit their 'freedom' as part of the gospel new creation to destroy their proper-self-respect and respect in the eyes of others by taking part in worship dressed like an 'available' woman. That is not love, for it brings 'shame' on themselves, their menfolk, and on God.[60]

An alternative interpretation of 1 Corinthians and 1 Timothy

5.3.21   A fourth argument concerns the two texts, 1 Corinthians 14.33-38 and 1 Timothy 2.12-15, which have traditionally been seen as prohibiting women from exercising ministry in church in the presence of men.

5.3.22   The first point that is made in this connection is that whatever the meaning of these passages we cannot hold that St Paul was opposed to women exercising authority over men in all circumstances. In the words of Trevor Hart:

> In fact we know the opposite is true. In Romans 16, for example, Paul refers to women holding the offices of deacon (Phoebe in verse 1), 'fellow worker' in Paul's ministry of the gospel (Priscilla in verse 3) and, strikingly, apostle (Junia in verse 7); and in 1 Corinthians 11 itself he alludes to women praying and prophesying in church, roles which, as one writer puts it, 'made them far more prominent and equal to men than they would have been in Judaism in this period' ... Clearly, then, Paul did not think women unsuited to roles of responsible and authoritative ministry within the church, and any interpretation of 1 Cor 14.33-35 and 1 Tim 2.11-14 must reckon fully with this fact and be consistent with it.[61]

5.3.23   The second point is that it is possible to interpret these two texts in ways which make them consistent with St Paul's overall teaching and practice.

- 1 Corinthians 14.33-38 is seen either as prohibiting women from talking inappropriately in Church, or as containing a non-Pauline interpolation, or as reflecting St Paul's indignant repudiation of the views of those who want women to keep silent.

For example, Thiselton argues that while these verses are not an interpolation and reflect St Paul's own views they are not a generalized command for women to be silent in church. Rather, they are an exhortation to women to observe the principle of order in their behaviour by not publicly weighing the words of Christian prophets:

> With Witherington we believe that the speaking in question denotes the *activity of* sifting *or weighing the words of the prophets, especially by asking probing questions about the prophet's theology or even the prophet's lifestyle in public.* This would become especially sensitive and problematic *if wives were cross-examining their husbands about the speech and conduct which supported or undermined the*

authenticity of a claim to utter a prophetic message, and would readily introduce Paul's allusion to reserving questions of a certain kind for home. The women would in this case (i) be acting as judges over their husbands in public; (ii) risk turning worship into an extended discussion session with perhaps private interests; (iii) militate against the ethics of controlled and restrained speech in the context of which the congregation should be silently listening to God rather than eager to address one another; and (iv) disrupt the sense for the orderliness of God's agency in creation and in the world as against the confusion which preexisted the creative activity of God's Spirit.[62]

Gordon Fee, on the other hand, argues in his commentary on 1 Corinthians that 1 Corinthians 14.34-35 must be seen as non-Pauline gloss that has been inserted into the text. He gives four reasons to support this argument.

(a) The fact that a number of early manuscripts place verses 34-35 after verse 40 indicate that they were a marginal gloss that was subsequently included in the text at two different places.

(b) These verses disrupt the flow of the argument in chapter 14 which otherwise runs smoothly from verse 33 to verse 36.

(c) These verses contradict what St Paul says in 1 Corinthians 11.2-16 where he accepts that women will pray and prophesy in the gatherings of the Christian community alongside men.

(d) The phrase 'as even the law says' in verse 34 does not reflect St Paul's thought.[63]

• Many of the major commentators on 1 Timothy have supported the traditional view that 1 Timothy 2.11-15 contains a general prohibition on women exercising teaching authority in the Church. This is true, for example, of the commentaries by C. K. Barrett, J. N. D. Kelly, G. W. Knight and W. D. Mounce.[64] However, an increasing number of writers have responded to this traditional approach either by arguing that these verses are non-Pauline and mark a decline from the apostle's egalitarian teaching, or by arguing that they only restrict the activities of women in the Ephesian church in response to a specific issue which that church was facing at the time when St Paul wrote to it.

Hayter maintains, for instance, that 1 Timothy is post-Pauline and that these verses represent a retreat from St Paul's equalitarian vision:

> internal and external pressures upon the Church, pressures which were largely culturally conditioned, led Christian leaders to resort to Jewish interpretations of Old Testament teaching on woman's place and to reimpose ancient subordinationist views about family order and rules of conduct for females.[65]

By contrast, Aune, in her essay 'Evangelicals and Gender' which we noted in Chapter 3, accepts that 1 Timothy was written by St Paul. In her view the key to understanding the verses in question is to note that the problem which 1 and 2 Timothy address is the spread of heresy in the Ephesian church (1 Timothy 1.3, 1.6, 6.20-21, 2 Timothy 3.6). Women, including many young widows, were playing a significant role in the spread of the heresy in question, which included the teaching that marriage and childbearing were forbidden (1 Timothy 4.3). 1 Timothy 2.11-15 addresses this situation:

> Instead of teaching heresy, Paul tells women to learn. Women at that time had little or no education, which may be one reason why they were so easily influenced by false teaching. In verse 12 the tense of 'I do not permit' is the present continuous, rendering the meaning 'I am not *presently* permitting;' this is a culture dependent prohibition. If the heresy is Gnosticism, verses 13-14 show Paul countering the Gnostic myths about women's superiority. No, Eve wasn't created *before* Adam but *after*, he says. Furthermore, Eve was the first sinner, which negates any claim that women are spiritually superior. But even if the heresy was not Gnosticism, the verses must still be read as a culture-dependent prohibition. The word translated 'authority' is not the normal New Testament word for authority. It means something like 'domineer' and points to the activity of the women spreading false teaching. Paul then recalls the Fall; just as Eve was deceived by the serpent, these women had been deceived by false teachers. This cannot be made to imply that women are inherently more deceivable than men. A claim for the reverse could just as easily be made with reference to Romans 5.12, where Paul makes a similar point but this time only attributes blame to Adam: 'Just as sin entered the world through *one man*.' The thrust of 1 Timothy 2.11-15 is that the women must do the opposite of what they had been doing. They must stop their noisy, domineering, false teaching, and turn back to marriage and bearing children. This would be how they would keep their salvation. This prohibition against women teaching or having authority is not for all time.[66]

The theory that 1 Timothy 2.12-15 is a response to heretical teaching is now an argument that is often put forward to explain why St Paul restricted women's ministry in Ephesus.[67] Other explanations that are put forward are that women were preaching when they lacked the necessary education to do so, or that they were seizing authority in a way that would have harmed the Church's witness in a tense social situation.[68]

The evidence for women's ministry in the Early Church

5.3.24 A fifth argument is that there is evidence from epigraphic and other sources that women were extensively involved in the ministry of the Early Church. For example, in her study *Women Officeholders in Early Christianity* Ute Eisen looks at what we can learn about the activity of women in early Christianity, both in smaller sectarian groups such as the Montanists and in the mainstream 'Great Church'. She surveys literary evidence, such as the writings of the Fathers, and liturgical and canonical material, and epigraphic evidence, such as inscriptions on tombstones, and although she acknowledges that this evidence has traditionally been interpreted differently her conclusion is that it indicates that

> women were active in the expansion and shaping of the Church in the first centuries: they were apostles, prophets, teachers, presbyters, enrolled widows, deacons, bishops and stewards. They preached the Gospel, they spoke prophetically and in tongues, they went on mission, they prayed, they presided over the Lord's Supper, they broke the bread and gave the cup, they baptized, they taught, they created theology, they were active in the care of the poor and the sick, and they were administrators and managers of burial places.

5.3.25 If it is asked why the role of women became restricted in the subsequent history of the Church, the answer that is given is that this was the result of a growing fear of female sexuality and a belief in the intellectual and emotional weakness of women. As John Wijngaards puts it in his book *No Women in Holy Orders?*, research has shown that the reasons that women were gradually excluded from ministerial office

> were cultural: mainly the dominance of men and the fear of menstruation. In the course of time these cultural grounds were justified with spiritual explanations: 'Women are punished for Eve's sin.' 'Jesus did not choose a woman among the apostles.'

'Paul forbade women to teach.' 'Being imperfect human beings, women cannot represent Christ', and so on. Of great influence was also Roman Law according to which women could not hold any public responsibility, a principle that became part of Church law.[69]

5.3.26 In a contribution to the Working Party Christopher Hill argues that the point about Roman law made by Wijngaards can be developed further. Following Campbell, he argues that Roman law did allow women to be heads of households and in this role women were able to lead household churches as the New Testament indicates. However, Roman law did not permit women to exercise public office so when the household churches came together and sought overall leadership in a particular city from a single leader (a *monepiscopus*) women were not eligible to perform this role since it was a public rather than a household one.

The argument from tradition

5.3.27 A sixth argument is that the claim that tradition is against the ordination of women is problematic for three reasons:

- The way that the tradition developed marked a departure from what is seen as the egalitarian trajectory of the biblical witness.

There is evidence in the early history of the Church of the kind referred to above for the acceptance of women ministers and as Jane Shaw puts it:

> That this history is not an 'official' part of the Christian tradition is not a sign that women should not be ordained as priests and bishops today but rather a corporate sin of the Church which must be admitted, repented of and remedied. Furthermore, if the place of women in the apostolic succession – that is, the line of women's ordained ministry – is broken, that too is a collective sin of the church. We need to reincorporate into the Tradition this lost history, looking at all the ways in which women, against all the odds, have exercised their calls to ministry through two thousand years of Christianity.[70]

- Tradition is not static but develops and therefore the fact that women have not been ordained in the past is not a valid reason for saying that they cannot be ordained today. To quote Shaw again:

At the heart of these arguments is our understanding of the nature of Tradition. Do we believe Christian Tradition to be static or dynamic? The idea that women cannot be ordained to the priesthood or the episcopate because they never have been springs out of an understanding of Tradition as static. But orthodox Christianity has always believed in a Trinitarian God and thus a dynamic notion of Tradition, for belief in a Trinitarian God assumes that God the Holy Spirit is still at work in the world.[71]

5.3.28 The argument that tradition can legitimately develop was put forward by Stephen Sykes in his meeting with the Working Party with reference to his 1990 essay 'Richard Hooker and the Ordination of Women to the Priesthood'.[72] In this essay Sykes draws attention to the fact that according to Hooker even laws given by God can be changed if the particular circumstances which led to their being instituted have changed.

5.3.29 As Hooker puts it in Book III of the *Laws of Ecclesiastical Polity* the biblical evidence regarding such things as the abrogation of the Jewish ceremonial law shows us that:

> Whether God be the author of laws by authorizing that power of men, or by delivering them made immediately from himself, by word only, or in writing also, or howsoever; notwithstanding the authority of their maker, the mutability of that end for which they are made doth also make them changeable.[73]

> ... God never ordained anything that could be bettered. Yet many things he hath that have been changed, and that for the better. That which succeedeth as better now when change is requisite, hath been worse when that which now is changed was instituted. Other wise God would had not then left this to chose that, neither would now reject that to chose this, were it not for some new-grown occasion making that which hath been better worse. In this case therefore men do not presume to change God's ordinance, but they yield thereunto requiring itself to be changed.[74]

5.3.30 As Sykes explains, Hooker would have opposed the ordination of women not only because it was contrary to specific New Testament teaching (what Hooker called a 'positive law'), but also because it was contrary to the belief, ultimately derived from Aristotle, that women were by nature inferior to men and so needed to be ruled by them. For Hooker this combination of a positive law and the law of nature (what he called a 'mixed positive law') would have been immutable. However, for us who no longer accept the Aristotelian belief in the natural inferiority of women the only barrier to the ordination of women would be positive law which, according to Hooker himself, is open to change. To quote Sykes, the relevance of all this is that

> it shows Hooker to be the architect of an understanding of church polity which can seriously consider the necessity of change, even in an institution as traditional as an all-male priesthood. It does not, of course, turn Hooker into an advocate of women's ordination. But on his own principles Hooker would undoubtedly have been ready to consider an argument which destroyed the status of the doctrine of women's subordination as a deliverance of natural reason. The point can be made more precisely. The issue is not patriarchy (the rule of the father in the household), but male dominance. Aristotelian physiology and psychology are entirely general in their application to womankind, and are the basis on which the impropriety of female dominance can be urged. Once this generalized basis was abandoned (and it must be said to have lingered in psychology long into the twentieth century), the support from 'natural reason' essential to Hooker's prescription for a mixed positive law evaporates. When generalized female subordination ceases to make sense medically or empirically, the route must be open for a reappraisal of the scriptural positive law concerning the impropriety of female teachers.[75]

5.3.31   Sykes' point that female subordination no longer makes sense medically or empirically was also illustrated in a paper presented to the working party by Fraser Watts entitled *Women and the Episcopate: A Brief Comment from the Perspective of the Human Sciences*. In this paper Watts makes four points.

5.3.32   First, some of the differences between men and women are related to culture and at the moment these culturally based differences seem to be reducing:

> Thus whatever basis there may have been for the claim that women are not suited to be bishops, the empirical basis for that claim may be shrinking. It may well have been the case, 200 years ago, that men were more suited to exercise religious leadership than women. However, as the roles of men and women in society change, the relevant differences may be narrowing or disappearing.[76]

5.3.33   Secondly, the psychological differences that can be observed between men and women tend to be probabilistic rather than absolute in character. That is, they are true of most but not all men and women. This means that

> Even if we allow that men and women differ on average in some way that is relevant to their suitability to be bishops, it would be a very rough way of selecting people with the required characteristic to select men rather than women. Whatever characteristic was sought, some men would be much poorer at it than some women (and vice versa).[77]

5.3.34 Thirdly, the biological differences that exist between men and women are of doubtful relevance:

> It is also doubtful whether biological differences on their own are relevant to ordination or consecration, though such arguments might conceivably be advanced. For example, only women menstruate, but there is great difficulty in constructing a valid argument that leads from that clear fact to the unsuitability of women for particular roles such as those of a bishop in the church.[78]

5.3.35 Fourthly, the suggestion in the first 1988 House of Bishops report on the ordination of women that the exercise of authority is characteristic of men rather than women is implausible:

> Some women are well able to exercise authority, and that could probably be demonstrated for any conceivable measure of aptitude for the exercise of authority. However, it may be that the House of Bishops was not suggesting that men have greater capacity for the exercise of authority, but just that in some other sense it was more appropriate for them to do so. But what basis can be found for such a claim? I cannot myself see that it can be made to follow from the undoubted biological differences between men and women.[79]

5.3.36 One final point is made in connection with tradition:

- In order for some aspect of the Church's theology or practice to be seen as part of the fundamental Christian message (Tradition with a capital T[80]) more than longstanding continuity is required. What is generally needed is for the Christian Church to have considered a particular question in a decisive fashion at some point in its history, as in the case of the Nicene doctrine of the Trinity which was recognized as part of Tradition after the Church wrestled with Arianism in the fourth and fifth centuries.[81]

5.3.37   Because the exclusion of women from the threefold ordained ministry has only been challenged comparatively recently, the issue of whether women should be ordained has not yet been decisively considered. This means that the Church cannot yet draw fully on tradition in relation to the role of women in the ministry of the Church, and that it is therefore premature to say that the exclusion of women from the episcopate is part of Tradition.

The need for both women and men to represent Christ

5.3.38   A seventh argument is that an episcopate that consists of members of both sexes is required in order for the Church to bear proper witness to Christ. Drawing on the work of R. A. Norris mentioned earlier in this chapter, Gillett argues, for example, that through baptism women as well as men are incorporated into Christ and thereby given the role of representing him. It follows, says Gillett,

> that male and female together not only represent the *imago dei* in all its fullness but also the ministry of Christ within the Church. And this leads immediately to a consideration of the episcopate as a focus/sign of unity within the Church. The exclusion of women from the episcopate vitiates its ministry of proclaiming unity and calling the Church back to its fundamental unity in Christ. This leaves a gaping hole within the apostolic ministry of the Church and is, increasingly, within our society a denial of the very message we preach.[82]

The right of the Church of England to develop its own orders

5.3.39   An eighth argument is that the Church of England has the right to develop its own orders to bring them more in line with its developing theological understanding or to meet new circumstances, and this is in fact what took place at the Reformation in faithfulness to Scripture and apostolic tradition. There is therefore no need to wait for universal ecumenical agreement before moving ahead on the issue of women bishops.

5.3.40   This is a line of argument that was developed, for example, by Paul Avis in the context of the debate about the ordination of women to the priesthood. He makes two points.

● The first is that:

> While the Churches remain tragically divided they must perforce act 'unilaterally'. What that pejorative term means in practice is that

each branch of the Church must act responsibly, in accordance with its conscience, and through its structures of conciliarity and decision-making in fulfilment of its mission.[83]

- The second is that the very basis of Anglicanism is the action taken by the Church of England at the Reformation without waiting for the consent of the Church of Rome:

> The Churches that were shaped by the Reformation insisted that a particular Church has the authority to reform itself without tarrying for Rome. That is the very *raison d'être* of Anglicanism. It is implied in the logic of the Reformation itself. At that time the structure of the ministry was modified in the light of a deeper understanding of what was and was not required by the gospel, by Scripture and by primitive tradition. The jurisdiction of the pope was removed; clergy were permitted to marry; some minor orders were abolished.

> Just as the sixteenth-century English Church acted in accord with the continental Lutheran and Reformed Churches, so the Church of England today has acted in accord with many sister Churches of the Anglican Communion. The precedent of the Reformation does not of course justify the particular decision regarding women priests – which has to be assessed on its merits – but it does, I think, establish the principle that unilateral action is sometimes justified. It certainly shows that no Anglican can condemn unilateral action *tout court* without condemning their own standing ground as an Anglican.[84]

The significance of the 1992 decision to ordain women priests

5.3.41 A ninth argument is that in terms of the traditional Anglican church order the issue of whether women should be ordained as bishops was decided in principle when General Synod voted to ordain women as priests in November 1992. This is because in the Church of England those in priest's orders have always been eligible to be bishops and there is no reason for it to be different in the case of women.

5.3.42 Thus the submission sent to the Working Party by Women and the Church in October 2001 states:

> Our theological understanding of the three-fold orders of ministry – bishop, priest and deacon – is that ordination to the presbyterate admits of ordination to the episcopate. It therefore follows that if women have been ordained priest, sharing equally with their male counterparts, they are eligible to be ordained bishop also.[85]

5.3.43   The tenth argument is that if women are ordained as bishops then the Church will benefit more fully from the particular gifts that women have to offer. This was a point that was made in a large number of submissions to the Working Party and can be illustrated from the submission made to the Working Party from the Barking Episcopal Area of the Diocese of Chelmsford. This declares:

> The consecration of more women bishops will enrich the church because:
>
> - They will make the church more truly representative
>
> - They will give the church greater credibility and therefore make mission more effective (people outside the church will see it as a proper equality/justice issue)
>
> - Many women are good at making connections between life and faith, between theory and practice. They are also good at juggling life's demands and multi-tasking and with these skills will bring valuable benefits complementary to the work of men bishops
>
> - All have valuable, life-long experience to bring, modelling the commonwealth of God
>
> - They work with generative (i.e. birth/life giving) values and the nurture and enhancement of gifts and relationships rather than institutional concepts of products and projects
>
> - Their presence gives a wider recognition of the qualities and gifts of the women who are emerging as leaders, e.g. women priests, leaders of oppressed communities, women professionals, etc.
>
> - They are more naturally inclusive
>
> - They prefer to work collaboratively[86]

5.3.44   Evidence about the kind of difference a woman bishop might make was provided for the Working Party when it met with Victoria Matthews, the Bishop of Edmonton in the Anglican Church of Canada.

5.3.45   In discussion with the Working Party Bishop Victoria said that as a suffragan bishop in Toronto and as a diocesan bishop in Edmonton, being a woman had enhanced her role. When the Anglican Church of

Canada accepted the ordination of women to the episcopate, it brought the Church much media coverage, and this gave her a voice in a number of places and on a number of issues, which would not otherwise have been available to her. For example, she chose to live in the inner city of Edmonton and could speak at first hand about the problems in her district and draw attention to the needs of the poor.

5.3.46 After Bishop Victoria had been elected, she had received many letters from people who had been physically or sexually abused by priests, but the bishops had not listened. Because she was a woman, she was seen as more accessible to come to with experiences of abuse and some came to her who would not have come to a male bishop. From her time on, the victims of abuse were listened to for the first time.[87]

The missiological need for women bishops

5.3.47 A final argument picks up a point that we have already noted in the quotation from Gillett illustrating argument seven, and which is also made in the Barking area submission, which is that the ordination of women as bishops is required in order to give credibility to the Church's proclamation of the gospel in today's society. As we noted in Chapter 4, a belief in equality of opportunity between men and women has become a part of the prevailing ethos of our society (4.2.29-31), and the argument that is put forward is that in this context the Church of England's present position on women bishops is damaging to its presentation of the gospel.

5.3.48 For example, in her submission to the Working Party Amiel Osmaston notes:

> Recently on a train I spoke to a young mum who was not a churchgoer. On hearing that I was a priest, she raised the issue of women bishops. Her conclusion was, 'Well, if they really think that God doesn't want women bishops, then he's not the God I would want to have anything to do with'. The implications for mission speak for themselves.[88]

5.3.49 A similar point is made in the submission to the Working Party from St James', Piccadilly:

> A Church that supports Sex Discrimination (by opting out of the Sex Discrimination Act) and does not insist on Equal Opportunity practice, is an unconvincing carrier of the Gospel. In fact this stance

results in institutionalising the abuse of women just as individual women are abused. The Church's traditional teaching is that women are second-rate, need to be under headship and cannot take responsibility; this results in the Church being in a poor position to minister and challenge society. The Church sets a poor example in relationships between women and men. So it is that, at best, society ignores the Church on this issue and also, sadly, ignores the Gospel of justice, costly love and freedom of spirit that the Church proclaims. Men still represent women in the House of Bishops and in many Churches in England. This is restrictive imagery.

The Church of England is the State Church, but we note the fact that we do not speak in our nation's cultural language of justice. We will not attract others into the Community of God's people, or have much of a future, while we enshrine 'isms' (sexism, racism, classism) within our legislation. Secular society hears us debating and squabbling about sexual and gender issues instead of engaging with the pains and injustice of poverty.[89]

5.3.50 The issue of the missiological consequences of consecrating women as bishops is one that has become more prominent as the Church of England generally has begun to make mission a prime objective. The key question that is raised is what would be the missiological consequences of *not* consecrating women bishops? Those who have grown up since the sex discrimination legislation of 1975, and who live within our current British legal frameworks, have become accustomed to operating with general assumptions of equality of opportunity. This includes members of Church of England congregations, who, spurred on by the debates about the priesting of women and the experience of their ministry, see equality as a theological concept. Thus Ian Jones, in his research into the impact of the first decade of the ordination of women to the priesthood, notes that respondents to his research made assumptions about equality in a church context which did not imply sameness between the genders, but rather equal status before God, and equal value in gifts offered to the ministry of the Church.[90]

5.3.51 This understanding is seen as having been hard won; Ann Loades contends, for instance, that the sense that women are at fault unless they are subordinate to men is deeply rooted in Christianity, is still prevalent and still powerful.[91] It is against the weight of this traditional theological anthropology that many in the Church now use the word 'justice' as shorthand for equality of opportunity for women in the Church.[92] They are aware that institutions and groups which have exclusions from sex discrimination legislation are treated by most people in our culture as curiosities at best, and as scandalous at worst. This is the context within which the Church of England now preaches the gospel, and, as is noted above, the argument is that the absence of women bishops makes this preaching much more difficult.

5.4 Is it enough to ordain women bishops?

5.4.1   The main arguments presented to the Working Party have concentrated on the question of whether it would be right for the Church of England to ordain women as bishops. However, there have been some contributions to the Working Party that have raised the issue of whether the proposal to ordain women as bishops goes far enough.

5.4.2   For example, a number of members of the Working Party have throughout its deliberations believed that the particular questions relating to the ordination of women to the episcopate could not realistically and properly be addressed because there was a prior underlying question which had not been resolved, namely the lack of a corporately accepted Christian anthropology, which might provide the necessary theological understanding of the relationship of men and women in the redeemed community. Without such an understanding, there is little shared basis for decision making, for when all arguments for and against have been laid out, there is no clear means of deciding which of them should have the greater weight. In a paper for the Working Party, 'Towards the Transformation of the Episcopate: Proposal for a Reinvigorated Process', Ann Loades and Christine Hall drew attention to the need for consideration of the position of women as a whole in the Church, as a prior step to any discussion on any particular order or ministry:

> At every level of ecclesial life, paradigms constructed for males are regarded as normative and stand uncriticized, and, at every level, males who live exclusively in terms of these paradigms regard women as problematic. The ordination issue has unfortunately become symbolic of all the many other issues that the Church of England is not prepared to face in male/female relationships. Focusing on ordination, whether to the diaconate, priesthood or episcopate, effectively obscures the fact that the overall position of women in the Church needs urgent consideration, and enables men to avoid addressing a variety of issues of discrimination.[93]

5.4.3   The authors of this paper further suggest that the present situation, whilst it marginalizes women, is also damaging to men. The Church of England has not addressed the known fears of some men that changes in the position of women in the ecclesial community might result in redistribution of roles and power with possible consequent male redundancy. There seems to be little acknowledgement of the opportunities for enrichment for everyone that such change would in fact provide. Serious engagement is required in a much more thorough re-examination of the relationship between men and women in the kingdom, drawing particularly on perspectives from psychology and the natural and social sciences and also endeavouring to undertake an assessment of the freighting and value of traditional symbolic gender/role relations that is surely required by an incarnational religion which has hitherto found symbolic and differentiated sacramental expression.

5.4.4   In similar fashion Anne Richards states in her contribution to the Barking Episcopal Area submission to the Working Party:

> I am very concerned that women priests and deacons are badly treated by the institution of Church and that, notwithstanding the ordination of women, women's vocation and exercise of ministry is often treated without proper seriousness, or as a second class ministry to be glossed over in terms of appointment and affirmation. This is necessarily damaging to mission, as the ministry of men and women unequally valued and affirmed in this way cannot model kingdom. I am somewhat concerned therefore that the consecration of women as bishops could be used to mask this difficulty (look what we're doing to affirm women), could be used to make women into honorary male bishops (silenced and sidelined) and could be used to entrench the very things which women should be able freely to challenge and change (hierarchy etc). That is why I ask the question about how far change in episcopacy goes beyond the act of consecrating women.[94]

5.4.5   Richards asks whether women should refuse to become bishops if the House of Bishops does not first acknowledge the need for reform of the episcopate, and how, if the need for reform were to be accepted, the presence of women 'could transform the episcopal function into something representative of what it means to be fully expressive of being human under God'.[95]

5.5 Critical questions raised by the arguments about the ordination of women bishops

5.5.1   The critical questions that arise from the material we have considered in this chapter include the following:

Questions concerning biblical interpretation

- Does Scripture make a link between the submission of the Son to the Father and the submission of women to men? The traditional link between the two is St Paul's teaching in 1 Corinthians 11.3:

> I want you to understand that the head of every man is Christ, the head of a woman is her husband, and the head of Christ is God.

The argument is that what St Paul is doing here is drawing a parallel between the ordered relationship between Christ and the Father in the life of the Trinity and the submission of women to men. The issues that have to be considered are whether the term 'head' does carry connotations of authority in this verse and whether St Paul is intending to describe a hierarchy with God the Father at the top and women at the bottom.[96]

- Do the creation narratives in Genesis 1 – 2 teach that women are to submit to men or do they teach equality between women and men?

- Does the New Testament teach that the inequality between men and women has been overcome by the work of Christ, or does it teach that men and women are equal in respect of salvation but that women are still to submit to male authority? In particular, is Galatians 3.28 a passage that enunciates a general principle of equality between women and men or is it only concerned with declaring that they are equal in respect of being heirs of the blessing promised to Abraham?

- Do the three key passages appealed to in the New Testament (1 Corinthians 11.12-16, 1 Corinthians 14.34-38, 1 Timothy 2.8-15) (a) really teach the subordination of women and (b) if they do so, is it as a matter of universal principle or as a response to particular circumstances that may no longer apply?

- Is there evidence that women exercised ministerial authority in New Testament times and were even recognized as apostles? If they did exercise authority what form did this take and was it restricted in any way because they were women?

- With reference to the above, how should the Church respond to the fact that there is continuing disagreement between competent scholars about how the relevant material should be understood? How should it handle this lack of scholarly consensus?

Questions concerning tradition

- Is it clear that the Early Church did forbid women exercising ministerial authority or has fresh reading of the relevant evidence called this idea into question? As we have seen, the work of scholars such as Eisen and Wijngaards has called the traditional view of the matter into question, but the evidence to which they appeal has been questioned by other scholars.[97]

- In addition to the question about the interpretation of the evidence to which they appeal there is also the wider question of why, if their reading of the evidence is correct, the ministry of women became restricted in the Church in both East and West. Was this a result of the influence of cultural prejudice, as Wijngaards suggests, or was it a question of the Church coming to discern the mind of God more clearly on the matter, in the same way that it came to see which books properly belonged in the New Testament canon and discarded other texts which had previously been accepted in some churches?

- How should we relate the proposal to ordain women as bishops in the Church of England to the issue of tradition? Should we say

    (a) Tradition is against the proposal and this is an indication that the proposal is wrong? The argument here would be that the fact that for most, if not all, of the history of the Church only men have been bishops is in itself an indication of God's will that should not be ignored.

    (b) In this area tradition has been distorted by sin and we need to reclaim the Church's original practice of sexual equality? The argument here would be that in the New Testament we have a picture of a community in which, within the cultural constraints of the day, there was sexual equality and women and men exercised leadership together. The fact that this

equality was eventually lost and women became subordinate
once again is an example of the way in which human beings
reject God's will in favour of traditions of their own devising,
and the duty of the Church today is to restore equality
once again.

(c) Tradition is dynamic rather than static and so we are free to
develop the practice of the Church in a new way in our day
under the guidance of the Spirit? The argument here would be
that the dynamic nature of tradition which we noted in Chapter
3 means that the Church is free to adapt the tradition of having
a male-only episcopate in order to respond to the requirements
of our own cultural situation in the same way that, as we noted
in Chapter 2, the episcopate has already adapted in other ways
down the centuries.

Questions concerning ecclesiology

- Does the maleness of Christ mean that he can only be represented by
male bishops? Or are both female and male bishops required in order
to represent the fact that the human nature assumed by Christ at the
incarnation was for the salvation of both men and women ('what he
has not assumed he has not healed . . .') and that the risen and
ascended Christ assumes both women and men in his glorified
humanity (Ephesians 2.1-22)?

- Would the ordination of women as bishops in England truly
undermine the integrity of Anglican orders, or could it be argued
that traditional Anglican theology indicates that reforming these
orders to bring them in line with God's will would enhance their
integrity?

- If women were to be ordained as bishops in the Church of England
would this call sacramental assurance into question, or is this not
an issue, either because women bishops would be validly ordained,
or because the efficacy of the sacraments is not tied to the validity
of ministerial orders but to the action of God and the faith of
God's people?

- Is the likelihood of disunity, both within the Church of England
and in its ecumenical relationships, resulting from a decision
to ordain women bishops an argument against proceeding

in this direction or are the theological and missiological imperatives for this move so significant that the pain of this disunity must be discounted? Might not a female bishop still be able to promote unity through her ministry even in a situation where there was disunity?

- Is it enough for women simply to be ordained as bishops or does a major reconsideration of the episcopate and of the relationship between men and women in the Church of England as a whole need to take place either prior to or alongside their ordination?

Broader theological questions

- Have almost all societies been patriarchal as Goldberg has argued? If so, is this to be seen as a reflection of God's creative intention, or as an example of how this intention has been frustrated by sin?

- In debates about the relationship between men and women the traditional arguments relating to the supposed natural inferiority of women to men have now been almost universally abandoned. In this situation is it possible to hold that God has ordained that women should submit to men without giving the impression that God has decreed this arbitrarily? If so, how?

- The risen and ascended Christ is the symbol of the way in which the divisions of humanity have been overcome by the action of God (Ephesians 2.1-22). Is the existence of distinctive roles for men and women an example of the kind of divisions that have been overcome in Christ or is the unity established by Christ one that embraces distinctive gender roles within it?

- If it is held that women should submit to the authority of men is this something that should be consistently applied over all areas of the life of society or only within the family and the life of the Church?

- How should we assess the growth in the demand for female emancipation and equality since the nineteenth century? Is this to be seen as an act of rebellion against the order placed into creation by God, as a movement of the Spirit leading society and the Church forward into truth, or as a mixed phenomenon with some good and some bad aspects?

chapter 6

The issue of timing

6.1 Introduction

6.1.1   As we noted in Chapter 3, pressure for the Church of England to ordain women bishops has been increasing ever since the first women were ordained as priests in 1994. The decision of the Scottish Episcopal Church to permit the ordination of women bishops will only serve to increase this pressure given the close ties that exist between the Anglican churches north and south of the border

6.1.2   However there are people in the Church of England who feel that this is not the right time for the Church of England to proceed on this matter. In this chapter we shall look at the arguments put forward to support this position and the arguments of those on the other side who feel that further delay would be inappropriate.

6.2 Arguments for delay

(a) Arguments concerned with the Church of England

6.2.1   The first argument is that while there are those in the Church of England who have no problems with the Church of England ordaining women as bishops there are still a large number of people who have conscientious doubts about the matter and the requirements of Christian love mean taking their conscientiously held views into account.

6.2.2   In Romans 14.13-23 and 1 Corinthians 8.1-13 St Paul addresses the question of what Christians should do if other Christians feel that the food that they are eating is unclean or has been polluted by being offered to pagan idols. The answer he gives is that Christians should respect the scruples of those who have conscientious objections to eating this kind of food since for them it would be a sin to consume it while believing this to be against the will of God.

6.2.3   St Paul sums up his argument in 1 Corinthians 8.9-13 as follows:

> Only take care lest this liberty of yours somehow become a stumbling block to the weak. For if any one sees you, a man of knowledge, at

table in an idol's temple, might he not be encouraged, if his conscience is weak to eat food offered to idols? And so by your knowledge this weak man is destroyed, the brother for whom Christ died. Thus, sinning against your brethren and wounding their conscience when it is weak, you sin against Christ.

6.2.4   As Gordon Fee notes in his commentary on 1 Corinthians, the real concern that motivates St Paul in this passage, and also in the parallel passage in Romans, is that

> Personal behaviour is dictated not by knowledge, freedom, or law, but by love for those within the community of faith. Everything one does that affects relationships within the body of Christ should have care for brothers and sisters as its primary motivation.[1]

6.2.5   The application of this to the current situation in the Church of England, it is argued, is that those who favour the ordination of women as bishops are like the 'strong' Christians in Romans 14 and 1 Corinthians 8 who had no problem with eating all kinds of food, while those who object to their ordination are like the 'weak' Christians in those passages who had conscientious problems with eating certain kinds of food.

6.2.6   Just as the principle of love for other members of the Christian community meant that the 'strong' Christians in Rome and Corinth should refrain from eating certain foods to avoid hurting their sisters and brothers so also those who favour women's ordination should refrain from going down this route while there are still members of the Church for whom this would create conscientious problems.

6.2.7   A second argument is that although there might be a majority in favour of ordaining women bishops there is no consensus about the matter and since ministerial orders, particularly episcopal orders, are intended to act as a means of unifying the Church it would be wrong in principle to act until such a consensus has been achieved. As the Reform submission put it, to ordain women bishops

> would deepen the divisions and alienations that already exist, by pouring salt into the wounds. The episcopate, instead of being a focus of unity, would become a focus of division.[2]

6.2.8   A third argument is that when it was decided to ordain women as priests it was agreed, in line with the recommendations of the Eames Commission, that there should be an 'open period of reception' in order to discern whether the decision was the right one. As we saw in the previous chapter, those who oppose the ordination of women as bishops ask whether it is right to proceed with their ordination while the question of women priests is still meant to be in this process of reception. Thus, the second submission from Forward in Faith declares:

> Before embarking upon the ordination of women to the episcopate (and the additional, overlapping 'period of reception' which that additional innovation will undoubtedly entail) the Church of England needs to take time to evaluate the gift and promise which came with the ordination of women to the priesthood: to decide whether the gift was worth the expense and if the promise will ever be fulfilled.[3]

6.2.9   In similar fashion Toon declares:

> The House of Bishops is currently committed to the testing of the innovation and experiment of the ordaining of women to the first two orders and to these alone. For the House to add the ordination of women to the third order to this complex state of affairs of testing and discernment would be, I believe, to act dishonestly, hastily and prematurely, going back upon and contradicting its own clear words.

> What I state holds I believe even if the Working Party on Women in the Episcopate reports that the theological arguments in favour of elevating women to the episcopate are compelling (that is compelling as they are seen at this point of time in the life of the Church and the situation in western culture where the dignity of women is emphasized). A commitment to reception has been made and it must on moral and theological grounds be kept to and allowed to be an open process.[4]

6.2.10   A fourth argument is that if the Church of England wants to justify a move to ordain women bishops on the basis of sound theological scholarship it ought to continue to wait. This is because the scholarly discussion about the interpretation of the relevant passages of Scripture and the historical evidence from the Early Church is still inconclusive. Just as there is no consensus in the Church in general so also there is no consensus among scholars on these issues. Scholars are still producing arguments in favour of the Church's traditional position and until it can be convincingly shown that these arguments are invalid then the Church ought not to proceed further on the matter.

6.2.11   An example of this point is provided, for example, by the continuing scholarly discussion about the interpretation of 1 Timothy 2.8-15. As Thiselton argues in a review of recent literature on this subject presented to the Working Party, there exists a spectrum of views about the interpretation of these verses. At one end of the spectrum there are those who propose a new egalitarian reading of them; at the other end of the spectrum there are those who still argue for a traditional reading, and in the middle there are those who take a nuanced but still generally traditional point of view.

6.2.12   Thiselton's conclusions are twofold:

- He notes that recent more egalitarian readings 'place at least a serious question mark against the more traditional interpretations' but that 'they do remain hypothetical and speculative, and the major commentators appear in general to remain unconvinced'.

- He also argues that 'What emerges most clearly is that none of the three groups of views on the spectrum can simply be brushed aside as unworthy of respect and of due attention.'[5]

6.2.13   Given that this is the case, the argument runs, should not the Church hesitate to innovate further unless and until the scholarly uncertainty is resolved and there is a consensus that the egalitarian reading of 1 Timothy 2 is the correct one?

(b) Ecumenical arguments
6.2.14   There are two arguments here.

6.2.15   First, although there are three Anglican provinces that have women bishops (ECUSA, The Anglican Church of Canada, and the Anglican Church in Aotearoa, New Zealand and Polynesia) and three more (The Church of Ireland, the Episcopal Church of Scotland and the Church of the Province of South Africa) that have voted to make their ordination possible, the vast majority of the Communion does not have women bishops and has not accepted them in principle. Reception has yet to take place.

6.2.16   This means, it is argued, that if the Church of England were to ordain women bishops this would increase the impairment of communion that already exists within the Communion over women priests, women bishops and other issues. It would exacerbate the process whereby the Communion ceases to be in any meaningful sense a communion of churches with common and interchangeable orders and becomes instead merely a loose federation of churches with a shared history but different and incommensurable polities.

6.2.17 The question of the role of the Archbishop of Canterbury is particularly significant here. Being in Communion with the Archbishop of Canterbury is a defining mark of an Anglican church. If provinces could no longer be in communion with the Archbishop either because the Archbishop ordained women bishops or was herself a woman then the unity of the Communion as a whole could be threatened. Would it not be better to wait until there was a consensus across the whole Communion about this matter?

6.2.18 Secondly, the two traditions that encompass the vast majority of Christians around the world, the Roman Catholic[6] and Orthodox traditions,[7] do not ordain women as either priests or bishops and at present show no sign of changing their position and receiving this development.

6.2.19 In the case of the Roman Catholic Church the *Catechism of the Catholic Church* declares, for instance:

> 'Only a baptized man (*vir*) validly receives sacred ordination.' The Lord Jesus chose men (*viri*) to form the college of the twelve apostles, and the apostles did the same when they chose collaborators to succeed them in their ministry. The college of bishops, with whom the priests are united in the priesthood, makes the college of the twelve an ever-present and ever-active reality until Christ's return. The Church recognizes herself to be bound by this choice made by the Lord himself. For this reason the ordination of women is not possible.[8]

6.2.20 The Apostolic letter *Ordinatio Sacerdotalis* issued by Pope John Paul II in 1994 makes the same point in more detail. Quoting the 1988 Apostolic letter *Mulieris Dignitatem*, it declares:

> In calling only men as his Apostles, Christ acted in a completely free and sovereign manner. In doing so, he exercised the same freedom with which, in all his behaviour, he emphasized the dignity and vocation of women, without conforming to the prevailing customs and to the traditions sanctioned by the legislation of the time.[9]

6.2.21   It then goes on to say:

> In fact, the Gospels and the Acts of the Apostles attest that this call
> was made in accordance with God's eternal plan: Christ chose those
> whom he willed (cf Mk 3.13-14; Jn 6.70), and he did so in union
> with the Father, 'through the Holy Spirit' (Acts 1.2) after having
> spent the night in prayer (cf Lk 6.12). Therefore in granting
> admission to the ministerial priesthood, the Church has always
> acknowledged as a perennial norm her Lord's way of acting in
> choosing the twelve men whom he made the foundations of his
> Church (cf Rev 21.14). These men did not in fact receive only a
> function which could thereafter be exercised by any member of the
> Church; rather they were specifically and intimately associated in the
> mission of the Incarnate Word himself (cf Mt 10.1, 7-8; 28.16-20;
> Mk 3.13-16; 16.14-15). The Apostles did the same when they chose
> fellow workers who would succeed them in their ministry. Also
> included in this choice were those who, throughout the time of
> the Church, would carry on the Apostles' mission of representing
> Christ the Lord and Redeemer.[10]

6.2.22   In the case of the Orthodox Church there is no agreed pan-
Orthodox statement about the matter. However, there are clear
indications that at the moment the Orthodox churches are not likely
to move towards the ordination of women. Two examples will illustrate
where the Orthodox, officially at least, currently stand on the matter.

6.2.23   The communiqué issued after the Athens meeting of the
Anglican–Orthodox Theological Commission in 1978 sets out the
Orthodox position as follows:

(1) God created mankind in his image as male and female, establishing
     a diversity of functions and gifts. These functions and gifts are
     complementary but, as St Paul insists (1 Corinthians 12), not
     all are interchangeable.

(2) The Orthodox Church honours a woman, the Holy Virgin Mary,
     the Theotokos, as the human person closest to God. In the
     Orthodox tradition women saints are given such titles as
     'megalomartyrs' (great martyr) and 'isapostolos' (equal to the
     apostles). Thus it is clear that in no sense does the Orthodox
     Church consider women to be intrinsically inferior in God's eyes.
     Men and women are equal but different, and we need to exercise
     this diversity of gifts.

(3) While women exercise this diversity of ministries, it is not possible for them to be admitted to the priesthood. The ordination to the priesthood is an innovation, lacking any basis whatever in holy tradition.[11]

6.2.24   In his paper *The Ordination of Women to the Priesthood* which was presented to the International Commission of the Anglican–Orthodox Theological Dialogue in 2002, Bishop Basil of Sergievo draws the same conclusion as the 1978 Athens communiqué, explaining that the basis for this is the distinction between men and women at the heart of the liturgy, and therefore the spiritual life, of the Orthodox churches:

> It may well be true that there is no clear theological reason for not ordaining women. It may be true that the Scriptures do not explicitly exclude it. But the tradition of the Church – at least of the Eastern Church – would seem to exclude it simply through the way it has for centuries structured the Liturgy. The polarity between men and women, male and female, has been used to express the deepest aspects of the work of Christ, his overcoming division while preserving difference at all levels of creation. It is hard to see how the Byzantine Liturgy could survive as a coherent symbol system if women were to be ordained. Perhaps it needn't be preserved. But the Orthodox faithful will be hard to convince of this. The Liturgy, as they experience it, is the very heart of the Church.[12]

6.2.25   Not only is it the case that the Roman Catholic and Orthodox Churches show no sign at present of receiving the ordination of women. It is also the case that they have made it clear that the ordination of women by the Church of England places a serious obstacle in the development of ecumenical relationships.

6.2.26   To take the Roman Catholic Church first of all, in 1975 Pope Paul VI wrote to Archbishop Donald Coggan declaring that the 'new course taken by the Anglican Communion in admitting women to the ordained priesthood' could not fail to introduce 'an element of grave difficulty' into the work of the Anglican–Roman Catholic Commission and its attempt to develop doctrinal agreement between the Anglican and Roman Catholic churches.[13] In 1976 in a further letter to Archbishop Coggan Paul VI described the proposal to ordain women priests in the Anglican Communion as 'so grave a new obstacle and threat' on the path to reconciliation between Anglicans and Roman Catholics.[14]

6.2.27   In 1984 Pope John Paul II wrote to Archbishop Robert Runcie and declared that 'the increase in the number of Anglican Churches which admit, or are preparing to admit, women to priestly ordination constitutes, in the eyes of the Catholic Church, an increasingly serious obstacle' to the 'progress towards reconciliation between our two communions'.[15]

6.2.28   In 1986 Cardinal Willebrands, the President of the Vatican Secretariat for Promoting Christian Unity, wrote to Archbishop Runcie stating that

> The Catholic Church takes very seriously the considerable progress that has been made towards our eventual goal of full communion of faith and sacramental life. Our greater unity must be a fundamental concern, and it has to be stated frankly that a development like the ordination of women does nothing to deepen the communion between us and weakens the communion that currently exists. The ecclesiological implications are serious.[16]

6.2.29   In 1988 Pope John Paul II wrote to Archbishop Runcie in connection with the decision of the Lambeth Conference to respect the right of Anglican provinces to decide to ordain women bishops and expressed his

> concern in respect of those developments at Lambeth which seem to have placed new obstacles in the way of reconciliation between Catholics and Anglicans. The Lambeth Conference's treatment of the question of women's ordination has created a new and perplexing situation for the members of the Second Anglican/Roman Catholic International Commission to whom, in 1982, we gave the mandate of studying 'all that hinders the mutual recognition of the ministries of our Communions'. The ordination of women to the priesthood in some provinces of the Anglican Communion, together with the ordination of women to the episcopacy, appears to pre-empt the study and effectively block the path to the mutual recognition of ministries.
>
> The Catholic Church, like the Orthodox Church and the Ancient Oriental Churches, is firmly opposed to this development, viewing it as a break with tradition of a kind we have no competence to authorize. It would seem that the discussion of women's ordination in the Anglican Communion has not taken sufficiently into account the ecumenical and ecclesiological dimensions of the question. Since the Anglican Communion is in dialogue with the Catholic Church –

as it is with the Orthodox Church and the Ancient Oriental
Churches – it is urgent that this aspect be given much greater
attention in order to prevent a serious erosion of the degree of
communion between us.[17]

6.2.30   In regard to Anglican–Orthodox relations, the Athens meeting
of the Anglican–Orthodox Joint Doctrinal Commission in 1978
declared that

> (9) The action of ordaining women to the priesthood involves not
> simply a canonical point of Church discipline, but the basis of the
> Christian faith as expressed in the Church's ministries. If the
> Anglicans continue to ordain women to the priesthood, this will have
> a decisively negative effect on the issue of the recognition of Anglican
> orders. Those Orthodox Churches which have partially or
> provisionally recognized Anglican orders did so on the ground that
> the Anglican Church has preserved the apostolic succession; and the
> apostolic succession is not merely continuity in the outward laying-
> on of hands, but signifies continuity in apostolic faith and spiritual
> life. By ordaining women, Anglicans would sever themselves from
> this continuity, and so any existing acts of recognition by the
> Orthodox would have to be reconsidered.

> (10) If one member of the body suffers, all the other members suffer
> with it (1 Cor 12:26). We Orthodox cannot regard the Anglican
> proposals to ordain women as a purely internal matter, in which the
> Orthodox are not concerned. In the name of our common Lord and
> Saviour Jesus Christ, we entreat our Anglican brothers not to proceed
> further with this action which is already dividing the Anglican
> Communion, and which will constitute a disastrous reverse for
> all our hopes of unity between Anglicanism and Orthodoxy.[18]

6.2.31   Although the Athens statement refers only to the ordination of
priests the centrality of the episcopate for Orthodox ecclesiology means
that the ordination of women bishops could only make the situation
more difficult.

6.2.32   The attitude of the Roman Catholic and Orthodox churches
raises two questions in the minds of those who are arguing for a delay.

- As was also the case with regard to the ordination of women to the
  priesthood, the first question is whether the Church of England has
  the authority to change Catholic orders without the ecumenical

consent of the two largest groups of Christian churches. This is a particularly important issue because the claim of the Church of England has always been that its ministry is the same as that of the ancient churches of the West and East and as such is a sign and instrument of the Church of England's apostolicity and catholicity. To change this ministry without the consent of those other churches would be ecclesiologically and dogmatically significant since it would mean that this claim could no longer be made.

- The second is whether it would it be right for the Church of England deliberately to introduce what would be a further impediment to the development of unity with them.

6.2.33   If the answer to either of these questions is 'No', then the further question has to be asked whether now is the right time to ordain women bishops in the Church of England even if it were right in principle to do so. Once again, as with the issue of women priests, it can be argued that the proper course would be to wait until there was an ecumenical consensus involving the Roman Catholic and Orthodox Churches that this was a legitimate development.

6.2.34   Although the argument about ecumenical consent has focused on the position of the Roman Catholic and Orthodox churches, mention also has to be made of those Protestant churches in this country and around the world who object to the ordination of women because they consider it to be against biblical teaching. Examples of such churches would be the churches belonging to the Fellowship of Independent Evangelical Churches (FIEC) in this country, the Evangelical Lutheran Church in Latvia and the churches belonging to the Southern Baptist Convention and the Lutheran Church, Missouri Synod in the United States. If the Church of England is committed to the pursuit of all-round ecumenical unity then their concerns must be taken into account as well.

6.3 Arguments for ordaining women bishops now

6.3.1   The first argument that is made for acting now is that there is evidence that there is a widespread desire within the Church of England for such a move as shown, for example, by the growing number of Diocesan Synod Motions that have asked General Synod to take action on the matter. There is still opposition but total agreement is unlikely to be achieved and there is sufficient agreement to proceed, both in terms of the likelihood of getting legislation through the synodical process and in terms of it being possible to say that the Church of England as a whole has a generally agreed mind about the matter.

6.3.2   To put it another way, women priests have now been sufficiently 'received' to make it legitimate to move on to ordain women bishops. Furthermore, because the ordination of women bishops is an issue which goes to the heart of what the gospel is all about (the working out in history of the reconciling work of Christ) the theological imperative to ordain women as bishops makes it necessary to take this step, particularly if some kind of arrangement can be made to ensure that the consciences of those opposed to it are respected.

6.3.3   A second argument is that although there is still scholarly disagreement about the issues of biblical and historical interpretation involved, complete scholarly agreement is something that is unlikely ever to be achieved and there are sufficiently weighty scholarly arguments to make ordaining women bishops a legitimate step to take. A parallel case would be that of infant baptism. There is continuing scholarly disagreement about whether or not the practice of infant baptism can be supported from the New Testament evidence and yet the Church of England feels that there are sufficiently good scholarly arguments to justify it continuing to maintain its traditional practice.

6.3.4   The key requirement is not that there is complete scholarly unanimity on a particular issue, but that those who support a particular position are confident their position can be justified using the sort of responsible approach to biblical interpretation set out in Chapter 3 of this report. Those who support the ordination of women as bishops in the Church of England argue that this is the case.

6.3.5   Furthermore, following the long-established principle of interpreting the less clear parts of Scripture in the light of those parts that are more clear, they would say that uncertainty about the interpretation of particular texts such as 1 Timothy 2.9-15 has to be seen in the light of the overall trajectory of the Bible which points towards an egalitarian understanding of the relationship between men and women and the possibilities of ministry and leadership for them both.

6.3.6   A third argument is that the experience of women's ministry since 1994 has shown that women would be capable of serving as bishops and it would be both unjust and a waste of their God-given talents not to give them the opportunity to do so. In the words of the WATCH submission to the Working Party:

> Women priests are now a reality and have been widely accepted throughout the Church of England. Indeed, the widespread, grass-roots appreciation of women's priestly ministry leads us to conclude that women's episcopal ministry would be a blessing not just to the Church but to our secular society also. Our own experience of the ministry of ordained women in the Church of England is that their God-given gifts and ability make them as fitted for episcopal consideration as their male colleagues.[19]

6.3.7 This is a point that was also made very strongly to the Working Party by the representatives of the National Association of Diocesan Advisers in Women's Ministry when they met with the Working Party in December 2002. They spoke from their own experience of women priests who they felt would be ready to serve as bishops.

6.3.8 A fourth argument is that while women are not permitted to be bishops women priests will continue to be discriminated against and treated as second class and we need to act as soon as possible to bring this situation to an end. This was a point that was made in several meetings of the Working Party.

6.3.9 A fifth argument is that while the Church delays its decision on this matter argument about it will, in the words of Amiel Osmaston,

> continue to deflect the Church's energies from focussing on the primary purposes of the Church such as worship and mission.[20]

6.3.10 A sixth argument is that the longer the Church delays and so continues to discriminate against women the more incredible its witness to the gospel will be in our society where equality of opportunity is taken as a given. We have already noted material to this effect in the previous chapter.

6.3.11 A seventh argument is that, in contrast to the issue of homosexuality, it has been accepted within the Communion that it is legitimate for provinces to move forward on this matter without the agreement of the Communion as a whole. Thus in 1988 the Lambeth Conference resolved:

> That each province respect the decision and attitudes of other
> provinces in the ordination or consecration of women to the
> episcopate, without such respect necessarily indicating acceptance
> of the principles involved, maintaining the highest possible degree
> of communion with the provinces which differ.[21]

Indeed the reports of the Eames Commission have discussed how the
highest possible degree of communion might be maintained within the
Communion between provinces that differ on this matter while the
period of discussion and reception continues.

6.3.12   It could also be argued that there would be gains as well as
losses in terms of the impairment of communion with other Anglican
provinces. In order not to pre-empt the decision of the Church of
England in the matter of the ordination of women to the episcopate,
since the election of the first woman bishop in the Anglican
Communion in 1988 the Archbishops of Canterbury and York have
declined to exercise their discretion under the *Overseas and Other
Clergy (Ministry and Ordination) Measure 1967* to permit women
bishops to perform episcopal functions here. Nor have the Archbishops
been willing to give permission under the 1967 measure to those
ordained by women bishops to officiate in the Church of England.
A decision by the Church of England to ordain women bishops would
mean that this particular form of impaired communion would come
to an end.

6.3.13   An eighth argument is that the wider ecumenical issue is more
complex than opponents of women bishops suggest, and that there
would be ecumenical gains as well as losses.

● There are already signs that a debate has started among the Orthodox
on this issue.

For example, while acknowledging that many Orthodox Christians
are very conservative in this area, the Orthodox philosopher and
theologian Elisabeth Behr-Sigel nevertheless writes as follows in a
book written with Bishop Kallistos Ware entitled *The Ordination
of Women in the Orthodox Church*:

> The door does seem ajar in the Orthodox churches for an intelligent
> creative restoration of the diaconate of women accompanied by a
> comprehensive rethinking of this ministry. Perhaps we should push

that door open, while at the same time still thinking together, in a free and conciliar way, on the question being asked by the churches which do ordain women to the ministry. The attitude of the Orthodox churches to them should be modest, friendly and expectant, open to the possibility expressed towards the end of the Lima document *Baptism, Eucharist and Ministry* 'that the Spirit may well speak to one church through the insights of another'. The desire for the unity of the Lord's followers in obedience to him should encourage the Orthodox churches – and other traditional churches – to face the question of women's ordination to a full ministry within the Church. It is a difficult problem, to be approached in the light of the mystery of God, who became human so that humankind as a whole, in its communion with the Divine/Human Person by the Spirit, should be saved, sanctified and transfigured.

While awaiting that agreement to be achieved through ecumenical dialogue, perhaps it would be possible for the Orthodox churches to admit the legitimate existence of different disciplines in this area of ordination within the Universal Church. That would be to acknowledge (in the words of Fr Jean-Marie Roger Tillard) a Church *kat' holon*, a 'communion of communions', with differing historical and cultural traditions.[22]

Even more strikingly, an informal 1996 Old Catholic–Orthodox consultation on the issue concluded that

The participants in the consultation were not able to recognize any 'compelling dogmatic or theological reasons' for not ordaining women to the priesthood. This means that the ordination of women could not fundamentally call in question or destroy the communion or unity of the church or the moves toward restoring broken communion and unity. Difficulties might occur in practice, because the ministries of priests might not always be interchangeable.[23]

Although this consultation had no official standing in the eyes of the Orthodox churches, the conclusion it reached indicates that some at least of the Orthodox have moved a long way from the position taken at Athens in 1978 and, if built upon, might lead to the conclusion that there were no dogmatic objections to women bishops from an Orthodox perspective.[24]

- In spite of the official prohibition of discussion of the issue within the Roman Catholic Church, it is clear that there are Roman Catholics who would like to see the issue opened up for discussion and would indeed favour the ordination of women priests and bishops. For example, Nicholas Lash has questioned whether *Ordinatio Sacerdotalis* should be regarded as the final word on the matter,[25] and other Catholic theologians such as John Wijngaards are questioning the theological basis of the traditional Roman Catholic position.

In his book *No Women in Holy Orders?* Wijngaard argues, for instance, that there are 'three powerful factors' that should lead the Roman Catholic Church to 'overcome ancient prejudice and admit women to all holy orders'.[26]

The first factor is that

> Scripture teaches unambiguously that all the faithful, men and women, are made children of God and carry Christ's image. All partake in the general priesthood of Christ through one and the same identical baptism. ... This fundamental identification with Christ through baptism gives every Christian, whether man or woman, the fundamental openness to receive all the sacraments, including holy orders.[27]

The second factor is that

> The full content and meaning of Revelation is carried in the hearts of ordinary members of the Church. It is known as the *sensus fidelium*, the 'awareness of the faithful'. ... Well, with regard to women priests, research has abundantly documented that, in countries where people receive a proper education, two-thirds of Catholics feel there is no conflict between Catholic faith and the ordination of women to the priesthood. This applies equally to practising Catholics, teachers at Catholic schools, parish workers, members of religious communities, and, when they are free to speak, priests.[28]

The third factor is that the historical evidence shows that

> For at least eight centuries bishop after bishop laid his hands on woman after woman, invoking the Holy Spirit on her, and imparting the full sacramental diaconate with all the ceremonies that designated it as such. Tens of thousands of women deacons served their parish churches. A fragmentary record of their life and work can be found

on tombstones, in written documents, in feasts celebrated in their honour. This undeniable historical precedent proves to the Church that women *can receive holy orders*.[29]

Those in the Roman Catholic Church who take this view, it is argued, would welcome a decision by the Church of England, the mother Church of the Anglican Communion, to ordain women bishops, as this would increase the pressure on Rome to reconsider its own position.

- It is also pointed out that in spite of dire warnings about what would happen to Anglican–Orthodox and Anglican–Roman Catholic relations if women were ordained in Anglican churches, the ordination of women priests and bishops has not in fact brought these relationships to an end. Dialogue and the building of good ecumenical relationships have continued and would continue even if the Church of England were to ordain women bishops.

- Furthermore, ordaining women bishops would remove an anomaly in our relationship with the Lutheran churches in Norway and Sweden with whom we have only partial inter-changeability of ministry since the Church of England does not recognize the orders of their women bishops. In addition, it would improve ecumenical relations with a range of other churches who do ordain women to all levels of their ministry.

- In particular, ordaining women as bishops in the Church of England would remove an obstacle to the development of Anglican–Methodist relations under the terms of the Anglican-Methodist covenant. The fact that the Church of England places restriction on the ministry of women is explicitly identified as a major stumbling block in the way of the development of an interchangeable ministry between the Anglican and Methodist churches:

> All posts and positions within the Methodist Church that are open to men are also open to women. There are women District chairs and there have been women Presidents of Conference. The report to Conference 2000 on *Episkope and Episcopacy*, Guideline 6, made it clear that an episcopate in the Methodist Church would be open to women as well as to men. This principle is regarded as something that the Methodist Church has received from God and wishes to share with the wider Church. For many Methodists, any failure to

recognize and accept the full ministry of women would constitute a serious theological obstacle to full visible unity.[30]

Ordaining women bishops in the Church of England would remove this obstacle.

6.3.14 There are thus arguments both for and against this being the right time to ordain women as bishops in the Church of England and a decision will have to be made as to which arguments carry more weight.

chapter 7

The theological and practical issues raised by possible options for the future

7.1 Introduction

7.1.1   The purpose of this chapter is to consider the options facing the Church of England in the light of the material considered in the previous chapters of this report. We shall look in turn at each of the options facing the Church and examine the theological and practical issues raised by each option.

7.2 Issues raised by maintaining the status quo

7.2.1   The assumption is often made that the only issue facing the Church of England is in what way to move towards the ordination of women as bishops. What must not be overlooked, however, is that another option open to the Church of England is not to proceed in this direction at all, but to maintain the status quo either permanently or for the time being. This would mean that women could be priests and could serve as archdeacons and deans but would continue to be ineligible to be either suffragan or diocesan bishops.

7.2.2   The arguments in favour of maintaining permanently the status quo are the theological and ecclesiological arguments set out in section 2 of Chapter 5; and those in favour of maintaining it on at least a temporary basis are those set out in section 2 of Chapter 6. As we have seen, these arguments revolve around the question of whether such a move could be seen as justified on the basis of Scripture and tradition and whether it would be right to undertake such a move in the face of continuing doubts within the Church of England and the absence of wider ecumenical agreement.

7.2.3   If any or all of these arguments are thought to be valid, either individually or cumulatively, then maintaining the status quo would be the right course for the Church of England to take. However, going down this road would raise a number of issues.

7.2.4   First, it would have to be realized that a decision simply to maintain the status quo would be unlikely to bring the argument in the Church of England concerning the ordination of women to an end. This is for four reasons:

(a) Those who support the ordination of women as bishops would view any decision by General Synod to maintain the status quo as a temporary setback rather than as the end of the matter. They believe that admitting women to the episcopate would be a significant expression of gospel values and they are not going to give up on campaigning for change. Therefore, as in the case of the campaign for the ordination of women to the priesthood, the result of a decision to maintain the status quo would simply be intensified campaigning for the decision to be reversed.

(b) On the ecumenical front it seems likely that pressure for the ordination of women to all ministerial offices in the Church will continue to grow across the ecumenical spectrum. If this proves to be the case, then the Church of England will come under pressure to reconsider its position, not only from churches in the Anglican Communion, the Lutheran Churches of the Porvoo agreement and the Methodist Church, but also, in the longer term, from within traditions such as Roman Catholicism and Orthodoxy which have hitherto resisted the idea of the ordination of women and it will risk ecumenical isolation if it does not do so.

(c) It seems certain that, for the foreseeable future at least, acceptance of gender-blind equality of opportunity will remain a central feature of Western society. This means that the Church's position will appear increasingly isolated and anachronistic and there will be continuous pressure on the Church to reconsider its decision for missiological reasons and that the Church of England will not be able to commend the gospel effectively if its structures embody sexism in a way that contemporary society no longer finds acceptable.

(d) On the other side of the argument, it is clear from the submissions from bodies such as Reform and Forward in Faith that many of those who are opposed to the Church of England deciding to ordain women bishops also continue to be opposed to the 1992 decision to ordain them as priests. It seems likely, therefore, that there would be those who would seek to persuade the Church of England to follow the path taken by the Evangelical Lutheran Church in Latvia and the Presbyterian Church in Australia and reverse that decision.[1]

7.2.5   The fact that for these four reasons a decision to maintain the status quo will not mark the end of the debate about the ordination of women does not, of course, mean that this might not be the right decision to make. Those taking the decision would simply need to be aware that it would be a mistake to vote for the status quo in the hope that this would be an end to the matter.

7.2.6   As well as accepting the fact that a decision to maintain the status quo is unlikely to bring the debate about women's ordination to an end the Church of England would also need to think about the theological implications of the grounds for taking such a decision.

7.2.7   If it is held that there are fundamental theological reasons why *in principle* women can be priests but not bishops then these reasons will need to be spelt out. The problem is that in the evidence submitted to the Working Party this issue has not really been addressed.

7.2.8   Many of the objections to the ordination of women bishops that have been put to the Working Party have been concerned with the inability of women to fulfil the role of bishop in a situation where their ministry was not universally accepted,[2] the impact of the ordination of women bishops on the internal unity of the Church of England and upon its ecumenical relationships[3] and the issue of whether it is right to ordain women bishops when the ordination of women priests has not yet been 'received'.[4] These are important objections, but they are all contingent on continuing opposition to the ordination of women in the Church of England and in other churches. If this opposition ceased to exist then these objections would cease to have any force. They are thus not *fundamental* objections to women bishops in the sense of being theological objections that would rule out women bishops in all circumstances as a matter of theological principle.

7.2.9   Most of the objections to the principle of having women bishops have been objections on the grounds of Scripture, tradition and the Church of England's authority to act unilaterally that apply equally to the priesthood and to the episcopate. One of the few new arguments

that has been submitted to the Working Party has been the argument
put forward by the Master and Guardians of the Shrine at Walsingham.
As we saw in Chapter 5, they argued that an exclusively male episcopate
is required because the episcopate is called to be a sign of unity and an
episcopate that was both male and female would signify duality rather
than unity.[5]

7.2.10   Another possible argument from the evangelical side would
be that women priests are acceptable since they are under the authority
of male incumbents or male bishops and thus the principle of male
headship is maintained, whereas women bishops would not have a men
in authority over them and thus the principle of male headship would
be violated. This argument has been raised in the meetings of the
Working Party, but has not actually featured in any of the submissions
that have been made to it.

7.2.11   The fact that most of the objections in principle to women
bishops have been the same as those to women priests raises the
question as to why, if the Church of England as a whole thought that
these were not cogent objections to having women priests, it should
now regard them as cogent objections to having women bishops?

It is, of course, open to the Church of England to revisit these
objections and to discover that it now finds them valid, but this would
then mean that not only should it not have women bishops, but that
it should not have women priests either.

7.2.12   Another issue that needs to be considered is the argument
about reception. As we have explained, a number of those who oppose
the ordination of women bishops in the Church of England hold that
it would be improper to proceed to the ordination of women bishops
while there is still an open process of reception in regard to women
priests. The force of this argument depends on accepting a particular
understanding of what the concept of reception means.

7.2.13   If reception is understood to mean that the Church of England
is unsure about whether it should have women priests and is
experimenting with having them in order to try to discover if they are
what God wants for his Church then the argument has weight. It would
clearly be wrong for the Church of England to pile one degree of
uncertainty upon another by experimenting with women bishops at

the same time that it was still experimenting with women priests. If it has doubts about the orders of its women priests, then it cannot in good conscience go on to make some of them bishops.

7.2.14   If women cannot be priests then they cannot be bishops. Doubts about the orders of women priests would therefore necessarily lead to doubts about the orders of women bishops. This would in turn lead to doubts about the validity of the episcopal functions performed by women ministers, which would lead to doubts about the orders of any priests (even male priests) whom they ordained, which would eventually lead to questions about the validity of ministerial orders and sacramental assurance becoming endemic throughout the Church of England.

7.2.15   However, it is possible to see reception in a different light. It could be argued that what reception means is that the Church of England as a corporate body, while acknowledging that there were those who thought differently, decided in 1992 that it was God's will that there should be women priests. However, being aware of its own fallibility, it submitted its decision to the long-term judgement of the universal Church. This judgement may cause the Church of England to rethink its decision, but at the moment it still thinks ordaining women priests was the right thing to do and has to act on this basis, holding that the orders of its women priests are not in doubt.

7.2.16   If this second view of reception is accepted then the issue of reception would not be a valid reason for not ordaining women bishops. It is only if the first view is accepted that reception poses a problem.

7.2.17   If it is held that the need to uphold unity within the Church of England and unity between the Church of England and other churches rules out the ordination of women as bishops in the Church of England, then the issue becomes one of how to understand the meaning of unity. Both sides in the debate about women bishops would agree about the importance of unity given that according to St John's Gospel Christ himself prayed for the unity of his followers on the night before he died:

> I do not pray for these only, but also for those who believe in me through their word, that they may all be one; even as thou Father art in me, and I in thee, that they may also be in us, so that the world may believe that thou has sent me.[6]

Where there is disagreement is about what the importance of unity means in terms of the issue under discussion.

7.2.18   On the one hand, it can be argued, as we have seen, that the ordination of women bishops would further disrupt the internal unity of the Church of England and would also damage the prospects of unity with the Roman Catholic and Orthodox churches and with many Protestant churches as well.[7]

7.2.19   On the other hand, the argument can also be put forward that, in spite of continuing opposition, there is now widespread agreement in the Church of England about the desirability of ordaining women bishops.[8] Furthermore, their ordination would strengthen the relationship between the Church of England and ecumenical partners such as the Methodist Church and the Lutheran Churches of Norway and Sweden. There would be ecumenical gains as well as losses.[9]

7.2.20   More fundamentally, it can also be argued that if one accepts an equalitarian reading of Galatians 3.28 this points to unity of women and men being fundamental to the unity of the Church.[10] This would in turn mean that we have to strive for a united worldwide Church in which all ministerial offices are open to both men and women. The ordination of women bishops in the Church of England would be a step towards this goal and might eventually encourage more conservative Christian traditions to move in the same direction.[11]

7.3 Issues raised by the other options facing the Church of England

7.3.1   There are a number of different options for the appointment of women bishops in the Church of England. Each of these raises different issues and we shall look in turn at each option and the specific issues it raises.

(I) Simple, single clause legislation

7.3.2   If the arguments for proceeding with the ordination of women bishops set out in section 3 of Chapter 5 and section 3 of Chapter 6 are thought to be convincing, the first option would be for them to be appointed on a par with male bishops. This would require the deletion of Canon C 2(5) and the relevant section of the *Priests (Ordination of Women) Measure* and their replacement by a single clause stating that the ordination of women to the episcopate is lawful.

7.3.3 This is the option advocated by WATCH who declare in their submission to the Working Party:

> we consider it essential that when legislation is drawn up for women to be consecrated as bishops there be no conditional clauses that would distinguish or discriminate between male and female bishops on the basis of sex. Women should be able to be bishops on exactly the same terms as their male colleagues, just as the 1993 Code of Practice described them as fully equal priests.[12]

7.3.4 The first and most obvious attraction of this option is that it is clear and straightforward. Theologically, it would be an unambiguous statement of the equality of men and women in the life and ministry of the Church of England. Practically, it would mean that women would simply be bishops and that would be that.

7.3.5 It has also been argued by Vivienne Faull and Joy Tetley in a paper for the Working Party that women bishops need to be appointed without restrictions in order for bishops to fulfil their prophetic and unifying role.

7.3.6 On the first of these points they argue that

> Bishops are called, as part of their missionary task to be the voice of conscience in society, a prophet proclaiming God's justice. As the episcopate in the Church of England has, over the last generation, been opened to those from outside traditional English elites (those from working class and non-English and non-white backgrounds), so members of the House of Bishops have spoken effectively and powerfully on behalf of the poor, and the migrant, and those who are black. Yet while women are excluded from the House of Bishops or included only on a restricted basis, these prophetic statements are heard by those raised in a culture of gender equality as ringing hollow.[13]

7.3.7 It is important to note they are contending that the prophetic ministry of *all* bishops, and not just female ones, will be adversely affected unless women bishops are appointed on the same basis as their male colleagues.

7.3.8 On the second point, they argue that a key part of the bishop's role is to act as a focus for unity both in the Church and in wider society. They note that in today's society 'women are now widely regarded as unifying public figures' and then go on to say:

> These women[14] have no statutory inhibition on their role as compared with their male counterparts. If women who were consecrated bishops were faced from the start with inhibitions on the exercise of their ministry (for example through the provision of extended or alternative episcopal oversight), would their potential role as unifying public figures be undermined either by questions about their authority, or by their own internalization of restrictions?[15]

7.3.9 Faull and Tetley also contend that there needs to be no restriction on the role of women bishops because experience of the provisions of the *Priests (Ordination of Women) Measure* and the *Episcopal Ministry Act of Synod* has shown that provision for those opposed to women's ordination has in practice enabled them to 'pull up the drawbridge' and not engage with those of a different view. As they put it:

> What seems obvious to many, especially to women clergy after their experience of nearly a decade of the provisions under which they were priested, is that the institution of the church ought not, through pastoral provisions or legal constraints, further institutionalize (and thus ossify) that disunity.[16]

7.3.10 It has also been put to the Working Party that it has proved difficult to persuade women to apply for the senior posts within the Church that are currently open to them and that it would prove equally if not more difficult to persuade women to agree to become bishops if they could only operate as bishops on some kind of restricted basis (although of course male bishops who ordain female clergy already have to live with a restriction of their ministry in that there will be some parishes in which their ministry is not welcome as a result).

7.3.11 If women were to be appointed as bishops with no restrictions on their role and no provision for those who could not accept their appointment, a number of issues would, however, have to be faced.

7.3.12 First, there would be the question of how women bishops might be received as part of the episcopal college of the Church of England and as part of the House of Bishops. There are two distinct issues that need to be considered in this regard.

(a) If, as was suggested in section 4 of Chapter 5, women bishops might want to develop a distinctive style of episcopal ministry would their fellow bishops be prepared to adapt the way that they currently operate in consequence? If one of the reasons for having women bishops is in order to allow episcopal ministry to develop in new directions would existing male bishops be willing to allow this to happen?

(b) It is likely that there would be male bishops in the Church of England who would be conscientiously unable to recognize women bishops as being truly bishops and who would therefore be unable to be in communion with them as such. This is a point made by Forward in Faith whose submission declares:

> bishops who could not endorse the ordination of women to the episcopate would be unable to recognize women bishops as members of the college of bishops, and the House of Bishops would therefore become a church leaders' meeting rather than an episcopal college.[17]

In terms of traditional Anglican ecclesiology this would be an extremely grave situation because the collegiality and inter-communion between the bishops has been one of the means by which the Church of England has been held together as a single Church rather than each diocese constituting a church in its own right. If a bishop were unable to recognize a bishop of another diocese as being a validly ordained bishop and was in consequence unable to recognize episcopal actions performed by him or her, then the communion of those dioceses with each other would be very seriously impaired. This would also have important practical consequences in terms of matters such as the transferability of clergy between dioceses.

7.3.13 Secondly, as was noted earlier in this report, in addition to the bishops just mentioned, there would also be a significant number of other people in the Church, both clergy and laity, who would not be able to accept the validity of their ordination or, in the case of some of these objectors, the ministry of those bishops who were in communion with them.

7.3.14 As the Forward in Faith submission puts it:

> If women were ordained to the episcopate ... a significant minority of clergy and laypeople would be unable to recognize a woman as

being the diocesan bishop or to make oaths of canonical obedience to her. Such clergy would be able to accept neither institution or licensing by a woman bishop nor institution or licensing undertaken by a male bishop on her behalf. Not only would clergy and laypeople be unable to receive her own sacramental ministrations; they would also be unable to receive those of priests ordained by her, whether male or female.[18]

7.3.15 The Forward in Faith submission goes on to add that not only would these people be unable to accept the ministry of a woman bishop, those acting on her behalf, or those ordained by her, but they would also be unable to accept 'the ministry of bishops who continue in communion or "full visible unity" with those women'.[19]

7.3.16 A very similar forecast is made from an evangelical perspective by David Banting in his submission to the Working Party on behalf of Reform:

Anglo-Catholic clergy have already broken communion with bishops who ordain women presbyters, on the grounds that they have performed heretical acts. Evangelical clergy have on the whole not done this, contenting themselves with being out of communion with the women presbyters concerned. But the advent of women bishops would change matters. We believe that many, if not all, members of Reform would be unable conscientiously to accept confirmation, ordination, institution or licensing from a woman bishop, or to make an act of canonical obedience to her, since this would be to recognize the headship which she was improperly exercising; also that they would be unable to regard as truly ordained the clergy, male as well as female, whom a woman bishop had ordained.[20]

7.3.17 If no provision were made for them to opt out from having to accept the ministry of a woman bishop or recognize the validity of her episcopal actions, those opposed would seem to be left with three options:

● Refuse to recognize the legislation and break Church law.

● Leave the Church of England.

● Act in ways they conscientiously believed to be wrong.

7.3.18 The question is whether it would be right and in accordance

with the principles set out by St Paul in Romans 14.13-23 and
1 Corinthians 8.1-13 to force people into a situation in which they had
to choose between these options. It was noted in Chapter 6 that these
verses show that Christians need to avoid offending the conscientious
convictions of their fellow believers; it could be argued that this is
exactly what would be happening in the situation described above.

7.3.19   Thirdly, one of the key principles set out in the reports of the
Eames Commission and endorsed by the Lambeth Conferences of 1988
and 1998 was that provision should be made for those conscientiously
unable to accept the ordination of women bishops.

7.3.20   Thus Resolution 1.4 of the Lambeth Conference of 1988
declares that

> in any province where reconciliation on these issues is necessary,
> any diocesan bishop facing this problem be encouraged to seek
> continuing dialogue with, and make pastoral provision for, those
> clergy and congregations whose opinions differ from those of the
> bishop in order to maintain the unity of the diocese.[21]

7.3.21   Similarly Resolution III.2 of the Lambeth Conference of
1998 calls upon the provinces of the Communion 'to affirm that
those who dissent from, as well as those who assent to, the ordination
of women to the priesthood and the episcopate are both loyal
Anglicans' and to 'make such provision, including appropriate
episcopal ministry, as will enable them to live in the highest degree
of Communion possible'.[22]

7.3.22   In the *Episcopal Ministry Act of Synod* the Church of England
explicitly declared that 'the integrity of differing beliefs and positions
concerning the ordination to the priesthood should be mutually
respected and recognized'[23] and the 1994 Code of Practice stated:

> The House of Bishops and the General Synod have recognized
> that there have been and will continue to be deeply held differences
> of conviction about the ordination of women to the priesthood and
> that some, bishops, clergy and lay people, find it unacceptable.
> Christian charity and the exercise of true pastoral care require that
> careful provision be made to respect as far as possible their position
> while doing as little as possible to prejudice the full exercise of
> priestly ministry.[24]

7.3.23   The inclusion of resolutions A and B as part of the main measure and the provision for extended episcopal oversight in the *Episcopal Ministry Act of Synod* were attempts to honour the theological principles set out in these statements.

7.3.24   A decision simply to permit women to be bishops with no restrictions and no provisions would seem to go against the spirit of the Lambeth resolutions and the decisions taken and promises made by the Church of England in 1993 and 1994.

7.3.25   Fourthly, there is the issue that, because of the kind of problems just outlined, proceeding down this route might mean a substantial delay in women being appointed as bishops, and this is a fact which has been recognized by those who are supportive of this approach. For example, Faull and Tetley write:

> The main risk of this approach is that it delays decisions on consecration of women as bishops. The necessary majorities would be difficult to achieve in General Synod, and the Ecclesiastical Committee might not find the Measure expedient (though it would be foolish to second-guess the views of this committee some years hence). Simple legislation might also delay the appointment of a woman as a bishop in a diocese with no pastoral provisions, a very high level of agreement would be wise and necessary before an appointment would be acceptable either to the diocese or to the women concerned.[25]

The issue here is whether supporters of women's ministry would be willing to pay the price of delay in order to achieve the prize of the appointment of women bishops with no restrictions.

7.3.26   It has been suggested that in order to make provision for the needs of those opposed to women bishops single clause legislation could be accompanied by a code of practice, perhaps similar to the *Statement of Intent* put forward by the College of Bishops of the Scottish Episcopal Church, or along the lines of the provision for extended episcopal oversight contained in the legislation for the ordination of women bishops proposed in the Anglican Church of Australia. The Scottish *Statement of Intent* states that:

> Should a diocese of the Scottish Episcopal Church call a woman to the office of Diocesan Bishop, the College of Bishops:

- Recognizes unreservedly her jurisdiction within the diocese to which she is called, as set out in the Canons of the Church.

- Commits itself to being available to that bishop should there arise matters concerning pastoral provision and sacramental care within her diocese which through their assistance she might be able to address.

- Would respond to a request from her to assist episcopally when an issue of pastoral provision and or sacramental care needs to be addressed in a special way due to the current diversity within our Communion.

- Would also hope that any such bishop appointed and called to a diocese would be available to them should particular issues arise within their dioceses which she would be able to help them in addressing.[26]

The Australian proposals are set out in 7.3.33–35 below.

7.3.27   Many of those who are campaigning for the ordination of women bishops are strongly opposed to the introduction of anything resembling the 1993 arrangements. As they see it, the 1993 legislation simply institutionalized division and prejudice. In the words of the WATCH submission to the Working Party:

> Our experience of the workings of Resolutions A and B in the legislation and the damaging and divisive effect of the Act of Synod has led us to conclude that instead of bringing the two sides together to work harmoniously, they have encouraged division, bitterness and isolation.[27]

7.3.28   Those arguing for a code of practice believe that it would make provision for those opposed to the decision to ordain women bishops without running the danger of institutionalizing division in this way. However, the point has also been made very strongly to the Working Party that a code of practice would not be sufficient for many of those opposed.

7.3.29   To put the matter at its starkest, they simply do not believe that there is sufficient goodwill on behalf of those supporting the ordination of women bishops to make their position in the Church of England viable in the long term if it is not underwritten by binding legislation.

As they see it, the marginalization of opponents of women's ordination in ECUSA and the Church of Sweden would also happen in the Church of England. From their perspective the 1993 arrangements are what has enabled them to survive and indeed continue to flourish in the face of what they have experienced as misunderstanding and marginalization within the Church of England, and therefore they would want to see it continued and developed.

(II) There could be explicit provision of some form of extended or alternative episcopal oversight, within the present provincial and diocesan structure of the Church of England, for those opposed to the ordination of women bishops

7.3.30   There are two possible options here, both of which have parallels with the provision currently made under the terms of the *Episcopal Ministry Act of Synod* for parishes who wish for extended episcopal oversight.

7.3.31   The first option is that in each diocese there should be at least one male bishop opposed to the ordination of women to the episcopate who could minister to dissenting parishes while still remaining under the overall jurisdiction of the diocesan bishop.

7.3.32   The second option would be for a provincial system in which male bishops opposed to the ordination of women would minister to dissenting parishes on the authority and under the jurisdiction of the Archbishop of the Province.

7.3.33   This is the option that is proposed, for example, in the legislation for the ordination of women bishops that is currently being discussed by the Anglican Church of Australia.

7.3.34   This legislation provides that when, after following a set procedure, a parish requests 'episcopal ministry by a bishop other than a female bishop'[28] then the diocesan will refer the case to either the Metropolitan bishop of the province or, in the case of a non-provincial diocese, to the Australian primate who will either:

(a) invite a bishop in accordance with an arrangement previously made between the diocesan bishops of the province or, in the case of a non-provincial diocese, an arrangement previously made between the primate and the diocesan bishop;

(b) convene a meeting of the diocesan bishops of the province, or of the primate and the diocesan bishop, as the case may be, who will then decide to invite a bishop to enter the diocese to minister with the diocesan bishop's permission to officiate as bishop to the parish concerned.[29]

7.3.35 It is also stated that

> The bishop to be invited ... will, as far as possible, be from the province concerned, or failing that, from elsewhere in the Anglican Church of Australia.[30]

7.3.36 The case for extended or alternative oversight along the lines of either of these two options has been strongly argued by Mike Ovey. He argues that some kind of provision that builds on the precedent set by the 1993 Act of Synod is necessary because:

> It seems quite clear that without protective provisions, certain classes of churchmanship, at least in terms of presbyteral ministry, will start to disappear from certain dioceses.
>
> This process can be envisaged happening in at least two ways. First as certain areas acquire women bishops, these will tend to become no-go areas for priests who feel in all conscience that they should not submit to female oversight. Secondly, such priests will be less attractive to train because they will be more inflexible in terms of location after training, an argument with primary application to those contemplating stipendiary ministry.
>
> This process will be more, not less, significant ultimately for the laity of the Church of England. After the 1992 Measure, dissentients could no doubt often find some church in the vicinity that reflected their own views on the issue. This will be less possible when an entire diocese or episcopal area is under female oversight.
>
> To this extent the effect in terms of churchmanship will be to eliminate progressively strong Anglo-Catholics and conservative Evangelicals from various areas. This effect is not difficult to predict. It is perhaps true that some do not foresee this result, but such people should be acutely aware that this is widely perceived as the likely result in those constituencies mentioned. Some in them feel that they are facing not just marginalization, but elimination, albeit over a period. Faced with that, some will perhaps simply leave,

as happened in 1992. Others perhaps will feel that they cannot faithfully accept female oversight and will accordingly look for male oversight from bishops in the communion who feel able, or even obliged, to provide it.[31]

7.3.37 His solution to this problem is the establishment of some form of 'differential oversight' within the present diocesan and provincial framework. Ovey envisages some form of permanent delegation of the oversight normally exercised by a diocesan bishop to a bishop acceptable to those opposed to the ordination of women. As he sees it, such a bishop would need to have the ability 'not just to ordain and discipline, but also to consider and adopt ordinands for training, as would happen with a geographically defined bishop.'[32]

7.3.38 Ovey's proposal would work within either the diocesan or provincial frameworks noted above. He talks about the permanent delegation of authority by a diocesan bishop[33] but presumably this could either be to a bishop from within the diocese or to a bishop from another diocese within the province.

7.3.39 The advantage with Ovey's proposal is that it would provide clergy and parishes unable to accept women bishops with a form of episcopal oversight which they would be able to accept in good conscience and which would allow them to see a permanent future within the Church of England for those of their persuasion. It would also prevent them from seeking overseas episcopal oversight and thus preserve the territorial integrity of the Provinces of Canterbury and York.

7.3.40 The issue raised by Ovey's proposal is that, as he himself admits, the bishop to whom oversight was delegated would 'in reality be another diocesan, or something like it'.[34] It would undermine the hitherto accepted principle of the oversight of the diocesan bishop as ordinary over all clergy and parishes of a diocese, it would, as he says, 'represent a significant rupture in Anglican church polity',[35] and it would certainly be felt by many that his proposal would, in the words of the first Eames report, 'amount to institutional schism by the creation and transfer of parishes in which the diocesan bishop is not recognized'.[36]

7.3.41 An alternative proposal to Ovey's would be for episcopal oversight that was 'extended' rather than 'alternative' in the sense that oversight would explicitly remain with the diocesan bishop.

7.3.42 For example, the first Eames report examined a proposal for episcopal visitors, under which the episcopal visitors would provide sacramental acts for congregations that requested them under the authority of the diocesan bishop. At the time this was a proposal for dealing with this matter within ECUSA (though not subsequently adopted by them, although strikingly similar to what was to emerge in the Church of England under the *Episcopal Ministry Act of Synod*). Eames concluded that

> From an ecclesiological perspective such a scheme can be defended, as a necessary and strictly extraordinary anomaly in preference to schism, if certain conditions are met. Dissenting priests and congregations must, for their part, not go so far as to refuse canonical recognition to their diocesan bishop or to say that they are not in communion with their ordinary. This would mean that their position would have to fall short of maintaining that the Church could never admit women to the priesthood or episcopate while the matter is in debate in a continuing process of reception within the Anglican Communion and the universal Church. Bishops and dioceses who accept and endorse the ordination of women to the priesthood and episcopate would need to recognize that, within a genuinely open process of reception, there must be room for those who disagree … Understood in this way, we recommend such a proposal be further explored in Provinces in which there is serious dissent.[37]

7.3.43 This model could operate with either diocesan or provincial arrangements, and its advantage is that it would cater for those unable to accept the sacramental acts of a woman bishop while at same time preserving the principle that a woman bishop must be recognized by everyone as possessing full canonical oversight in her diocese.

7.3.44 However, there are issues raised by this model as well which are spelt out by Faull and Tetley in their paper for the Working Party mentioned above. They write:

> The Church of England already has (mixed) experience of this kind of arrangement through the provisions of the 1993 Act of Synod. Could it bear another 'extraordinary anomaly'? And if agreement could be reached on the precise form of such an anomalous

expression, would it witness to the possibility of graciously living with major difference, whilst maintaining the truth of fundamental communion in Christ? Or would it speak, rather, of further institutionalising division, of encouraging and fostering entrenched positions, of an institution in avoidance, not to say denial mode? Indeed, in purely practical terms, would it be workable?

If there is to be some form of *extended* (rather than alternative) Episcopal ministry, then the recognition of the jurisdiction of the diocesan bishop becomes very much a key issue – particularly, of course, where that diocesan is female. There is a debate to be had as to whether, for an incarnational faith, the power of order and the power of jurisdiction should *in principle* be separable. Certainly for those who believe that the Bible forbids women to have authority over men, it would be very difficult to accept the canonical jurisdiction of a woman bishop. For others, the challenge might be to accept from any form of extended episcopal oversight a sacramental ministry which has been 'delegated' by someone they consider not to have the right to exercise such a ministry in the first place. Full account should also be taken of those for whom this kind of provision undermines the integrity and authority of properly constituted episcopal ministry. For those who believe that the inclusion of women in the episcopate is God's will and God's way, institutionally-sanctioned opt-out routes are a serious affront to unity and godly justice. It should be remembered, perhaps, that profound concern for issues of unity and truth is not confined to any particular groupings. It most certainly crosses the 'position' barrier. In that light, careful consideration should be given when coming to any decision on this option to its effect on women bishops themselves, who would have to exercise a pioneering ministry in the context of institutional ambivalence. They would be serving a Church which is facing two ways – a Church which in saying 'yes' also sanctions an official 'no.' Having been canonically and properly ordained as bishops, it seems that they would not even be able to rely on Article XXVI (Of the Unworthiness of the Ministers, which hinders not the effect of the Sacrament … 'forasmuch as they do not the same in their own name, but in Christ's, and do minister by his commission and authority').

The question does therefore have to be asked as to whether the 'pastoral provision' of extended episcopal oversight is, in fact, truly 'pastoral' for any of the parties concerned. And it does, of course, beg all sorts of further questions as to the proper recognition of authority, whether spiritual or temporal or both.[38]

(III) A third province with its own bishops and archbishop could be established within the Church of England. It would have an exclusively male episcopate and priesthood to which clergy and parishes opposed to the ordination of women could then opt to belong

7.3.45 In recent years this option has become increasingly prominent in discussions about the possibility of ordaining women bishops in the Church of England. The Third Province Movement explicitly campaigns for the acceptance of this option[39] and it is also looked on with favour as a real possibility for the future by both Forward in Faith and Reform. It is suggested that it could be seen as equivalent to the forms of non-territorial jurisdiction that already exist in the Anglican churches in Australia, New Zealand, South Africa and the United States.

7.3.46 A clear example of what its proponents think such a province might look like is provided by Geoffrey Kirk in an article in *New Directions* for January 2003.

7.3.47 He writes that

> its parishes would share the privileges and responsibilities of mission and service expressed through the parochial structures with Church of England parishes. It would also be 'of' the Church of England in the sense that its canons and formularies would derive 'from' those of the Church of England, and consequently bear that 'family resemblance' which marks the Anglican identity worldwide.[40]

7.3.48 Kirk compares such a province to the Church in Wales following its break with the Church of England and resists the notion that such a province would be a 'parallel church', cognisant, no doubt, of Eames' strictures against such a development.

7.3.49 The possible advantages of the establishment of such a province are set out by Andrew Burnham in his article 'A New Province For England?' in *New Directions* in April 2003.

7.3.50 Admitting to being 'a fairly late convert' to the idea he argues that he can now see that it has advantages for both 'Mainstream Anglicans' and 'Anglo-Catholics'.

7.3.51 For the former he thinks the advantages are:

- It would provide a chance to end the arguments about gender issues and thus release a lot of missionary energy and it would allow there to be provinces where women could be either bishops or archbishops without any restriction.

- It would fit inside the existing Anglican Communion framework which accepts the idea that there are provinces with different approaches to the question of the ordination of women.

- It would help promote Protestant ecumenism in the sense that the Church of England provinces which admitted women to all levels of ministry could pursue unimpaired the quest for unity with other Protestant churches in this position.

- Because the new province had a coherent Catholic identity it would be able to act as a bridge between Anglicanism and Orthodoxy.

7.3.52 For Anglo-Catholics the advantages would be the establishment of a province that had ecclesiological coherence and, because it was smaller, this province could be less bureaucratic and more flexible than the present Church of England. Its bishops would be able to give more time for pastoral care. Since it would be a province in which it was settled that women could not be priests or bishops there would be the freedom to develop other forms of lay ministry for women such as the roles of catechists, acolytes and readers.

7.3.53 However, a number of issues in connection with the proposal have also been identified by a number of commentators.

7.3.54 First, there is the theological objection that it would be wrong in principle to establish a province which excluded women from the priesthood and the episcopate in the same way that a province that did not allow people of a particular ethnic origin to be priests or bishops would be. Those who support the idea of a Third Province make the point that it would not be a single issue province but would seek to preserve the traditional Anglican consensus on a number of issues (of which women's ordination is only one). Nevertheless, critics of the idea insist that the reason for setting up such a province is opposition to the ordination of women and the creation of a province on this basis is simply unacceptable.

7.3.55 Secondly, there is the theological objection that one of the important features of the Church of England (and indeed of the Anglican tradition) is that it models an ability to live with difference in a creative rather than a destructive fashion. An important part of this witness would be lost, so it is argued, if the Church of England had officially to divide over the issue of the ordination of women.

7.3.56 Faull and Tetley write, for example, that the challenge facing the members of the Church of England is to seek to 'live out in our contemporary context the truth that, in Christ, all things hold together in all their blending and clashing diversity' and to 'demonstrate in our ecclesiological life the reality of Christ's gospel of reconciliation'.[41] As they see it, the creation of a Third Province would mean the Church of England ducking this challenge by eliminating the need to learn to live with difference.

7.3.57 In addition to these theological difficulties, there are also a number of practical issues raised in connection with the idea of a Third Province.[42]

- How would a separate province hold together (particularly in the long term) when its only strong commonality is an objection to a particular ecclesiological development? It is likely to consist of those of 'conservative Catholic' and 'conservative Evangelical' persuasions. Is one significant negative enough to make viable a close union of those with very different theological and ecclesiological persuasions?

  Andrew Burnham's article majored on the significance of the new province as an opportunity for Anglo-Catholics. If it were predominantly Anglo-Catholic in nature how would evangelicals feel about this? If it turned out not to be the case or if in the long term the province became dominated by large evangelical parishes and thus became evangelical in flavour how would Anglo-Catholics feel about this?

- In order to remain Anglican in any formal sense the new province would have to be in communion with the Archbishop of Canterbury. What would happen if the incumbent Archbishop of Canterbury were to take part in the consecration of women bishops – or, indeed, were herself a woman?

- If such a province were to be part of the Church of England, in the same way that the non-territorial jurisdictions mentioned above are part of their respective churches, then its bishops would need to be in communion with the other bishops of the

Church of England. Would this be possible if some of those bishops were women?[43]

- How far would provincial structures be taken? Would this be in all respects a province parallel to those of Canterbury and York? Would it have its own archbishop? Its own dioceses, diocesans and archdeacons, with all their legal, administrative and financial implications?

- Who is going to pay for all this? There would surely be strong objections from parishes up and down the land if the provinces of Canterbury and York had to meet *that* financial burden.

- Would the numbers involved really justify such structural provision? Would a non-geographical *diocese* be an alternative and more proportionate possibility? It would not, however, resolve most of the issues raised.

(It should be noted that supporters of the Third Province idea argue in response that a PEV such as the Bishop of Ebbsfleet has more stipendiary clergy looking to him for extended oversight than exist in some dioceses and that a Third Province would be much larger than the Scottish Episcopal Church and possibly larger than the Church in Wales.)

- What would be its synodical arrangements? If it were to remain part of the Church of England then presumably representation on General Synod (and the level of this representation) would need to be negotiated. If the province were to have its own synod the question would then be whether it was not in fact a separate church and not part of the Church of England at all.

- How would it be constituted in terms of canon law? Would it operate according to the same body of canon law as Canterbury and York? Or would it develop its own corpus? If so, what is that saying about its membership of the Church of England?

- How would its own membership be determined? This really is of critical significance. It would need to be made very clear to the community of the whole parish that opted-out parishes would no longer form part of the diocesan jurisdiction in which they were geographically situated. This is not just a matter for the PCC. It affects all who live within the boundaries of the parish. It would be fitting, therefore, for the decision to be taken (after extensive explanation and discussion, both leading up to and during the meeting) by a special general meeting of the parish and with the requirement of more than a simple majority (two-thirds?). There should also be provision for a possible reversal of any decision to opt out.

- How would the particular issue of Church schools be resolved? Is it proposed that they would become part of the new province? If so, what if the staff, parents or LEA objected to such a move? In any event could a new province afford to resource Church schools adequately? (In response it is argued that such schools might for instance be transferred to the local deanery with certain parochial rights reserved if this proved to be a problem and that money to finance Church schools would have to be part of the financial arrangements for the new province.)

- Would the setting up of a Third Province encourage those holding strongly to 'single issues' to press for similar provision, thus leading to the gradual break-up of the Church of England into a whole series of small groupings institutionally divided from each other? Could this be guarded against?

7.3.58   As an alternative to a Third Province and in the light of such issues, a number of less radical versions of the same basic idea have been put forward.

7.3.59   It has been suggested, for example,

- That there could be another diocese in the Church of England. This diocese would have an exclusively male episcopate and priesthood and would either be transferred to whichever of the provinces always had a male archbishop or, if that were to vary, it could be extra-provincial but under the metropolitical jurisdiction of whichever archbishop was a man.

- That clergy and parishes opposed to the ordination of women could form a distinct 'religious order' under the oversight of the Archbishop of Canterbury. This option would depend, of course, on the archbishop always being a man.

- That there could be some form of 'apostolic administration' providing for their needs but with existing diocesan ties maintained.

- That the parishes concerned could form group ministries which would be under the oversight of the archbishops of Canterbury and York though geographically in the middle of other dioceses. This again would depend on one of the archbishops being a man.

- That a 'peculiar jurisdiction' could be created akin to Westminster Abbey, St George's Windsor and the Oxbridge colleges that would be within the Church of England but would have a great degree of independence and would be free from local episcopal jurisdiction.

7.3.60   A number of issues have been identified with these proposals, the most obvious of which are that they would restrict the oversight of a female diocesan bishop and that all but the last of them would depend on one or both of the two archbishops not being women (and possibly on one or both of them not consecrating women bishops). As yet they do not seem to have attracted much support.

(IV) There could be some form of restriction on the exercise of the episcopal office by women
7.3.61   In the submissions that have been made to the Working Party the following suggestions have been made about how the exercise of the episcopal office by women might be restricted.

(a) Women could be appointed as diocesan bishops but with the office of archbishop restricted to men
7.3.62   The three possible advantages of this approach are that

- It might be attractive to some evangelicals since women bishops could be seen as ultimately under male headship and so the headship principle would still be maintained.

- It might provide the basis for some kind of provincially based episcopal oversight for those unable to accept a woman bishop. This is an option which is explored in more detail below.

- Given current Anglican polity, it might be helpful in terms of maintaining the unity of Anglicanism if the Archbishops of Canterbury and York were men. This would make it easier for

provinces that did not ordain women to remain in communion
with the mother church of the Anglican Communion.

7.3.63   The issues raised by this approach are that

- It would still involve the ordination of women bishops who would
  exercise the office of bishop in the normal fashion and would thus still
  raise conscientious difficulties for those who believed that the ordination
  of women as bishops would be contrary to biblical teaching and
  Catholic order. These people would still be unable to accept the
  ministrations of a woman bishop or anyone ordained by her.

- It would not address the ecclesiological problem of diocesan bishops
  being in a state of at least impaired communion with each other.

- It would still entail the existence of a 'glass ceiling' in the Church of
  England and would therefore create severe difficulties for those inside
  and outside the Church of England who believed that *any* discrimination
  against women was wrong as a matter of theological principle.

(b) Women could be appointed as suffragan or area bishops but not as diocesan bishops
7.3.64   The advantages of this approach are that

- As in the case of the previous suggestion it might allow the argument
  that a woman bishop was under male headship.

- As in the case of the previous suggestion it would ensure that
  Archbishops of Canterbury were always men.

- It might enable at least some of those who had conscientious difficulties
  concerning women bishops to accept the ministry of their diocesan
  bishop if this bishop were a man.

- It might provide a basis for maintaining communion between
  diocesan bishops if these were still all male.

7.3.65   The issues raised by this approach are that

- It would still not solve the problem of Anglo-Catholics for whom a
  woman bishop of any kind would be a violation of Catholic order.

- It would still not solve the problem for many Evangelicals, because women would still be exercising an episcopal role, restricted though this might be, and this would necessarily involve women in the exercise of authority over men and thus violate the theological principle of male headship.

- As with the previous option it would be unacceptable to those opposed as a matter of theological principle to any discrimination against women both within the Church of England and amongst the Church of England's ecumenical partners. As we noted in Chapter 6, the Methodist Church, for example, would find what it would see as continued discrimination against women by the Church of England very hard to accept.

- As Forward in Faith point out:

> It would raise serious questions about the episcopal credentials of suffragan bishops. Suffragans presently belong to the order of bishops no less than diocesans (indeed suffragans are only suffragans by analogy with the relationship of diocesans to metropolitans). A suffragan who could not in principle be preferred as a diocesan would arguably (cf. a priest who could not, in principle, be authorized to exercise the cure of souls) not be a bishop at all.[44]

(c) Women could be appointed as bishops within a reformulated episcopate which would have a team of bishops in each diocese, at least one of whom would always be male

7.3.66 The advantages of this approach are that

- It would involve a move towards a collegial style of episcopacy and this would arguably be a good development in and of itself (see the discussion of this point in 2.7.34–53).

- It would provide a basis for those unable to accept women bishops to relate within their own diocese to a male bishop. This would make provision for those opposed to women bishops while at the same time preserving the principle of the territorial integrity of each diocese – a principle which has traditionally been seen as fundamental to Anglican ecclesiology.

7.3.67 The disadvantages of this approach are that

- It would still involve the ordination of women bishops and, as we have already said, many in the Church would continue to object to this in principle.

- It might conceivably involve the creation of a completely 'flat' team of co-equal bishops in each diocese. In this case there would be a huge breach with Catholic tradition which has always insisted from at least the second century (and arguably from the end of the first) that there should be a single personal focus of unity and authority within each diocese.

- Alternatively it might mean that there was a team of bishops with one exercising a leadership role as *primus inter pares*. This would be more in accordance with Catholic tradition, but in this case either the primacy could be exercised by a woman (in which case there would still be questions about whether it was right for a woman to exercise leadership and authority over male episcopal colleagues) or it could only be exercised by a man (in which case there would be questions about continued discrimination against women).

(V) There could be financial provision for those clergy who left the Church of England because they could not accept the ordination of women bishops

7.3.68   The argument in favour of this proposal, which could run alongside any of the other options mentioned above, is that if it were right to provide compensation for those clergy who left the Church of England over the ordination of women priests it would be right to provide similar compensation for those who left over the ordination of women bishops. Indeed, it would be unjust not to do so.

7.3.69   The arguments against this proposal are that

- In its present financial state the Church of England would simply not be in a position to afford such financial provision.

- Any clergy who object to the ordination of women on principle have already had the opportunity to leave the Church of England and receive financial provision.

7.3.70   In response to this latter point it is argued that the ordination of women bishops does raise new theological problems of the kind outlined in this report. For evangelical clergy there is the issue of a woman bishop exercising 'headship' over them and for Catholic clergy there is the issue of being unable to recognize the bishop as the focus of unity and source of sacramental life. A new situation has thus arisen which was not covered by the 1993 arrangements.

7.4 The questions that have to be faced

7.4.1   Faced with these options the questions the Church of England has to face are the following:

7.4.2   In the light of the theological issues discussed in this report as a whole would it be right to proceed with the ordination of women as bishops or should it remain with the status quo?

7.4.3   If it does seem right to proceed with their ordination the question that must be faced is which, if any, of the options II–V should be followed. In deciding this the key issues that will need to be borne in mind are:

- Which option(s) would allow respect for the genuinely held conscientious convictions of those on both sides of the debate in accord with Romans 14 and 1 Corinthians 8?

- Which option(s) would be in accordance with the established principles of Anglican church order and the resolutions of the 1988 and 1998 Lambeth Conferences?

- Which option(s) would be practical within the theological and legal constraints under which the Church of England has to operate?

- Which option(s) would enable those in the Church of England to remain in the 'highest possible degree of communion' with each other as those who share a common faith in Our Lord Jesus Christ and who together are part of the one body of Christ through their common baptism (1 Corinthians 12.12-13)?

- Which options(s) would give most assistance (or do least damage) to the ability of the Church of England to continue to bear effective witness to the gospel in the life of our nation?

chapter 8

Would the ordination of women as bishops be a legitimate development in the Church of England?

8.1.1   As we have seen in the course of this report, there are serious differences within the Church of England and the wider Church about whether it is right for women to be ordained as bishops.

8.1.2   In order to see this disagreement in its proper theological context it is useful to begin with those points in the debate about the ordination of women as bishops on which almost all mainstream Christians would agree. These points are helpfully set out by Bishop Kallistos Ware as follows:

> At his human birth Christ did not only become man in the sense of being human (*anthropos, homo*), but he also became man in the sense of becoming male (*aner, vir*). Certainly Christ is the saviour of all humankind, of men and women equally; at his incarnation he took up into himself and healed our common humanity. But at the same time we should keep in view the particularity of the incarnation. Christ was born at a specific time and place, from a specific mother. He did not just become human in an abstract or generalized sense, but he became a *particular* human being; as such he could not be both a male and a female at once, and he was in fact a male.
>
> Secondly, men and women are not interchangeable, like counters, or identical machines. The difference between them ... extends far more deeply than the physical act of procreation. The sexuality of human beings is not an accident, but affects them in their very identity and in their deepest mystery. Unlike the differentiation between Jew or Gentile or between slave and free – which reflect man's fallen state and is due to social convention, not to nature – the differentiation between male and female is an aspect of humanity's natural state before the Fall. The life of grace in the Church is not bound by social conventions or the conditions

produced by the Fall; but it does conform to the order of nature, in the sense of unfallen nature as created by God. Thus the distinction between male and female is not abolished in the Church.

We are not saved *from* our masculinity and femininity, but *in* them; to say otherwise is to be Gnostic or Marcionite. We cannot repent of being male and female, but only of the *way* in which we are these things. Grace co-operates with nature and builds upon it; the Church's task is to sanctify the natural order, not to repudiate it. In the Church we are male and female not sexless. Dedicated virginity within the church community is not the rejection of sex, but a way of consecrating it.[1]

8.1.3   When he talks about the 'sexuality' of human beings, Ware means their existence as male and female and over the centuries the majority of the Christian Church has seen the implication of the fact that God created men and women to be different from each other as being that women should not be part of the ordained ministry.

8.1.4   The theological argument has been that God chose to become human in a male form at the Incarnation. He also chose twelve male apostles to represent him. This choice of male ministers was not arbitrary but reflects the fact that when God created men and women he created men to lead and to exercise authority and women to submit to men and to exercise a supportive and nurturing role, primarily, though not exclusively, within the domestic context. Respecting God's creation of human beings as male and female means accepting these different roles assigned by God and reflecting them in the way that the Church and its ministry is organized and structured.

8.1.5   As we noted in sections 5.2.5–52 of Chapter 5, there are still those in the Church of England who would accept some or all of this argument. However, as we noted in sections 5.3.1–51 of the same chapter, in recent years this line of argument has been challenged, without a rejection of either the maleness of the Incarnation or the God-given difference between men and women. An alternative line of argument has developed that suggests that the important thing about the Incarnation was Christ's assumption of humanity rather than maleness and that the combination of equality and difference that marks God's creation of human beings as male and female is best reflected not by men and women having different roles within the Church but by their exercise of these roles in appropriately differing ways.

8.1.6 This second line of argument, and the suggestion flowing from it that women can legitimately be bishops, represents a potential development of Christian doctrine, and the theological question at the heart of the debate about the ordination of women as bishops in the Church of England is whether it would be a *legitimate* development.

8.1.7 At the end of the discussion of the development of doctrine in Chapter 3 of this report (3.5.20–24) it was suggested that a permissible development is one that:

Is biblically based in the sense that it

- Has explicit or implicit support in specific biblical texts.

- Enables us to make coherent sense of the overall biblical picture.

- Takes the logic of the biblical material and applies it in a new cultural and historical context.

Takes tradition seriously in the sense that it

- Shows understanding of what the traditions of the Church (as manifested in the totality of its life) have been concerning a particular matter.

- Shows that it has understood the reason(s) for the existence of these traditions.

- Builds on the Church's existing traditions rather than simply rejecting them.

Takes reason seriously in that

- It can be shown in a rational and coherent fashion that such a development is rooted in Scripture and tradition in the ways outlined above.

- Such a development will enable the Church to respond creatively and persuasively to the issues raised by contemporary culture and contemporary Christian experience.

8.1.8   What has become clear from the material considered by the Working Party and surveyed in this report is that there is a fundamental difference of opinion on all these three aspects of a permissible development.

Scripture

8.1.9   Those who argue for the status quo contend that the present position in which women cannot be bishops is biblically based in that it is supported by the practice of the New Testament Church and is the explicit teaching found in texts such as 1 Corinthians 11.2-16;14.33-8 and 1 Timothy 2.9-15. They also maintain that it best conforms to the overall biblical picture of the relationship between men and women ordained by God (described as the principle of 'headship' by Conservative Evangelicals). As they see it, the way to apply the biblical material in today's context is to find appropriate ministries for women that give scope to women's talents and abilities while respecting the traditional, biblical ordering of the Church.

8.1.10   Those who hold that women should be bishops are equally clear that their position is biblically based because it reflects the way in which, according to the New Testament, women played an equal role alongside men in leading the Early Church and teaching about the fundamental equality of women and men contained in Galatians 3.28. It also best conforms to the biblical picture of an original equality between men and women disrupted by sin but restored through the saving work of Christ. As they see it, the way to apply the biblical material in today's context is to open up all ministries equally to both women and men.

Tradition

8.1.11   Those who argue for the status quo hold that their position is the one that best respects tradition as it reflects the consistent pattern of Christian belief and practice maintained down the centuries under the guidance of the Holy Spirit in almost all parts of the Church. In their view, a decision to ordain women as bishops would not be evolution but revolution, the repudiation of the considered mind of God's people over the past two millennia and the mind of most of the Church of Christ in the present day. It would call into question the claim of the Church of England that its form of ministry is a sign and instrument of the catholicity and apostolicity of the one Church of God across space and time.

8.1.12   Those who hold that women should be bishops see their position as consonant with tradition, not only because they think that there is evidence for the presence of women in the ministry of the Church in the early centuries, but, more fundamentally, because they think that the development of tradition on this matter has been skewed by the effects of a patriarchal culture that has prevented the Church from fully reflecting the egalitarian approach of the Bible itself. In our day, the Church has the possibility of a true development of tradition in this area, a development that will retain the Catholic threefold order of ministry as a sign and instrument of catholicity and apostolicity, but will allow it to be a more faithful representation of the biblical revelation by being opened up to women as well as men.

Reason

8.1.13   Those who argue for the status quo see their position as supported by reason. They hold that it can be rationally shown that their position is the one that has the support of Scripture and tradition and is the one that will be most beneficial to the Church of England. Not only will it preserve the Church of England's theological integrity, but it will also preserve internal and ecumenical unity, and give space for the agreed process of open reception of the ordination of women as priests to take place. As they see it, the Church of England can best address the questions about the relations of men and women raised by contemporary culture by remaining faithful in this way to the biblical teaching about equality of status but diversity of role.

8.1.14   Conversely, those who favour the ordination of women as bishops also see their position as having the support of reason. For the reasons outlined above they believe that their position is demanded by Scripture and consonant with attentiveness to tradition. As they see it, the Church of England has already accepted the principle that women should be ordained alongside men and the ordination of women as priests has been widely accepted. The time is therefore right to take the next logical step, which is to open the episcopate up to women as well. This will benefit the Church of England because of the distinctive gifts that women will bring to episcopal ministry, and it will enhance its mission by showing the wider world that it is serious about its message concerning the equality of men and women before God.

How should the Church of England proceed?

8.1.15 Given these arguments on both sides how should the Church of England proceed?

8.1.16 What all should be able to agree is that the calling of the Church of England is to pursue the path of justice. As we saw in Chapter 3, what this means is helping people to live lives in obedience to God by enabling them to fulfil the roles which God laid down for men and women when he established human sexual differentiation as part of his good creation. This in turn means not just asking the narrow question 'should women be bishops?', but also addressing the wider relationship of men and women in the Church, exploring how the Church of England can develop structures and attitudes that enable *all* women and men to flourish together and to exercise fully the varying gifts that God has given them.

8.1.17 The difficulty facing the Church of England is how to discern what this should mean in practice, given that people of equal integrity and godliness within the Church of England continue to hold contradictory views on the matter.

8.1.18 There is no easy solution to this difficulty. Both sides in the debate are arguing on the basis of views which seem to them to be axiomatic but which are not accepted by those on the other side of the debate and this has resulted in the impasse referred to in Chapter 1. However, the twin Christian constraints of the pursuit of truth and the pursuit of charity point in the direction of a continuing dialogue in which both sides seriously and prayerfully seek the will of God together as they listen to what the other thinks God is saying to his people.

If the Church of England decides to ordain women bishops, there will have to be a development of structures which first come to terms with the basic ecclesiological principles of the Church of England that

- All bishops in the Church of England are in communion with the Archbishops of Canterbury and York and with each other.

- Diocesan bishops, although operating in a collegial manner and sharing their oversight with other bishops as and when appropriate, retain oversight over the whole of their dioceses.

- All clergy and laity are in communion with their bishops.

Secondly, people of differing views will have to be enabled to live together in the highest possible degree of communion, fostering courteous relationships which enable people of different views to continue to pray together and to work together for justice, peace and the integrity of creation.

Thirdly, both the conscientious difficulties that many people still have with regard to the ordination of women and the need for women ministers to exercise their vocation in as full and unrestricted manner as possible will have to be addressed.

In Chapter 7 we looked at some suggestions as to what such structures might look like and the various issues which these suggestions raise.

8.1.19   Above all, perhaps, we need to bring an eschatological perspective to bear on all these things. This world will one day pass away and the ecclesiastical structures on which we expend so much time and energy, important though they are, will pass away with it. In the light of this fact, we need to give the highest priority to deepening the quality of our love for the other members of the body of Christ, perhaps especially those with whom we most strongly disagree on issues such as the ordination of women to the episcopate. All else may pass away, but the love we have shown to our sisters and brothers will remain and will bear fruit in eternity.

> For now we see in a mirror dimly, but then we will see face to face. Now I know only in part; then I will know fully, even as I have been fully known. So, faith, hope, love abide, these three; and the greatest of these is love. (1 Corinthians 13.12-13)

> I therefore, a prisoner of the Lord, beg you to lead a life worthy of the calling to which you have been called, with all humility and gentleness, with patience, bearing with one another in love, eager to maintain the unity of the Spirit in the bond of peace. There is one body and one Spirit, just as you were called to the one hope of your calling, one Lord, one faith, one baptism, one God and Father of us all, who is above all and through all and in all. (Ephesians 4.1-4)

Sanctify them in the truth; your word is truth. As you have sent me into the world, so I have sent them into the world. And for their sakes I sanctify myself, so that they also may be sanctified in truth. I ask not only on behalf of these, but also on behalf of those who will believe in me through their word, that they may all be one. As you, Father, are in me, and I am in you, may they may also be in us, so that the world may believe that you have sent me. (John 17.17-21)

Ordination of women in the Anglican Communion and other Churches (as at February 2004)

1. The Anglican Communion (and United Churches in Full Communion):

Status	*Province*
No women's ordination	Central Africa
	Jerusalem and the Middle East
	Korea
	Melanesia[1]
	Nigeria
	Papua New Guinea
	South East Asia
	Tanzania
Diaconate only	Indian Ocean
	Southern Cone
	Congo
	Pakistan
Diaconate and presbyterate only	Australia
	Burundi
	England
	Hong Kong[2]
	Kenya
	Rwanda
	South India
	Uganda
	Wales
	West Africa
	West Indies

Diaconate, presbyterate and episcopate (women bishops canonically possible but none yet ordained)	Bangladesh
	Brazil
	Central America
	Ireland[3]
	Japan
	Mexico[4]
	North India[5]
	Philippines[6]
	Scotland[7]
	Southern Africa[8]
	Sudan[9]
Women bishops have been ordained	Aotearoa, NZ and Polynesia[10]
	Canada[11]
	United States[12]

2. Other churches in communion with the Church of England

No women's ordination	Mar Thoma Syrian Church of Malabar
Diaconate and presbyterate	Old Catholic Churches of the Union of Utrecht
Information not available at present	Philippine Independent Church

3. The Communion of Porvoo Churches

The Evangelical-Lutheran Church of Finland
The Evangelical-Lutheran Church of Iceland
The Church of Norway
The Church of Sweden
The Estonian Evangelical-Lutheran Church
The Evangelical-Lutheran Church of Lithuania

Of the churches covered by the Porvoo agreement Norway and Sweden have women bishops. The following description has been received:

The Church of Norway

Women are fully recognized in all ministerial offices.

When the Church permitted women pastors, it was a logical consequence that women could also become bishops. Nevertheless, it took some time before the first woman bishop was elected. The Church of Norway currently has two women bishops.

There is a provision that one is not required to celebrate the service together with a woman pastor/bishop in front of the altar if it is against one's own conviction.

The Church of Sweden
Women can occupy all ministerial offices without restriction.

When the law was introduced in the 1950s to open the presbyteral office to women, there was a possibility for women to be consecrated as bishops – in this respect, no distinction is made between men and women, priests and bishops.

There was a provision for those priests who did not want to work alongside a female colleague, but that provision was removed in the 1990s. A deacon, priest or bishop has to confirm their willingness to serve together with a colleague irrespective of their gender.

4. The Meissen Declaration: The Evangelical Church in Germany (Evangelische Kirche in Deutschland – EKD)
The EKD has women pastors and also a number of women bishops. It has no specific provision for those opposed to women's ordination.

5. The Anglican-Methodist Covenant: The Methodist Church of Great Britain
The Methodist Church of Great Britain allows both women and men to exercise all forms of authorized ministry. There are women superintendents, women district chairs, and there have been women presidents of Conference.

6. The Fetter Lane Agreement: The Moravian Church in Great Britain
Women eligible to all ministerial offices, including bishops.

7. The Reuilly Agreement: French Lutheran and Reformed Churches
The French Lutheran and Reformed Churches have women pastors in equality with men.

Annex 2

Possible pastoral arrangements – a summary

Option	Principal features	Advantages	Disadvantages
◆ No provisions	N/A	❖ Ecclesiological clarity ❖ Women's ministry fully recognized ❖ No need for legislation for special pastoral provisions for those opposed	❖ Departure from principles of 1988 and 1998 Lambeth Conference resolutions, and the Eames Report, and the General Synod's 1993 legislation re women priests ❖ Likely to lead to significant defections, with possible high short-term cost of special financial provisions ❖ Even if acceptable to the General Synod, questions would remain as to whether the Ecclesiastical Committee of Parliament would find such a Measure expedient
◆ Code of Practice agreed by the House of Bishops	❖ Similar to 'extended episcopal ministry' model but without formal synodical provision	❖ Avoids the requirement for formal synodical agreement ❖ Potentially more flexible	❖ Dependent on episcopal goodwill ❖ Probably not regarded as adequate provision by those opposed (see also considerations above)
◆ Extended episcopal ministry	❖ Parishes would petition their diocesan bishop for *extended* episcopal ministry ❖ Diocesan bishop remains the ordinary	❖ Follows precedent of the 1993 Act of Synod ❖ Does not break with jurisdiction of diocesan bishops	❖ Might not fully meet the pastoral needs of those opposed, especially as they would need to accept the canonical authority of women bishops (and the basis on which bishops providing such episcopal care were consecrated) ❖ Would perpetuate the pastoral strain of the current arrangements

Option	Principal features	Advantages	Disadvantages
◆ Extended provincial episcopal ministry	❖ As above but parishes would petition *the archbishop of the province* (with the permission of the diocesan bishop who remains the ordinary)	❖ Reduces potential difficulties arising if the diocesan bishop is a woman	❖ Dependent on recognition of the archbishop's authority, even if he consecrated women bishops (would not work if either archbishop were a woman) ❖ Does not sit easily with the ecclesiological model of the diocesan being the ordinary (see also first bullet point above)
◆ 'Third (or Free) Province'	❖ Parishes would – by some new synodical provision – petition for *alternative* episcopal oversight ❖ Episcopal care would be outside the framework of territorial diocesan jurisdiction	❖ Meets perceived pastoral needs of some of those opposed ❖ Might remove a source of friction within the 'mainstream' Church of England	❖ Those opposed would still need to remain in communion with the See of Canterbury to remain Anglican ❖ Break with traditional Anglican ecclesiology re the territoriality of dioceses: perception that it would be legislating for schism ❖ Potential practical and legal difficulties re finance, administration, etc. ❖ Sets a precedent for separate jurisdictions on other issues

What does a bishop do?

The material in this annex has been included in response to those who have said to the Working Party that they knew little of what bishops did at present. It consists of illustrative examples of the work of two bishops on the Working Party, one a diocesan bishop and the other a suffragan bishop.

A diocesan bishop
The Bishop of Rochester

Bishops minister to a very large number of people, both publicly and privately, in local, national and even international contexts. There is, nonetheless, a widespread lack of knowledge about the *detail* of what bishops do.

As I write this, important issues from parishes having to do with pastoral care, worship and appointments are all waiting to be considered. This alerts me to a bishop's role as the principal minister in the diocese. Such a role involves a considerable teaching ministry, both directly and indirectly. Through lectures, informal talks and writing, as well as sermons, a bishop is constantly engaged in a teaching ministry. There is, however, indirect engagement as well in the oversight of ordinands, the delivery of integrated schemes for lay training and in the care and development of ministers, both lay and ordained.

As the principal minister in the area of worship, the bishop has a responsibility not only for specifically episcopal services (such as ordinations, institutions, commissionings and confirmations) but also for the coherence, good order and liveliness of worship in the parish churches, chapels and new ways of being Church throughout the diocese.

As I have said already, the bishop is involved in the pastoral care of the clergy and in their ministerial development and also in attempting to resolve particularly difficult concerns which reach the episcopal desk because 'the buck stops here'.

Many of these issues can be opportunities for mission just as worship and teaching can be. The bishop is not, though, just the pastor of the pastors, or even of all the congregations in the diocese. The canons refer to the bishop as 'chief pastor of all that are within his diocese, as well laity as clergy, and their father in God' (C 18). The local aspect of the work involves spending a great deal of time and effort in the wider community. This means maintaining relationships with civic authorities, participating in the development of plans for local communities, supporting local initiatives, working in a huge range of areas from conflict resolution in neighbourhoods to international development. Personally, I am involved, in one way or another, with 64 charities.

The bishop helps to relate the local church to the wider. This means participation in national bodies and their work; the House of Bishops and General Synod spring most readily to mind. Such participation is not, of course, limited to these bodies but extends to their committees and often involves leadership of such groups. Quite often, too, bishops take the lead in the work of the Church's voluntary organizations. Because bishops are active in local communities, they are sometimes called upon to take part in national initiatives, conferences and organizations. The actual or potential membership of diocesan bishops in the House of Lords is symbolic of their considerable involvement in national affairs.

We live in a rapidly shrinking world and sometimes local or national concerns develop an international dimension. Bishops get drawn into European, trans-continental and worldwide discussions on questions such as the role of religion in peace-making, the emergence of government by consent in particular parts of the world, fundamental human freedoms, immigration and refugee issues and a whole host of others besides.

At every level, bishops have a responsibility for promoting unity among Christians. This *does* involve gathering people in the diocese around a common understanding of the faith of the apostles which we have received and have a duty to pass on to others. It also means that bishops often have to take the lead in promoting unity between different Christian churches. This may be in the local context, in terms of Churches Together groups, LEPs, covenants and Sharing Agreements, it may be nationally in terms of schemes of unity or it may be internationally, in the context of dialogue between world communions.

There is also a responsibility to promote understanding and good relationships among people of different faiths. Again, this can have a local, national and international dimension. This is an aspect of the bishop's ministry which is likely to become more and more prominent.

Just before I began to work on this piece, I did a radio interview about a forthcoming visit to a partner diocese in the North of England. Working with the media – local, Christian, national and international – is a recurrent aspect of episcopal ministry. Sometimes this is 'trouble-shooting' but at other times it may be an intervention on topical questions in medical ethics, conflict or the state of religious belief. From time to time, this involves writing articles as well as personal appearances or interviews.

Apart from preparing lectures, seminars, etc., there is also the writing of articles for journals and of books. The preparation time needed for these is considerable and often not enough account is taken of it. Books and articles by bishops are still noticed by the general public and the time and effort spent on them is usually worthwhile.

Whether it is leadership in worship, teaching and preaching or the chairing of numerous committees, local, national or international, bishops need to be aware of their 'connecting' task. They gather the people of God in a particular locality, they relate them to other communities of faith, nationally and throughout the world, and they ensure the passing on of the faith from one generation to another. As leaders in mission, they must make sure that the word and the work of God is being proclaimed in every parish, in every church plant, in the nation as a whole and throughout the world. As 'servant of the servants of God' the bishop has a responsibility for those in any kind of need, for the voiceless and the oppressed and for those who are denied their freedom. Any influence or access which the bishop may have to those with power must be used to fulfil this aspect of episcopal ministry.

It is impossible in such a brief overview to give the full flavour of what a bishop does. To help people in this diocese, I publish a monthly diary but even this cannot take account of confidential meetings and interviews or of the time for prayer, preparation and correspondence which is required in significant amounts.

A suffragan bishop
The Bishop of Bolton

One of the marked features of a bishop's ministry is the enormous variety from day to day. There are many opportunities each month to commend the Christian faith and the contribution of the Church to those in the community at large as well as ministering in a whole host of church contexts. The day begins with prayers in chapel and then, as with all in full-time ministry, there is a fair amount of correspondence and administration in which I am ably helped by my PA.

The following two-week diary aims to give a typical picture of the events that make up the remainder of the day-to-day ministry of one area bishop in a northern urban diocese. Perhaps the most regular feature is meeting with individual clergy, there is normally a bit more time for preparation, and I do take a few whole days several times a year to get in some specific study. Also, at certain times of the year, Sundays are a little less full with major services, especially when there are no confirmations.

WEEK ONE
Each day begins with prayer in chapel.

Sunday
Morning   Parish Eucharist for 150th anniversary celebrations followed by a parish lunch. On the way home, visit a priest who is in hospital for a hip replacement.

Evening   Confirmation for a Team ministry of three churches: twelve adult candidates and thirty young teenagers. Confirmations present me with one of the great mission opportunities of the week. There will be somewhere between 100 and 400 in church, a high percentage of whom will be non-churchgoers. It is an important shop-window for the Church and each year there are adults whom I confirm who have come to faith initially by attending last year's confirmation service to support a friend or relative.

Monday
Morning   Ministerial review. (This is a regular feature in the diary. One to two hours with a priest to look at life, ministry, spirituality, future, etc. – at the end of his/her three-yearly assisted self-appraisal.)
Spiritual direction for a priest from another diocese, followed by lunch.

Afternoon Interviews for a post of team rector.

Evening Meeting with leaders of the local Jewish and Muslim communities on community tensions in the light of the international situation.

Tuesday
Morning Team rector review (each year I meet with each team rector for a review of their team).
Meeting with the archdeacon (with whom I work closely in this part of the diocese).

Afternoon Speak at Diocesan Retired Clergy Fellowship (this is a yearly commitment with a group of people who continue to exercise an enormously important ministry and without whom the hard-pressed parochial clergy would be even more stretched than they are).
Meeting with executive officer and vice-chair of the Diocesan Board for Ministry and Society.

Evening Chair the Diocesan Board for Ministry and Society.

Wednesday
Morning Meeting with the principal and the development officer of our Diocesan Ordained Local Ministry Scheme (I chair the governing body). Lunchtime meeting with a team vicar after six months in post. This is a regular feature with all new incumbency-type posts.

Afternoon Meeting (together with the Methodist Chair of District) with the chief executive of one of our local Metropolitan boroughs to discuss Church representation on the Local Strategic Partnership and general issues of community cohesion.

Evening My wife and I host 25 clergy and spouses for dinner and an evening get-together.

Thursday

Morning   Meeting with community development officers in one of the local boroughs.

Afternoon   Host a meeting of area deans for Holy Communion, Lunch and meeting for business/mutual support.

Evening   'Celebration of Lay Ministry' in a team of five churches. I commission twelve new pastoral workers.

Friday   Day off.

Saturday

Morning   Time with a local MP to discuss community cohesion policy. Meeting with an area dean and lay chair, at their request, to discuss issues in their deanery.

Afternoon   Preparation.

Evening   Speak at annual dinner of a local music society.

WEEK TWO

Sunday

Morning   Confirmation and Parish Communion. The parish presents 15 teenagers and 6 adults.

Evening   Confirmation service for three churches, one an LEP, so share with Methodist and URC ministers in the laying on of hands.

Monday

Morning   Opening of church school buildings and tour of the school. In a diocese where there are many church schools such visits form an important strand within episcopal ministry. Visit a priest who is off work with a protracted illness.

Afternoon   Meeting with an OLM ordinand. Interview with reporter from local radio station.

Evening   Speaking on 'Developing relationships with other faith communities' at a deanery meeting.

Tuesday
Morning   Bishop's staff meeting.

Afternoon Meeting in connection with local town-wide mission.

Evening   Meeting with members in one of the local mosques
             followed by curry and talking with individual young
             Muslims till late.

Wednesday
Morning   Lord Mayor's prayer breakfast.
             Ministerial review meeting with local priest.
             Luncheon reception in town hall of one of the
             Metropolitan boroughs.

Afternoon Afternoon walking the parish with a local incumbent.

Evening   Give Bible exposition at a local church for their combined
             house groups' meeting.

Thursday
All day   Meeting in London of the Working Party on Women in
             the Episcopate (good time for preparation on the long
             train journey).

Friday   Day off.

Saturday Leading a prayer school for lay people within the diocese.

Submissions made to the Working Party

From provinces of the Anglican Communion
Anglican Church in Aotearoa, New Zealand and Polynesia
The Anglican Church of Australia
The Anglican Church of Canada
The Holy Catholic Church in Hong Kong (Hong Kong Sheng Kung Hui)
The Church of Ireland
The Anglican Church of Kenya
The Anglican Church of Papua New Guinea
The Scottish Episcopal Church
The Church of the Province of Southern Africa
The Church of the Province of Uganda
The Episcopal Church in the United States of America
The Church in Wales

From United Churches in full Communion
The Church of North India

From organizations, groups, and religious communities
250 priests and people gathered in the Parish Church of St John the Baptist, Our Lady and St Laurence, Thaxted, Essex, on 29 September 2001 [submitted by Ven. E. C. F. Stroud]
Barking Episcopal Area, Chelmsford Diocese [submitted by Rt Revd Roger Sainsbury]
Catholic Women's Ordination, National Core Group [submitted by Mrs Ianthe Pratt]
Chapter of St Aidan and St Oswin, Newcastle [submitted by Revd Richard Pringle]
Church Society, Council [submitted by David Phillips]
Church Society, Trust [submitted by Revd Canon Michael Walters]
Church Union, Chairman and Council [submitted by Mrs Jenny Miller]
Committee of Cost of Conscience [submitted by Revd Francis Gardom]
Community of the Holy Cross [submitted by Mary Luke, Mother Superior]
Edmonton Area Evangelical Fellowship [submitted by Richard Wood]

Forward in Faith, Birmingham Diocese Executive [submitted by
 Mrs Rosemary A. Parslow]
Forward in Faith, Hereford Diocese [submitted by Mr Ronald G.
 Woodhead]
Forward in Faith, Peterborough Diocese [submitted by K. J. Briers]
Forward in Faith, UK [submitted by Revd Geoffrey Kirk]
Group for Rescinding the Act of Synod (GRAS) [submitted by
 Revd Mary Robins]
Northern Ordination Course full-time staff [submitted by Christine
 McMullen]
Shrine of Our Lady of Walsingham, Master and Guardians [submitted
 by Revd Canon Martin Warner]
Society of the Holy Cross, Devon Chapter [submitted by Revd Jeremy
 C. Dowding, SSC]
Society of St Margaret, Walsingham [submitted by Joan Michael, SSM]
Third Province Movement [submitted by Mrs Margaret Brown]
Women and the Church (WATCH), Executive Committee [submitted by
 Jenny Standage]

From Church of England churches

(Note: PCC stands for 'Parochial Church Council')

43 signatories from the Parish of St Augustine's, Aldershot [submitted
 by Revd Keith Hodges]
PCC of St Helen, Auckland [submitted by Lady Jane Gore-Booth]
21 members of St Mary Magdelene's Church, Bradford [submitted
 by Mary Sanders]
PCC of Broughton, Marton and Thornton, Bradford Diocese [submitted
 by Robert Hall]
Priests of the Parish of St Michael and All Angels, Brighton [Revd
 Robert Fayers, Revd David Hewetson, Revd Geoffrey Cook,
 Revd Michael Dymock]
PCC of St Peter's, Bushey Heath [submitted by Revd Robbie Low]
PCCs of the United Benefice of Chacewater and St Day with Carharrack
 [submitted by Revd Andrew Gough]
PCC of the Parish of the Annunciation of the Blessed Virgin Mary,
 Chiselhurst [submitted by Mrs E. M. Clark]
PCC of the Parish of St Giles, Cripplegate with St Bartholomew, Moor
 Lane, St Alphage, London Wall, and St Luke, Old Street, with
 St Mary, Charterhouse, and St Paul, Clerkenwell [submitted by
 J. David Freeman]

District Council of the Church of St Alban, Coventry [submitted by Ralph Rayner]

Churchwardens of St Mary Steps, Exeter [Dr Tegwyn Harris and Miss Hilary Romans]

PCC of St Mary's Church, Farleigh [submitted by Revd Hugh Grear]

PCC of St Francis of Assisi, Friar Park [submitted by Mrs Wendy Buckby]

18 members of Anglican Parish of St Peter's, Greets Green [submitted by Revd Michael J Moulder]

Parish Church of St Oswald, King and Martyr, Hartlepool [submitted by Revd Brian R. Turnbull]

Clergy and six lay officers of the Parish of Higham [submitted by Revd James F Southward]

Parish of St Michael, Harbeldown, Kent [submitted by Revd Michael Morris]

PCC of St Stephen and St Mark, Lewisham [submitted by Wong See Hock and Olabisi Ogunbambi]

The people of St James' Church, Piccadilly, London [submitted by Revd Dr Charles Hedley]

St Stephen's Church, Newcastle upon Tyne [submitted by Mrs Edith Avery]

PCC of South with New Hinksey, Oxford [submitted by Mrs P. Hartman]

Parish Church of St Saviour, Raynes Park [submitted by Heather Aldridge]

PCC of the Parish of the Most Holy Trinity, Reading [submitted by Revd J. M. R. Baker]

PCC and congregation of St Thomas, Somercotes [submitted by G. M. Thor]

Clergy team of the Parish of Central Southend [submitted by Revd Alison M. Ward]

Parish of Swindon New Town [submitted by Revd John Lees]

PCC of St Mary the Virgin, Tottenham [submitted by Flora Bryant]

PCC of St Christopher's Church, Warlingham [submitted by Kathleen Bennett]

PCC of the Parish Church of St Giles, Willenhall [submitted by Revd Keith H. B. Johnson]

PCC of Emmanuel Church, Wimbledon [submitted by Nigel P. Stone]

From individuals
Titles are those given by the individuals in their letters.

Mrs Audrey Agnew
Revd Roy Akerman
Revd H. O. Alby
Bernard and Iris Alderson
Revd Alex Allardice, SSC
Mrs Gillian E. Ambrose
Mr A. C. Anderson
Mrs D. Andrew
Revd D. Apps
Caroline Armitstead
Edward Armitstead
Peter Arnold
Audrey Asbridge
Christopher and Carolyn Ash
Anne Ashton
Revd Mark Ashton
Dr Nigel Aston
Dr Susan A. J. Atkin
Revd Nigel Atkinson
Mr G. Attey
Revd Sallyanne Attwater
Marjorie and Roy Avery
Revd Sue Ayling
Mr J. D. Back
Pat Bake
David Baker
Revd Canon Neville D. Baker
Revd Tony Baker
Edwin D. Bale
Mrs Jane Bale
Wing Commander B. J. Ball
Thora Ball
Revd Canon Michael T. H. Banks
Revd Preb. Peter Bannister
Revd David Banting

Revd Elaine B. Bardwell
Donald Barford
Revd Kevin Barnard
Revd Preb. Donald Barnes
Rt Revd Edwin Barnes
Revd Canon John Barnes
Doreen M. Barrell
Beth Barrett
Martin Bartholomew
Alan Bartley
Revd John Barton
Revd Robert Bashford
Dr Daphne Baston
Dr John Baston
Revd Daphne J. Bayford
Revd R. W. F. Beaken
Mrs Alison Beardwood
Mrs M. I. Beck
Revd William Beer, SSC
Mrs M. E. Beevor
Revd Dick Begbie
Ann Bell
Father Brian T. B. Bell, SSC
John and Joan Bell
John R. Bell
Mrs Vera M. Bell
Rachel M. Bennetts
Revd Mrs Jill Bentall
Revd Angela Berners-Wilson
Mr Michael Berrett
Richard M. Berriman
Sq. Ldr Michael Berry
Valerie Berry
Revd D. Birch
Hugh J. A. and Marjorie J. Bird

Revd Canon David H. Bishop
Gillian Bishop
Susan Black
Mrs Helen Blaby
Kenneth and Pamela M. Blundell
Miss I. T. Boas
Revd Gordon Bond, SSC
Graham Bostock
Elisabeth Boughton
Fr Stephen Bould
Miss Eleanor Boulter
M. Wendy Bowen
Duncan Boyd
Mrs Jean A. Boyle
Anthony T. Bradfield
Revd Daphne Bradford
Ben Bradshaw, MP
Revd Matthew Brailsford
Revd Canon Beaumont L. Brandie
Revd Peter H. Breckwoldt
K. J. Briers
Revd Johanna Brightwell
Revd Canon Michael Brinkworth
Revd Martin Brion
Rt Revd John C. Broadhurst
Canon Ann Brooks
Cyril Brown
Revd Claire Brown
H. Brown
Peter R. Brown
Revd Rosalind Brown
Mrs Doreen Buckland
Mrs Lynne P Buckley
Revd Timothy Bugby, SSC
Mrs E. M. Bullock
Mr A. C. Bullock
Mrs Margaret Burbidge
Revd Anne Burden

Colin Burgess
Mrs Margaret Burgess
John Burn
Revd Canon John Burrows
Barbara Burt
Revd Roger Burt
Revd Edwin W. Butcher
Revd William Butt
Revd Graeme Buttery
Rachel Buxton
M. Byron-Thomas
Joan M. Calder
Mrs Hilary A. Campbell
J. G. Campbell
Revd Tony Cannon
Jean R. Capstick
Mrs Judith Carr
Roy M. Cashmore
Mrs E. G. Cass
Revd Victor Cassam, RD SSC
Miss Kathleen Castle
Mrs Barbara Cauaghan
Alison M. Caw
Margaret R. Cehayer and
   Lilian Langhyard
Revd Charles Chadwick
Carl Chambers
Revd Sylvia Chapman
Tim Chapman
Mrs Liz Chave
Revd Barbara Chillington
John Chilver
Mrs J. Chisholm
Revd Linda A. Church
Mrs Patricia Churchill
Revd Blanche Clancey
Fr Simon P. J. Clark
Jenny M. Clark

Canon Robin Clark and
  Mrs Pat Clark
Mrs Ann Clarke
Revd Fr Peter Clarke, SSC
Miss Rosalind Clarke
Mrs Ann Claydon
Mrs Sheila Clayton
Stephen Clegg
Mary Clifton-Everest
Revd Dr Jean Coates
Mrs Rosina E. Cochrane
Fr C. Collins
Revd Doug and Mrs Valerie
  Constable
Revd Alan Cooke
Mrs Annie Cooke
Miss Margaret W. Cooke
Bryan and Pearl Cooksey
Beverley Cooper
Revd Colin Cooper
Mrs Jenifer Cooper
Mrs Margaret Cooper
Mr Paul K. Cooper
Sir Patrick Cormack, FSA MP
Revd Canon Andrew Cornes
Fr David Cossar
Miss Ann R. Cottingham
Revd Terence R. H. Coyne, SSC
Alan Cox
Revd Elaine Cranmer
Revd Canon Ralph Crowe, SSC
Barbara Cullen
Dorothy W Culley
Lewis Currie
Revd George Curry
Peter Dale
Mr D. R. and Mrs R. E. Dalton
Very Revd A. H. Dammers

R. G. Daniel
Christopher R. Daubney
John Davall
Revd Peter T. W. Davies
Timothy Huw Davies
Revd Tony Davies
Revd Andrew Davis
Patricia Davis and Helen Davis
Ms Barbara Daykin
Mrs Karen Dean
Revd Canon Dr A. J. Delves
Michael Dent
Revd Dorothy Derrick
Stewart Deuchar
Joan Devaney
Revd J. R. Diaper
Mrs O. Dickings
Judith Dimond
Brigadier W. Ian C. Dobbie
Mr H. Humphrey
T. Dobson
Mrs Joyce Donoghue
Revd J. H. Dossor
Revd Gordon Dowden
Revd Colin Duncan
Revd Jane Durell
Richard Dwyer
Revd John Earwaker
Revd Canon Ann Easter
Robin Edlin-White
Susan Edwarde and Jennifer Pullig
Angela Edwards
Mr Joel K. Edwards
Revd Nigel Elliott
Revd Peter W. Elliott
Mrs Anne Ellis
Robin Ellis
Revd Simon Ellis

Jill Elltingham
Mr and Mrs C. B. Eminson
Revd Ian P. Enticott
Elizabeth M. Estlea
Richard K. C. Evans, OBE
Mrs M. J. Eveleigh
Mary A. Evered
Revd John Fairweather
Revd Simon Falshaw
G. Farmer
Mrs B. Faulconbridge
Father Robert Featherstone
David Fenton
Mr Lyn Ferraby
Revd Janet H. Fife
Mrs Sarah Finch
David Fletcher
Dave and Jess Flower
Mrs Mary E. Fookes-Williams
Mrs Elisabeth Ford
David and Pat Forman
Rt Revd Dr Peter Forster
Mrs Gill Foster
Shirley M. Fountain
Revd Jonathan J. Frais
Mrs Doreen Fraser
Revd Alison Froggatt
Mr A. S. Frost
Mr H. R. and Mrs J. D. Fuller
Monica Furlong
Mrs O. M. Gardner and
    Mr P. Gardner
Revd Anna Garvie
Simon J. Gell
Rt Revd Anselm Genders, CR
Daphne George
June Gibbon
Father Paul J. Gibbons, SSC

Judith Gibson
Mr T. Gilks
Edna Gill and Richard A. Gill
Hephzibah E. Gillard
Catherine A. Gilmore
Doris Goddard
Revd Giles Goddard
Rt Revd John W. Goddard
Mrs J. A. Goody
Mrs Margaret Goodrich
Miss Catherine Gordon
Mrs Kathleen Gordon
Sir Josslyn Gore-Booth, Bt
Lady Jane Gore-Booth
Revd Karen Gorham
Dr Graham Gould
Rosalind Graham
Hunt Revd Olivia Graham
Mrs B. O. Gray
Revd Dr Susan Lochrie Graham
Father Gregory, Superior,
    Community of the Servants of
    the Will of God
Ian Grevott
Gary Grief
Dr A. Sheila Grieve, MB ChB
Mrs Angela M. and Mr Peter
    Grieveson
Peter Griffiths
Revd Leslie Grimwade
Mrs Glenys Grimwood
Mrs Marina K. Gunn
Mrs Eileen Gurr
Philip H. Hacking
Revd Fr Brian William George
    Hackney, SSC
Cathie Hall
Mrs Marguerite Hall

Mrs Viviane Hall
Canon Nigel Harley
Revd M. J. Halsall, SSC
Revd P. Hancock
Revd Richard Hancock, TSSF
Revd Graeme Hands
Mrs Faith Hanson
Revd John H. Harper
M. Harper
Revd Rosie Harper
Betty A. Harries
Revd Dr Harriet Harris
Revd Jonathan Redvers Harris
Revd M. S. Hart
Peter D. Hart
Mrs Pauline Hartman
Miss Nona Harvey
G. T. J. Harwood
Mrs Diana Hasting
Revd Martin Hathaway
Lance Haward
Revd Andrew T. Hawes
Kenelm Hawker
Revd John Hawkins
Revd Steven Hawkins
Anthony Hayward
Mrs Gwen Hayward
Major James G. A. Heaney
Revd S. J. Heans, MA
Revd Cynthia Heath
R. J. Herd
Anne Heuon
John Eagle Higginbotham
Revd O. C. G. Higgs
Revd C. Ann Hill
Steven Hilton
Revd David Hitchcock
Revd Christopher J. P. Hobbs

Revd Peter Hobson
Revd David Hodgson
Steve Hoffman
Revd John Hollins
C. W. R. Holloway
Mrs J. N. Holloway
Revd David Holmes
Mrs Dorothy Holmes
Mrs Constance Holt, CBE
Harold W Holwell
Seraphim Alton Honeywell
Mr E. Hooper
Hilda M. Hopkins
Revd Keith Horsfall
J. E. Hotchin
John Hough
Fr Andrew Howard, SSC
Judy Howard
Sue Howard
F. Hulbes
Revd Jeremy Hummerstone
John Humphrey
Revd Lydia Humphreys
Peter F. Hunt
Revd Dr Judith M. Hunt, BVSC
A. B. Hunter
Gordon and Audrey Huntly
Revd John W Hunwicke
Rex Hurrell
Paul Hutchins
Mr Keith and Mrs Frances
    Hutchings
Revd G. John Hutchinson
Revd Paul Illingworth
Revd Dr Emma Ineson
Revd Kelvin Inglis
Mr Geoffrey Ireland
Mavis Jacobs

Revd Colin James
Revd Tom Jamieson
Fr Mervyn Jennings, SSC
José Johnes
Mrs M. G. Johnston
Dr C. A. Jones
Rt Hon. Tessa Jowell, MP
Mrs Susan M. Kanavan
Revd Ian G. Kay
Revd P. F. Keeling
Mrs Mary K. Kempster
John Kennedy
Revd Patsy Kettle
Revd Simon D. A. Killwick
Revd C. M. King
Revd J. S. King
Major Patrick King
Mrs Rosemary King
Mrs Winifred King
Revd Geoffrey Kirk
Revd Charles Knowles
Mary Laehman
Mrs Margaret Laird
Mrs Doreen Lambert
Mrs Anne Lane
Revd Paul S. Lansley
Mrs Emma Laughton
Revd Brian Lay, SSC
Fr Arthur R. Lewis
Jane Lewis
Mrs Kathleen Lewis
Miss L. Lewis Smith
Fr Michael Lewis, SSC
Revd Canon David F. Lickess
Fr John van der Linde,
    Mrs M. Brownbill and
    Mr P. C. Freke
Revd Christopher M. D. Lindlar

Basil K. Lindsey
Mrs Jill M. Lindsey
Revd J. E. Linton
Mrs D. P. S. Linton
David E. R. Lloyd
Revd Paul Lockett, SSC
John Lockyer
Mrs Sally Lowe
June and Gordon Robert Luck
Carol and Graham Lumsley
Rosalind Lund
Fred J. Lush
Miss Anne Lywood
Michael Macey
Revd Ann MacKeith
Angus MacLeay
Revd Kenneth E. Macnab
Revd David M. Maddock
Revd Canon Charmion Mann
Revd Michael J. F. Mannall,
    Obl. OSB SSC
Miss Lilian Marks
Mrs Patricia N Markwick, MCSP
    SRP
Brian J. Marley
B. D. Marlow
Revd Peter Marr
Revd Bob Marsden
Mrs Ann Marsh
Revd Bernard G. G. Marshall
Edward Martin
Mr David Mason
Freda Matchett
Revd James W. Mather, SSC
Revd David M. B. Mathers
Mrs Margaret Matthewman
Revd Jean M. Mayland
Revd Ann E. McKenzie

John McKenzie
Cllr Frank R. McManus
Mrs Hilary Megone
Canon M. A. Hugh Melinsky
Canon Ronald Meredith
Susan B. Meredith
Revd Mark Mesley, SSC
Fr P. B. Miall
Revd Steve Midgley
Miss Susan M. Miell
Mrs Julie Millar
Mrs Elizabeth A. Miller
John Miller
Revd John S. Miller
Fr L. J. Miller
Robert A. Miller
Anthony J. Mills
Mrs Lesley Mills
Revd David Milnes
Michael Minter
Mrs Sue Minton
Revd Richard J. A. Mitchell
Philip G. Mitchell
Mrs C. Moffat
Revd Edward Moll
Mrs Joanna Monckton
Miss G. Cécile Moore
Revd Darren Moore
Mrs Mary Moore
Revd Preb. Michael Moreton
Dr Gareth G. Morgan
Revd Marian Morgan
Father Peter J. Morgan
Sharon Morgan
Mrs Rachel Moriarty
Revd Mary Morris
Bryan Morris
Revd F. H. Mountney

Peter D. Mulley
Revd Dr Lawson Nagel, SSC
Revd Robin L Nash
Revd Peter Needham
Revd W. Nelson
Mrs Dorothy M. Netting
Revd Rosie Nixson
Revd Canon Keith Newton
Revd Dr Andrew Norman
Sherley Norman
C. J. Nowell
Deaconess Monica M. Obee
Gerald M. O'Brien
Mrs Elsie Ockford
Mrs Sadie Ockford
Mr A. P. and Mrs D. M. O'Dowd
S. V. Ogilvie
Revd Philip O'Reilly, SSC
Revd and Mrs S. Orme
Miss M. Osborne
Revd (Miss) Amiel Osmaston
Revd Michael Ovey
Mr Derek and Mrs Paula Owen
Revd John Paddock
Revd Jean Page
Mrs Gillian Pain
Revd Canon Marlene Parsons,
    Revd Dr Alison Joyce and
    Revd Canon Dr Brian Russell
V. J. and R. A. Parslow
Kevin Pask
Revd Douglas M. Paterson
Mrs W. Paul
Richard Payn
William S Payne
Revd Fergus Pearson
Mrs Marion Pegg
Revd John Peirce

Revd John Pelling
Revd Joanna Percival
Revd J. Martin Perris
Lord Phillips of Sudbury
Mrs Anne M. Phillips
David T. Phillips
Revd Canon F. E. Pickard
Miss Urszula Piotrowska
Revd John Pitchford
Revd Paul Plumpton
Revd Christine Polhill
Revd Canon Lambeth D. Poodhun
Revd James Poole
Joyce Pollock
Revd John E. Potter, SSC
Hugh Pratt
Revd James Price
Jennifer Price
Revd Canon Richard Price
Father Richard Pringle, SSC
Revd J Stephen Pullan
Prof. John J. Quenby
Mrs Mary L. Rawson
Alan Rayden
Christina Rees
Kathryn M. Reeve
Revd Mike Reith
Rt Revd John Richards
Father Shaun Richards, SSC
Revd Preb Douglas Richardson
Revd John Y. W. Ritchie
Revd Tana Riviere
Revd Judith Roberts
Mrs Veronica Roberts and Miss
    Joyce Spedding
Yvonne Roberts
Revd Ian Robins
A. J. Robinson

Eric Robinson
Miss Olive M. Robinson
Revd R. R. Robinson
Mary Rodger
Mrs Mary P. Roe
Revd Hugh Rom
Mrs Pauline Rook
Revd Alex Ross
John G. Ross Guy
Miss Jessie Rothera
Mrs J. A. Round and Elaine Round
Mrs Barbara R. Rowe
Miss B. M. Royle
Revd Katharine Rumens
Mrs Alison Ruoff
Jane Russell
Revd M. C. Rutter
Fr John Ryder
Revd C. W. Ryland
Revd Carrie Sandom
Mrs Ronna Saunders
Revd Dr Andy Saville
Michael Scaife
Revd Pam Schollar
Mrs Chris Scott
Revd Simon Scott
Revd Theresa Scott
Revd Stuart Seaton
Mr J. P. Serginson
Mrs E. M. Serginson
Revd Canon Bruce W. Sharpe
Revd David Sharpe
S. M. Sharples
Revd Dr Jane Shaw
Marian and Peter Shearan
Hazel Sheffield
Canon Tony Shepherd
Fr David Sherratt

Fr David J. Sherwood
James C. Siddons
Sylvia A. Simmonds
Mrs Carol Simmons
John G. Simmons
Kathleen Singleton
Sister Vivienne Joy, CHN
Fr Beresford Skelton, SSC CMP
Robert and Helen Slipper
Revd Simon Smallwood
D. E. Smeed
Dorothy Smith
Graham Smith
Miss Jean M. Smith
Michael Kinchin Smith, OBE
Mrs Gladys M. Smollea
Michael Snelling
Revd Colin Southall
Mrs Hilary Southall
Elizabeth M. Speight
Mrs Patricia Springett
Revd J. J. Stark
Wendy Steadman
Revd Penny Stephens
Rt Revd Dr Kenneth Stevenson
Revd Will Stileman
Granville V. Stone
Sir Kenneth Stowe, GCB CVO
Brian Strand
Revd Dr R. J. Stretton
Revd Canon J. R. Stringer
Canon Vincent Strudwick
Elizabeth M. Stuart
Mrs Elizabeth Studley
Revd Royston J. Such
Fr David Sutton, SSC SRC
Iris Sutton
Mrs Freida Sweet

Mrs G. Margaret Sweeting
Revd Clare Sykes
Miss L. Taconis
Mair Talbot
Jennifer M. Targett
Revd Jane Taylor
Victor H. Taylor
Revd William Taylor
L. F. Thacker
Revd Geoffrey T. Theasby
Revd Lucy Thirtle
Emily Thomas
Revd Dr F. H. J. Thomas, SSC
Revd Preb Pippa Thorneycroft
Revd J. A. Thurmer
Revd Dr Jane Tillier and
    Dr Ian Atherton
Revd Kevin Tingay
Mrs Heather Tinker
Revd Melvin Tinker
Revd Colin Tolworthy
G. Townsend
Revd Canon Dr John Toy
Mollie Toy
D. J. Tregidgo
Revd Alistair Tresidder
Revd Preb. Brian R. Tubbs
Canon Nicholas and
    Deacon Ann Turner
Revd Dr H. J. M. Turner
Revd Dr John F. Twisleton
Nicholas and Elizabeth Tyndall
Revd John E. Varty
Revd Simon Vibert
George-Daniel Vine
Revd Jane Virji
Nasir Virji
Sister Vivienne Joy, CHN

Mrs Mildred E. Vosper
Fr Gary Waddington
Revd Peter Walker
David Wall
Mrs M. Wallbanks
Stanley Wallis
Mr D. J. and Mrs C. A. Walton
Father Robin Ward, SSC
Peter and Sally Ward-Enticott
Dr Patricia Ward-Platt
Bevan Wardrobe
Revd Robert Warren
George Watson
Miss Katherine Collier Watson, SSB
Tony and Margaret Webb-Bowen
Ken and Eileen Welch
Mrs K. M. Weller
John and Maggie Webber
Mr John A. Wells-Cole
Mrs Pamela West
Tony Wharton
Mrs Cynthia M. E. White
Maureen Whitebrook
Revd Paul A. Whybrow
Mrs Margaret Wickstead
Revd Canon Malcolm Widdecombe
Revd G. D. V. Wiebe, SSC

Mike A. Wilkins
David Wilkinson
Br Mark William, CSWG
Anne Williams
Mr and Mrs O. A. Williams
Revd Richard Williams
Robert Ian Williams
Revd Sue Williams
Revd Paul S. Williamson
Dr Jonathan P. Wilson
Mr M. C. Wilson
Revd Gordon Winchester
Paul Winchester
Ms Christine Winnington
Jean Winter
Mrs Judith Woolcock
Revd Martin Wray
Miss Ann W. Wright
M. M. Wright and
   Miss Margaret Wright
John H. Wyatt
Mrs Joan Wyatt
June Wyton
Revd Ros Yates
Ian Yearsley
Albert E. Young
P. MacKenzie Young

The following attended a meeting of the Working Party and made a presentation in person:

Rt Revd Basil Osborne, Bishop of Sergievo – 2 April 2003

Revd Prof Gerald Bray – 25 June 2002

Revd Prof Sven-Erik Brodd – 2 April 2003

Representatives of the Catholic Group of General Synod – Revd Jonathan Baker, Revd David Houlding, Revd Dr Robin Ward – 18 June 2003

Representatives of Forward in Faith – Revd Geoffrey Kirk, Mr Stephen Parkinson, Revd Preb. Sam Philpott – 5 February 2002

Rt Revd Victoria Matthews, Bishop of Edmonton – 29 April 2002

Representatives of the National Association of Diocesan Advisers in Women's Ministry (NADAWM) – Revd Canon Penny Driver, Revd Canon Hilary Hanke, Revd Celia Thomson, Revd Frances Tyler – 12 December 2002

Representatives of Reform – Revd Nigel Atkinson, Revd David Banting, Revd Mike Ovey, Revd Carrie Sandom – 12 February 2003

Ven Judith Rose – 25 June 2001

Rt Revd Stephen Sykes – 12 December 2002

Representatives of the Third Province Movement – Revd Dr Roger Beckwith, Mrs Margaret Brown, Revd Canon Dr Terence Grigg, Revd Dr John Hall, Mr John Mitchell, Mr Trevor Stevenson – 18 June 2003

Representatives of Women and the Church (WATCH) – Revd Dr Judith Maltby, Revd Canon Patience Purchas, Revd Charles Reed, Mrs Christina Rees – 5 February 2002

Revd Dr Fraser Watts – 13 September 2002

Notes

HBWE designates a paper produced for the Working Party

chapter 1

1 *The Gift of Authority*, Anglican Book Centre and Church Publishing Incorporated, 1999, p. 17.
2 'Working Party on Women in the Episcopate – a Progress Report from the House of Bishops', GS 1457, General Synod, 2002.

chapter 2

1 *Baptism, Eucharist and Ministry*, WCC, 1982.
2 *The Meissen Agreement*, CCU, 1992.
3 *The Porvoo Common Statement*, CCU, 1993.
4 *Anglican-Moravian Conversations*, CCU, 1996.
5 *Called to Witness and Service*, CHP, 1999.
6 *An Anglican-Methodist Covenant*, CHP/Methodist Publishing House, 2002.
7 ARCIC, *The Final Report*, CTS/SPCK, 1982, pp. 29–39.
8 See for instance for ARCIC, *The Final Report*, CTS/SPCK, 1982, pp. 29–45, and for the Anglican–Orthodox Dialogue *The Dublin Agreed Statement*, SPCK, 1985 sections 21–30.
9 *The Porvoo Common Statement*, p. 20
10 *The Meissen Agreement*, p. 18.
11 For what the concept of oversight means in terms of the ministry of a bishop in the Church of England, see 2.7.16–17 and 2.7.29.
12 *Called to Witness and Service*, p. 29.
13 See 2.5.4–10.
14 *Baptism, Eucharist and Ministry*, p. 24.
15 R. Hooker, *The Laws of Ecclesiastical Polity*, VII.5.3, in *The Works of that Learned and Judicious Divine, Mr Richard Hooker*, OUP, 1841, vol.II, p. 341.
16 For details, see C. Gore, *The Church and the Ministry*, Longmans, Green and Co., 1919, pp. 156–61 and, 335–40. The arguments of these writers continued to be influential throughout the Middle Ages and eventually fed into the Reformation and Tridentine debates about the episcopate.
17 Jerome, *Epistle CXLVI* in *The Nicene and Post Nicene Fathers*, 2nd series, vol.VI, T. & T. Clark/ Eerdmans, 1996, p. 288.
18 John Chrysostom, *Homilies on Timothy XI*, in *The Nicene and Post Nicene Fathers*, 1st series, vol.XIII, T. & T. Clark/Eerdmans, 1994, p. 441.
19 Jerome, *Epistle CXLVI*, p. 289.
20 Jerome, *Epistle CXLVI*, p. 288.
21 Jerome, *Against the Luciferians 9*, in *The Nicene and Post Nicene Fathers*, 2nd series, vol.VI, T. & T. Clark/Eerdmans, 1996, p. 324.
22 A different person from Arius the originator of the Arian heresy.
23 Gore, *The Church and the Ministry*, pp. 147–8.
24 J. B. Lightfoot, *St Paul's Epistle to the Philippians*, Macmillan, 1891 p. 234. For the detailed argument, see pp. 186–234.
25 Clement of Alexandria, *Who is the rich man that shall be saved?*, XLII, in *The Ante-Nicene Fathers*, vol.II, T. & T. Clark/Eerdmans, 2001, p. 603.
26 Tertullian *Against Marcion*, Bk IV:5, in *The Ante-Nicene Fathers*, vol.III, T. & T. Clark/Eerdmans, 1997, p. 350.

27 Text in M. J. Routh, *Reliquae Sacrae*, vol.1, p. 394, cited in Lightfoot, *Philippians*, p. 212. In his work *Against Heresies*, written at the end of the second century, St Irenaeus of Lyons, who came from Asia Minor, writes concerning St Polycarp:

> Polycarp also was not only instructed by apostles, and conversed with many who had seen Christ, but was also, by apostles in Asia, appointed bishop of the Church in Smyrna. (Irenaeus *Against Heresies*, III.3, in *The Ante-Nicene Fathers*, vol.I, T. & T. Clark/Eerdmans, 1996, p. 416)

This evidence is best accounted for if we follow both Lightfoot (*Philippians*, p. 206) and Gore (*The Church and the Ministry*, pp. 257–8) in accepting that St John was one of a number of apostles who moved to Asia Minor after the fall of Jerusalem in AD70 and that these other apostles, including SS Andrew and Philip were associated with him in appointing bishops.

28 See his letters to the churches in Ephesus, Magnesia, Tralles, Philadelphia and Smyrna.

29 *Martyrdom of Polycarp* 16 in M. Staniforth, *Early Christian Writings*, Penguin, 1968, p. 161.

30 Eusebius of Ceasarea, *Ecclesiastical History*, III.36, V.19, V.24, in *Eusebius Ecclesiastical History*, vol.I, Harvard/Heinemann, 1980, pp. 281, 493, 505–9.

31 Lightfoot, *Philppians*, p. x.

32 For the references for this see J. Bingham, *Antiquities of the Christian Church*, vol.I, London, 1843, pp. 63–4. For a discussion of the precise role exercised by Timothy and Titus see Gore, *The Church and the Ministry*, pp. 221–2.

33 Eusebius, *Ecclesiastical History*, II.1.3, II.23.3, III.11, IV.22.4, in *Eusebius Ecclesiastical History*, vol.I, pp. 105, 171, 231–2, 375.

34 Lightfoot, *Philippians*, pp. 206–7.

35 See P. F. Bradshaw, *Ordination Rites of the Ancient Churches of East and West*, Pueblo, 1990, pp. 10ff.

36 G. Dix (ed.), *The Treatise On The Apostolic Tradition*, III.4–5, SPCK, 1968, pp. 5–6.

37 C. Kucharek, *The Sacramental Mysteries – A Byzantine Approach*, Alleluia Press, 1976, p. 277.

38 P. F. Bradshaw, M. E. Johnson and L. E. Phillips (eds), *The Apostolic Tradition*, Fortress Press, 2002, p. 34.

39 *The Apostolic Tradition*, XX.3–8 and XXII.1–4, in Dix, *The Apostolic Tradition*, pp. 31–2 and 38–9.

40 *The Apostolic Tradition*, XXVI.10, in Dix, *The Apostolic Tradition*, p. 47.

41 T. W. Manson, *The Church's Ministry*, Hodder & Stoughton, 1948, p. 67.

42 Because of this conviction the general rule was that there should only be one bishop in each city. Details of this rule are given in Bingham, *Antiquities of the Christian Church*, ch.XIII. Bingham notes,

> however, that the rule was not absolute and that where there was a 'reasonable cause', such as a bishop being unable to exercise his office, or the need to heal a schism, exceptions to the rule were permitted.

43 Lightfoot, *Philippians*, p. 235.

44 Ignatius of Antioch, *Epistle to the Magneians*, 6–7, in Staniforth, *Early Christian Writings*, pp 88–9.

45 Gore, *The Church and the Ministry*, pp. 152–4.

46 K. Ware, 'Patterns of Episcopacy in the Early Church and Today: An Orthodox View', in P Moore (ed.), *Bishops: But What Kind?*, SPCK, 1982, p. 17.

47 Cyprian, *Epistle XIII*, in *The Ante-Nicene Fathers*, vol.V, T. and T. Clark/Eerdmans, 1995, p. 294.

48 Cyprian, *The Seventh Council of Carthage under Cyprian* in *The Ante-Nicene Fathers*, vol.V, p. 565.

49 Irenaeus, *Against Heresies*, III.1, in *The Ante-Nicene Fathers*, vol.I, T. and T. Clark/Eerdmans, 1996, p. 415.

50 Irenaeus, *Against Heresies*, III.2–4, in *The Ante-Nicene Fathers*, vol.I, pp. 415–16.

51 Irenaeus, *Against Heresies*, IV.26:2, in *The Ante-Nicene Fathers*, vol.I, p. 497. In this context 'presbyter' means bishop rather than priest.

52 Tertullian, *On Prescription Against Heretics*, XXXII, in *The Ante-Nicene Fathers*, vol.III, T. and T. Clark/Eerdmans, 1997, p. 258.

53 See, for example, J. Zizioulas, *Being as Communion*, Darton, Longman & Todd, 1985, ch.6.

54 Bingham, *Antiquities of the Christian Church*, pp. 83–4.

55 John Chrysostom, *On the Priesthood*, IV.3, in *The Nicene & Post Nicene Fathers*, 1st series, vol.IX, T. and T. Clark/Eerdmans, 1996, p. 64.

56 *The Apostolic Tradition*, II.3–5, in Dix, *The Apostolic Tradition*, p. 3.

57 *The Apostolic Tradition*, VIII.1, in Dix, *The Apostolic Tradition*, p. 13.

58 *The Apostolic Tradition*, IX.1, 9, in Dix, *The Apostolic Tradition*, pp. 15, 17.

59 *The Apostolic Tradition*, IX.7–8, in Dix, *The Apostolic Tradition*, p. 17.

60 See Lightfoot, *Philippians*, pp. 231–2 and W. Telfer 'Episcopal Succession in Egypt', *Journal of Ecclesiastical History*, vol.3, no.1, April 1952, pp. 1–13.

61 Gore, *The Church and the Ministry*, pp. 119–21 and 315–20.

62 This latter practice was specifically ruled out by Canon III of the Seventh Ecumenical Council which was held at Nicaea in 787.

63 *The Martyrdom of Polycarp*, 12, in Staniforth, *Early Christian Writings*, pp. 159–60.

64 K. S. Latourette, *A History of the Expansion of Christianity*, vol.1, Eyre and Spottiswoode, 1938, p. 201,

65 L. Sherley-Price, *Bede – A History of the English Church and People*, II.9, Penguin, 1968, p. 115.

66 Price, *Bede – A History of the English Church and People*, II.14, p. 129.

67 Bingham, *Antiquities of the Christian Church*, ch.XIV.

68 Canon XXV of the Council of Antioch declares, for example:

> Let the bishop have power over the funds of the Church, so as to dispense them with all piety and in the fear of God to all who need.

Text in *The Nicene and Post Nicene Fathers*, 2nd series, vol.XIV, T. and T. Clark/Eerdmans, 1997, p. 121.

69 S. Lancel, *St Augustine*, SCM, 2002, chs XXIII–XXIV gives a good picture of the activity in both Church and society of a bishop of the early fifth century.

70 See for example Sermon III of Leo the Great in *The Nicene and Post Nicene Fathers*, 2nd series, vol.XII, T. and T. Clark/Eerdmans, 1997 pp. 116–17. For the development of the claim for papal primacy see K Schatz, *Papal Primacy*, Liturgical Press, 1996.

71 Hooker, *The Laws of Ecclesiastical Polity*, VII.II.1, in *Works*, vol.II, pp. 329–39.

72 See N. Edwards and A. Lane (eds), *The Early Church in Wales and the West*, OUP, 1992.

73 There were continuing tensions between the English monarchs and the papacy about the relationship between their respective spheres of authority throughout the Middle Ages, which were reflected in laws such as the *Statute of Praemunire* of 1352 and the *Statute of Provisors* of 1390 that sought to limit papal power. Furthermore, from the fourteenth century onwards the followers of John Wycliffe, the 'Lollards', rejected papal authority in principle. However, until the time of Henry VIII neither of these factors led to the authority of the pope over the English Church being seriously challenged.

74 *Baptism, Eucharist and Ministry*, p. 24.

75 It is worth noting that those Lutheran and Reformed churches who did not retain the traditional threefold order departed from it order to maintain their continuity with other aspects of the apostolic witness. As they saw it they upheld the threefold pattern of oversight, presiding ministry and service which they saw in the New Testament and the Fathers only in a different form.

76 J. Ayre (ed.), *The Works of John Jewel*, The Third Portion, Parker Society/CUP, 1843, p. 58.

77 Jewel, *Works*, p. 59.

78 S. Neill, *Anglicanism* 4th ed., Mowbray, 1977, p. 104. Italics his.

79 Neill, *Anglicanism*, pp,103–4.

80 See Jewel, *Works*, pp. 59–60.

81 E. Duffy, 'The Shock of Change: Continuity and Discontinuity in the Elizabethan Church of England', in S. Platten (ed.), *Anglicanism and the Western Christian Tradition*, Canterbury Press, 2003, p. 43.

82 G. Bray (ed.), *Documents of the English Reformation*, James Clarke, 1994, pp. 90–2.

83 C. Podmore, 'The Choosing of Bishops in the Early Church and the Church of England: An Historical Survey', in *Working with the Spirit: Choosing Diocesan Bishops*, CHP, 2001, pp. 120–1.

84 Neill, *Anglicanism*, p. 39.

85 J. Ayre (ed.), *The Works of John Whitgift*, vol.I, CUP/Parker Society, 1851, p. 185.

86 J. Moorman, *A History of the Church in England*, 3rd ed., Morehouse Publishing, 1980, p. 209.

87 For details see P. Collinson, *The Elizabethan Puritan Movement*, OUP, 1998, part 3.

88 See W. H. Frere and C. E. Douglas, *Puritan Manifestoes*, Church Historical Society, vol.LXII, pp. 1–40.

89 Hooker, *The Laws of Ecclesiastical Polity*, VII.1.4 in *Works*, vol.II, p. 330.

90 *Called to Witness and Service*, p. 31.

91 J. Findon, 'Developments in the Understanding and Practice of Episcopacy in the Church of England', in *Visible Unity and the Ministry of Oversight*, CHP, 1997, p. 90.

92 Findon, 'Developments', p. 83.

93 Findon, 'Developments', p. 85.

94 Hooker, *Laws of Ecclesiastical Polity*, VII.5.8, in *Works*, vol.II, p. 348.

95 Findon, 'Developments', p. 89.

96 Lightfoot, *Philippians*, p. 267.

97 Lightfoot, *Philippians*, p. 268.

98 Lightfoot, *Philippians*, p. 196.

99 For the evidence for this see Philippians 1.1, Acts 20.17, 28, 1 Timothy 3.1-7; 5.17-19, Titus 1.5-7, 1 Peter 5.1-2.

100 Lightfoot, *Philippians*, p. 196.

101 For the ministry of these prophets and teachers see Acts 11.27, 13.1, 15.32, 21.10.

102 Gore, *The Church and the Ministry*, p. 302.

103 Gore, *The Church and the Ministry*, pp. 302–3.

104 Gore, *The Church and the Ministry*, p. 59. It is important to note here the careful distinction that Gore makes between the pastoral role of the apostles which was transmitted to the bishops as their successors and their role as witnesses of the resurrection and founders of the Church under Christ which was not. This awareness of discontinuity as well as continuity between the apostles and the bishops goes back to the very earliest days of the Church. For example, as we have seen, St Ignatius of Antioch was someone with a high view of the episcopal office and yet he writes to the church in Rome: 'I am not issuing orders to you, as though I were a Peter or a Paul. They were apostles, and I am a condemned criminal.' (*Letter to the Romans*, 4, in Staniforth, *Early Christian Writings*, pp. 104–5)

105 Gore, *The Church and the Ministry*, p. 221.

106 M. Ramsey, *The Gospel and the Catholic Church* 2nd ed., SPCK, 1990, p. 69.

107 Ramsey, *The Gospel and the Catholic Church*, pp. 81–2.

108 Ramsey, *The Gospel and the Catholic Church*, p. 82.

109 Ramsey, *The Gospel and the Catholic Church*, pp. 82–3.

110 Ramsey, *The Gospel and the Catholic Church*, pp. 84–5.

111 H. W. Montefiore, 'The Historic Episcopate', in K. M. Carey (ed.), *The Historic Episcopate*, Dacre Press, 1955, p. 108.

112 J. Webster, 'The Self-organizing Power of the Gospel of Christ: Episcopacy and Community Formation', in J. Webster, *Word and Church*, T. and T. Clark/Continuum, 2001 pp. 206–7. Italics his.

113 Webster, 'The Self-organizing Power of the Gospel of Christ', p. 209.

114 This debate, about whether bishops and presbyters were originally one order or were always different is the same issue that is under discussion between Lightfoot and Gore.

115 A. Barratt, 'The Sacrament of Order and the Second Vatican Council: The Presbyter-bishop Relationship Revisited', HB WE (02) 28. The contemporary Roman Catholic debate focuses on the idea of presbyters as co-operators of the order of bishops with the precise point at issue being the nature of this co-operation.

116 *Episcopal Ministry*, CHP, 1990.

117 *The Porvoo Common Statement*, p. 27.

118 *Apostolicity and Succession*, CHP, 1998. A similar point is made in the ARCIC statement *Ministry and Ordination*:

> In the ordination of a new bishop, other bishops lay hands on him, as they request the gift of the Spirit for his ministry and receive him into their ministerial fellowship. Because they are entrusted with the oversight of other churches, this participation in his ordination signifies that this new bishop and his church are within the communion of churches. Moreover, because they are representative of their churches in fidelity to the teaching and mission of the apostles and are members of the episcopal college, their participation also ensures the historical continuity of this church with the apostolic Church and of its bishop with the original apostolic ministry. The communion of the churches in mission, faith, and holiness, through time and space is thus symbolized and maintained in the bishop. (*The Final Report*, pp. 37–8)

119 *Episcopal Ministry*, p. 160.

120 See Canons B 43 and B 44 for details.

121 *Bishops in Communion*, CHP, 2000, p. 50.

122 Manson, *The Church's Ministry*, p. 74.

123 Manson, *The Church's Ministry*, p. 75.

124 *An Anglican Methodist Covenant*, p. 29.

125 See 2.3.33–39.

126 *The Official Report of the Lambeth Conference 1998*, Morehouse Publishing, 1999, pp. 178–9.

127 *Resourcing Bishops*, CHP, 2001, pp. 227–49.

128 *Bishops in Communion*, p. 36.

129 *Baptism, Eucharist and Ministry*, p. 26.

130 *Bishops in Communion*, pp. 26–7.

131 See canon C 17.

132 *Bishops in Communion*, pp. 28–32.

133 *Episcopal Ministry*, p. 195.

134 *Episcopal Ministry*, p. 198.

135 *Suffragan Bishops*, GS Misc 733, 2004, p. 23.

136 See, for example, R. Banks, *Paul's Idea of Community*, 2nd ed., Hendrickson, 1994, pp. 49–63 and 149–58, E. Ellis, 'Paul and His Co-workers', in E. Ellis, *Prophecy and Hermeneutic in Early Christianity*, Eerdmans, 1978, pp. 3–22, and D. J. Harrington, 'Paul and Collaborative Ministry', *New Theology Review*, vol.3, 1990, pp. 62–71.

137 See, for example, E. Best, 'Paul's Apostolic Authority', *Journal for the Study of the New Testament*, 27, 1986, pp. 3–25, J. A. Crafton, *The Agency of the Apostle*, Sheffield Academic Press, 1991, pp. 53–103 and J. H. Schutz, *Paul and the Anatomy of Apostolic Authority*, Cambridge, 1975.

138 *Suffragan Bishops*, p. 23.

139 As was noted above, in the later patristic period the archdeacon was originally the head deacon and as such the chief assistant to the bishop. The role later came to be exercised by a presbyter but the idea that the archdeacon's role is to assist the bishop remains.

140 *Bishops in Communion*, p. 21.

141 *Bishops in Communion*, p. 15.

142 *Bishops in Communion*, p. 15.

143 *Bishops in Communion*, pp. 15–16.

144 *Bishops in Communion*, p. 16.

145 *Bishops in Communion*, p. 16.

146 *Bishops in Communion*, p. 16. Although the principle of representation is widely accepted in Anglican theology it also needs to be noted that in her paper *Representative?* presented to the Working Party Christina Baxter has argued that it is inappropriate to use such language of ordained ministers because it does not fit with the New Testament evidence or do justice to the fact that God is directly present to all Christian believers, indwelling them through the Holy Spirit. In this sense God does not require representation by bishops or anyone else. In the discussion of this paper in the Working Party it was argued in response that when we speak of 'representation' we do not mean representation in place of Christ as if he were absent and we are representing him, rather as Article XXVI indicates, we speak and act in his name.

chapter 3

1 Jewel, *Works*, p. 52.

2 Jewel, *Works* p. 69.

3 M. Tanner, *Towards a Theology of Vocation*, cited in M. Webster, *A New Strength, A New Song*, Mowbray, 1994, p. 35.

4 For the use of such arguments in the history of the Church see W. Webb, *Slaves, Women and Homosexuals – Exploring the Hermeneutics of Cultural Analysis*, IVP, 2001.

5 A. Flannery, *Vatican II: More Post Conciliar Documents, Volume II*, Eerdmans, 1982, p. 333. The point that the passage is making is that scholastic theologians in the Middle Ages, motivated by the desire to be faithful to the type of ministry ordained by Christ, used arguments in defence of this position that we could not or should not use today.

6 For an illuminating exposition of the early chapters of Genesis see P. Tribble, *God and the Rhetoric of Human Sexuality*, Fortress Press, 1978.

7 N. Sagovsky, 'A Note on "Justice" and "Equality": A Paper for the Working Party', HBWE (02) 14, 2002, p. 6.

8 The use of the term 'story' causes difficulty for some people because they see story as having no necessary connection with questions of truth as when we say that something is 'only a story'. However, for Christian theology the truth about God and the world is to be found in the story of the mighty acts of God in creation and redemption. As G. K. Chesterton observed, what Christianity did was bridge the age-long gap between the story-tellers and the philosophers:

> the sanity of the world was restored and the soul of man offered salvation by something which did indeed satisfy the two warring tendencies of the past; which had never been satisfied in full and most certainly never satisfied together. It met the mythological search for romance by being a story and the philosophical search for truth by being a true story. (G. K. Chesterton, *The Everlasting Man*, Ignatius Press, 1994, p. 248)

9 Text in J. H. Leith (ed.), *Creeds of the Churches*, Blackwell, 1973, p. 232.

10 *The Lambeth Conference 1958*, SPCK/Seabury Press, 1959, 2.12–2.13.

11 *The Lambeth Conference 1958*, p. 2.8.

12 *The Official Report of the Lambeth Conference 1998*, Morehouse Publishing, 1999, p. 32.

13 Dogmatic Constitution on Divine Revelation, *Dei Verbum*, 21.

14 R. Bauckham, *God and the Crisis of Freedom*, Westminster John Knox Press, 2002, p. 65.

15 W. Brueggemann, *Theology of the Old Testament*, Fortress Press, 1997, p. 200.

16 Bauckham, *God and the Crisis of Freedom*, p. 68.

17 For more details on 'behind the text', 'in the text' and 'in front of the text' issues, see M. Turner, 'Historical Criticism and Theological Hermeneutics of the New Testament', in J. Green and M. Turner (eds), *Between Two Horizons*, Eerdmans, 2000, pp. 44–70.

18 *The Interpretation of the Bible in the Church*, Editions Paulines, 1994 pp. 108–9 cf. Second Vatican Council, Dogmatic Constitution on Divine Revelation, *Dei Verbum*, nn.11–12.

19 I. Henderson, *Myth in the New Testament*, SCM Press, 1952, p. 3.

20 Bauckham, *God and the Crisis of Freedom*, p. 7.

21 Bauckham, *God and the Crisis of Freedom*, p. 7.

22 Bauckham, *God and the Crisis of Freedom*, p. 7.

23 Trible, *Texts of Terror*.

24 What is known as the 'regulative' principle.

25 For a useful introduction to the issues involved here see Webb, *Slaves, Women & Homosexuals*.

26 G. Gassmann (ed.), *Documentary History of Faith and Order 1963–1993*, WCC, 1993, p. 11.

27 *The Gift of Authority*, p. 17.

28 Bauckham, p. 109.

29 *The Truth Shall Make You Free – The Lambeth Conference 1988*, CHP, 1988, p. 288.

30 Specific New Testament support for the importance of tradition can be found in 1 Corinthians 15.1-11 where St Paul emphasizes the importance of the tradition concerning the Resurrection which he passed on to the Corinthian church and 2 Timothy 2.1-13 where St Timothy is exhorted to pass on the tradition of sound doctrine that he has himself received.

31 For this point see S. Holmes, *Listening to the Past*, Paternoster/Baker Academic, 2002, ch.1.

32 Canon A 5, for instance, declares that:

> The doctrine of the Church of England is grounded in the Holy Scriptures, and in such teachings of the ancient Fathers and Councils of the Church as are agreeable to the said Scriptures.

33 See 3.1.5-7.

34 For detailed examples of these arguments in the teaching of the Early Fathers, see P. Mitchell, *The Scandal of Gender*, Regina Orthodox Press, 1998. As Chapter 5 will show, these are not necessarily the reasons why people object to the ordination of women as bishops today. They may object to this idea for other reasons.

35 For this understanding of reason, see Hooker, *The Laws of Ecclesiastical Polity*, I.VI–VII.

36 Hooker, *The Laws of Ecclesiastical Polity*, III.VIII.11.

37 *The Virginia Report*, p. 244

38 As St Paul stresses in 1 Corinthians 13.9-12, it is only at the end of time that we shall attain to this kind of perfect knowledge.

39 J. Webster, *Holiness*, SCM Press, 2003, p. 10.

40 Webster, *Holiness*, pp. 11–12.

41 O. M. T. O'Donovan, *Resurrection and Moral Order*, 2nd ed., Apollos/Eerdmans, 1994, p. 89.

42 O. M. T. O'Donovan, *On the Thirty Nine Articles*, Paternoster Press, 1984, pp. 89–90.

43 For the argument for this last point, see, for instance, K. Aune, 'Evangelicals and Gender', in I. Taylor (ed.), *Not Evangelical Enough!*, Paternoster Press, 2003, pp. 89–91.

44 D. F. Sawyer, 'Feminist Interpretation', in R. J. Coggins and J. L. Houlden (eds), *Dictionary of Biblical Interpretation*, SCM Press, 1990 p. 231.

45 Sawyer, 'Feminist Interpretation', p. 232.

46 M. Daly, *Beyond God the Father*, Beacon Press, 1973.

47 D. Hampson, *Theology and Feminism*, Blackwell, 1990.

48 E. S. Fiorenza, *In Memory of Her: a Feminist Theological Reconstruction of Christian Origins* 2nd ed., SCM Press, 1997.

49 O. Chadwick, *From Bossuet to Newman*, 2nd ed., CUP, 1987.

50 Vincent of Lerins, *Commonitorium*, II.3. It should also be noted, however, that St Vincent does not argue for a totally static view of Christian belief. In Chapter XXIII of the Commonitorium he argues that Christian belief grows and develops in the same way that a child develops into an adult. The point of

this analogy is that while there is change there is also continuity and it is this basic continuity that the famous statement in Chapter II is intended to express.

51 One of the clearest illustrations of this belief is the legend found in the writings of Rufinus of Aquilea that the Apostles' Creed was literally the work of the apostles who had produced it word for word under the influence of the Holy Spirit on the day of Pentecost.

52 J. H. Newman, *An Essay on the Development of Christian Doctrine*, 8th ed., Longmans, Green and Co., 1891, p. 40.

53 Newman, *An Essay on the Development of Christian Doctrine*, p. 74.

54 Newman, *An Essay on the Development of Christian Doctrine*, p. 171.

55 Newman, *An Essay on the Development of Christian Doctrine*, pp. 169–206.

56 Newman, *An Essay on the Development of Christian Doctrine*, pp. 171–2.

57 Newman, *An Essay on the Development of Christian Doctrine*, p. 203. Italics his.

58 A. Nichols, *From Newman to Congar: The Idea of Doctrinal Development from the Victorians to the Second Vatican Council*, P. Toon, *The Development of Doctrine in the Church*, Eerdmans, 1979.

59 For the first approach, see, for example, J. Orr, *The Progress of Dogma*, James Clarke, 2002, and for the second, see M. Wiles, *The Making of Christian Doctrine*, CUP, 1967.

60 N. Lash, *Change in Focus*, Sheed & Ward, 1973, p. 72.

61 N. Lash, *Change in Focus*, p. 73.

62 Wiles, *The Making of Christian Doctrine*, p. 18.

63 Orr, *The Progress of Dogma*, p. 15.

64 Aune, 'Evangelicals and Gender', p. 84.

65 Aune, 'Evangelicals and Gender', p. 91.

66 Aune, 'Evangelicals and Gender', p. 91.

67 Orr, *The Progress of Dogma*, p. 31.

68 For details, see O. Rush, *The Doctrine of Reception*, Editrice Pontificia Universita Gregoriana, 1997, ch.III.

69 R. Gaillardetz, 'The Reception of Doctrine', in B. Hoose (ed.), *Authority in the Roman Catholic Church: Theory and Practice*, Ashgate, 2002, p. 96.

70 Y. Congar 'Reception as an Ecclesiological Reality', in G. Alberigo and A. Weiler (eds), *Election and Consensus in the Church – Concilium*, 77, Herder & Herder, 1972, p. 45.

71 W. Rusch, *Reception: An Ecumenical Opportunity*, Fortress Press, 1988, p. 31.

72 H. G. Gadamer, *Truth and Method*, 2nd ed., Sheed & Ward, 1989.

73 H. R. Jauss, *The Aesthetics of Reception*, University of Minnesota Press, 1982.

74 For examples of works that have made use of the idea of reception history, see U. Luz, *Matthew 1-7: A Commentary*, T. and T. Clark, 1990, and A. C. Thiselton, *The First Epistle to the Corinthians*, Eerdmans/Paternoster, 2000.

75 *Women in the Anglican Episcopate*, Anglican Book Centre, 1998, p. 26.

76 *Women in the Anglican Episcopate*, p. 115.

77 *The Ordination of Women to the Priesthood: A Second Report by the House of Bishops* (GS 829), General Synod, 1988, pp. 108–9.

78 *Bonds of Peace*, paragraphs 2–3, in *Ordination of Women to the Priesthood: Pastoral Arrangements*, General Synod, 1993, pp. 5–6.

79 P. Toon, *Reforming Forwards? The Doctrine of Reception and the Consecration of Women as Bishops*, Latimer Trust, 2004, p. 16.

80 Toon, *Reforming Forwards?*, p. 17.

81 *The Ordination of Women to the Priesthood: The Synod Debate*, CHP, 1993, p. 11.

82 Toon, *Reforming Forwards?*, p. 17.

83 Arguably this right is limited when, as in the case of human sexuality, a wider communion of churches (such as the Anglican Communion) to which a particular church belongs has decided that a particular

development is not permissible. This is not the case in regard to the ordination of women since it has been accepted by successive Lambeth conferences that this is a matter on which the provinces of the Anglican Communion should be free to determine their own policy subject to a continuing process of reception.

84 P. Avis, 'Reception: Towards An Anglican Understanding', in P. Avis (ed.), *Seeking the Truth of Change in the Church*, T. and T. Clark, 2004, p. 30.

85 Avis, 'Reception', p. 30.

86 'women duly ordained priests share equally with their male counterparts in the exercise of its ministry, in synodical government and in consideration for suitable appointments.' (*Priests (Ordination of Women) Measure Code of Practice*, 1993, Introduction).

87 A. C. Thiselton, 'Authority and Hermeneutics', in P. E. Satterthwaite and D. F. Wrights (eds), *A Pathway into The Holy Scripture*, Eerdmans, 1984, pp. 136–7.

88 Thiselton, 'Authority and Hermeneutics', p. 137.

89 *The Official Report of the Lambeth Conference 1998*, p. 394.

chapter 4

1 Neill, *Anglicanism*, pp. 413–21. In the text of his history a few women, such as Queen Anne and the evangelical tract writer Hannah Moore, appear who are not mentioned in the index. However, the point still stands that women are marginal to the point of invisibility in the bulk of his account of the Church of England's story.

2 Moorman, *A History of the Church in England*, pp. 461–85.

3 G. Cloke, *This Female Man of God: Women and Spiritual Power in the Patristic Age AD 350–450*, Routledge, 1995.

4 Neill, Anglicanism, pp. 402–3.

5 S. Gill, *Women in the Church of England*, SPCK, 1994.

6 C. M. Ady, *The Role of Women in the Church*, The Central Council for Women's Church Work, 1948, p. 11.

7 Gill, *Women in the Church of England*, p. 163.

8 B. Heeney, *The Women's Movement in the Church of England 1850–1930*, OUP, 1988, p. 68.

9 For details of the development of the ministry of deaconesses in the Church of England in the nintheenth century, see C. Robinson, *The Ministry of Deaconesses*, Methuen, 1914.

10 See Gill, *Women in the Church of England*, ch.7.

11 For details of this decision, see Heeney, *The Women's Movement in the Church of England*, pp. 95–8.

12 For details, see Gill, *Women in the Church of England*, ch.8. It is sometimes suggested that the mission field provided a major catalyst for the development of women's ministry since women were able to undertake work in the mission field that they were not permitted to undertake at home. There is some truth in this claim, but, as Gill explains, there were the same debates about the appropriate role for women among the various missionary societies as in the wider Church, and women missionaries were subject to many of the same restrictions as they were in Britain.

13 Dorothy L. Sayers' novel *Gaudy Night* (Victor Gollancz, 1935) provides an accessible introduction to the impact of these kinds of social change.

14 E. Storkey, *Created or Constructed – The Great Gender Debate*, Paternoster, 2000, p. 7.

15 See S. Fletcher, *Maude Royden – A Life*, Basil Blackwell, 1989.

16 *The Ministry of Women*, SPCK, 1919, p. 5.

17 *The Ministry of Women*, p. 19.

18 *The Ministry of Women*, pp. 19–20.

19 R. Coleman (ed.), *Resolutions of the Lambeth Conferences 1867–1988*, Anglican Book Centre, 1992, p. 60.

20 *Report of the Lambeth Conference 1930*, SPCK, 1930, p. 180.

21 *Report of the Lambeth Conference 1930*, p. 178.

22 *The Ministry of Women: Report of the Archbishops' Commission*, Church Assembly Publications Board, 1935, p. 47.

23 *The Ministry of Women* (1935), p. 10.

24 *The Ministry of Women* (1935), p. 29.

25 For an accessible account of what it felt like to minister as a woman in this context, see M. Cundiff, *Called To Be Me*, Triangle, 1982.

26 *Report of the Archbishops' Commission on Women and Holy Orders*, Church Information Office, 1966 p. 35.

27 Storkey, *Created or Constructed*, p. 8.

28 Storkey, *Created or Constructed*, p. 8.

29 A. Hastings, *A History of English Christianity 1920–1985*, Fount, 1987, pp. 580–1.

30 Storkey, *Created or Constructed*, pp. 24–25. Italics in the original.

31 For example, Constance Coltman became the first officially ordained female Congregational minister in 1917 and was followed by Elsie Chamberlain in 1941; women were ordained in the Church of Scotland in 1969 and in 1974 the first women were ordained by the Methodist Conference. For more details, see G. Rowell, 'Women and *Episcope* in the English Free Church Tradition'.

32 For example, Li Tim Oi was ordained priest in emergency wartime conditions by the Bishop of Hong Kong in 1944 and in 1971 the first two legal ordinations of women took place in Hong Kong. In 1976 eleven women were illegally ordained in Philadelphia and their ordination was then subsequently regularized by the ECUSA General Convention which adopted legislation to ordain women to all orders.

33 The voting figures were: House of Bishops 39 Ayes, 13 Noes (75 per cent), House of Clergy 176 Ayes, 74 Noes (70.4 per cent) and House of Laity 169 Ayes, 82 Noes (67.3 per cent).

34 The House of Bishops, *Manchester Statement*, 1993, p. 4.

35 House of Bishops, *Manchester Statement*, p. 5.

36 *Priests (Ordination of Women) Measure 1993 (No.2)*, HMSO, 1993.

37 *General Synod Episcopal Ministry Act of Synod 1993*, General Synod, 1993.

38 House of Bishops 39 Ayes, 0 Noes; House of Clergy 175 Ayes, 12 Noes; House of Laity 194 Ayes, 4 Noes.

39 *Priests (Ordination of Women) Measure*, pt II sections 3 and 4. Resolution A states: 'That this PCC would not accept a woman as the minister who presides at or celebrates the Holy Communion or pronounces the absolution in the parish.' Resolution B states: 'That this PCC would not accept a woman as the incumbent or priest-in-charge of the benefice or as team vicar of the benefice.'

40 *Episcopal Ministry Act of Synod*, p. 1.

41 *Episcopal Ministry Act of Synod*, p. 2.

42 Canon C 18(2)

43 See 6.2.26–29

44 6.2.30.

45 The history of the campaign for the ordination of women to the priesthood is detailed from the perspective of the Movement for the Ordination of Women by Margaret Webster in *A New Strength, A New Song – The Journey to Women's Priesthood*, Mowbray, 1994. A verbatim record of the November 1992 debate can be found in *The Ordination of Women to the Priesthood: The Synod Debate*, CHP, 1993.

46 I. Jones, *Women and the Priesthood in the Church of England Ten Years On*, CHP, 2004, p. 56.

47 The comparable figure for men is 7,920. The diocese with the highest number of stipendiary women clergy is Oxford with 72 and the only diocese with none at all is Sodor and Man.

48 The comparable figure for men, by contrast, is less than 600.

49 For a more detailed account of the objections to the Act of Synod, see M. Furlong (ed.), *Act of Synod – Act of Folly?*, SCM Press, 1998.

50 *Priests (Ordination of Women) Measure 1993*, Part I (2).

51 Jones, *Women and the Priesthood*, p. 56.

52 Figures taken from diocesan statistics supplied to the Working Party and contained in HBWE (04) 12 *Ordination of Women Resolutions/Petitions*. The comparative figures for 1999 when the previous survey was taken were 836 parishes that had passed resolution A, 980 had passed resolution B (6.3 per cent and 7.4 per cent respectively) and 296 parishes had petitioned for extended episcopal care (2.2 per cent).

53 See Jones, *Ministry of Women* for the evidence for this.

54 For the evidence for this latter point from an evangelical perspective, see C. Sandom, *Fellow Workers in Christ – An Analysis of the Development of Women's Ministries amongst Conservative Evangelicals since November 1992*, which is available from Reform. It is, of course, the case that there are permanent women deacons who are in favour of the ordination of women to the priesthood, but simply do not believe that they are called to be priests.

55 *Episcopal Ministry Act of Synod – Report of a Working Party of the House of Bishops* (GS 1395), General Synod, 2000, p. 15.

chapter 5

1 G. Kirk, 'Some Comments on a Meeting between Representatives of Forward in Faith and the Working Party on the Theology of Women in the Episcopate', 2002, p. 2.

2 Forward in Faith, 'By Their Fruits', 2002, p. 2.

3 D. Lickess, letter of 14 July 2001, p. 4.

4 Submission from the vicar, churchwardens and PCC of Holy Trinity, Reading, 28 October 2001.

5 Forward in Faith, 'By Their Fruits', p. 4.

6 S. Goldberg, *The Inevitability of Patriarchy*, Temple Smith, 1997.

7 Kirk, 'Some Comments', p. 5.

8 R. A. Norris, 'The Ordination of Women and the 'Maleness' of Christ', *Anglican Theological Review*, Supplementary Series 6, June 1976, pp. 69–90.

9 Forward in Faith, 'A Submission to the Rochester Commission', *2001*, p. 6.

10 Forward in Faith, 'A Submission to the Rochester Commission', p. 6.

11 'Submission by the Master and Guardians of the Shrine of Our Lady of Walsingham', 2003, p. 5.

12 R. A. Pesarchick, *The Trinitarian Foundation of Human Sexuality as Revealed by Christ according to Hans Urs Von Balthasar: The Revelatory Significance of the Male Christ and the Male Ministerial Priesthood*, Editrice Pontificia Universata Gregoriana, 2000, pp. 272–3.

13 Lickess, letter, p. 3.

14 Forward in Faith, 'A Submission to the Rochester Commission', p. 12.

15 Forward in Faith, 'By Their Fruits', p. 8.

16 Forward in Faith,'By Their Fruits', p. 8.

17 Forward in Faith, 'By Their Fruits', p. 9.

18 D. Houlding, 'Reception and Communion', 2003, pp. 10–11.

19 Houlding, 'Reception and Communion', p. 9.

20 Houlding, 'Reception and Communion', p. 10.

21 'Submission by the Master and Guardians of the Shrine of Our Lady of Walsingham', p. 4.

22 'Submission by the Master and Guardians of the Shrine of Our Lady of Walsingham', p. 8.

23 D. Banting, 'A Submission to the Rochester Commission on behalf of the Council of Reform', *Churchman*, Spring 2002, p. 74.

24 G. Bray, 'Bishops, Presbyters and Women', *Churchman*, Spring 2002, pp. 15–16.

25 Gordon Wenham writes, for example, in Volume 1 of his commentary on Genesis (Word, 1987, pp. 50–1): 'similarly, man's authority over woman is implied in his two fold naming of her (2.23; 3.20) but her superiority to the animals is manifest for only she is a perfect match for man.'

26 But the subordination of filial love is not a diminution of essence, nor does pious duty cause a degeneration of nature, since in spite of the fact that both the Unborn Father is God and the Only-begotten Son of God is God, God is nevertheless One, and the subjection and dignity of the Son are both taught in that by being called Son He is made subject to that name which because it implies that God is His Father is yet a name which denotes His nature. Having a name which belongs to Him whose Son He is, He is subject to the Father both in service and name; yet in such a way that the subordination of His name bears witness to the true character of His natural and exactly similar essence. (Hilary of Poitiers, *De Synodis*, 51) For a contemporary restatement of this position see W. Grudem, *Systematic Theology*, IVP, 1994, p. 251.

27 For a defence of this reading of 1 Corinthians 11 see W. Grudem, 'Does Kephale Mean "Source" or "Authority over" in Greek Literature?', *Trinity Journal*, 6 (1985), pp. 38–59.

28 M. Ovey, 'The Economy of Salvation and Ecclesistical Tyranny', *Churchman*, Spring 2002, pp. 36–7.

29 C. Sandom, 'Scripture and Good Practice', in *A Presentation from Reform to the House of Bishops' Working Party on Women in the Episcopate*, 12 February 2003, p. 5. It is important to note that those who argue in this way for the subordination of women to men in the family and the Church are insistent that men must exercise their headship in a loving fashion in accordance with Ephesians 5.21-33. John Stott writes, for example:

> The husband's headship of his wife, therefore, is a headship more of care than of control, more of responsibility than of authority. As her 'head' he gives himself up for her in love, just as Christ did for his body, the church. And he looks after her, as we do our own bodies. His concern is not to crush her, but to liberate her. As Christ gave himself for his bride, in order to present her to himself radiant and blameless, so the husband gives himself for his bride, in order to create the conditions within which she may grow into the fullness of her femininity. (J. Stott, *Issues Facing Christians Today*, Marshall, Morgan and Scott, 1984, p. 247)

30 M. Burkill, D. Peterson, and S. Vibert, *Latimer Trust Ministry Work Group Statement Concerning the Ministry of Women in the Church Today*, 2001, p. 3. For a detailed study of 1 Timothy 2.9-15 from a traditionalist perspective, see A. Kostenberger, T. R. Schreiner and H. Scott Baldwin (eds), *Women in the Church – A Fresh Analysis of 1 Timothy 2:9-15*, Baker, 2000.

31 Burkhill, Peterson and Vibert, *Latimer Trust Work Group Statement*, pp. 3–4.

32 Ovey, 'The Economy of Salvation and Eccelesiastical Tyranny', pp. 30–1.

33 Ovey, 'The Economy of Salvation and Eccelesiastical Tryranny', p. 51, referring to St Ignatius of Antioch, *Epistle to the Trallians*, 3: 'you should also look on the bishop as a type [icon] of the Father' (Staniforth, *Early Christian Writings*, p. 96). The question as to what we mean when we use sexually differentiated terms such as 'Father' to refer to God and whether it is appropriate to use both male and female imagery to refer to God is one that has been much discussed in modern theology. For examples of contemporary thinking about this matter, see *The Catechism of the Catholic Church*, p. 57, P. K. Jewett, *God, Creation and Revelation*, Eerdmans, 1991, pp. 323–5 and A. Carr, 'Feminist Theology', in A. E. McGrath (ed.), *Blackwell Encyclopedia of Modern Christian Thought*, Blackwell, 1993, pp. 223–4.

34 R. Beckwith, *The Question of Women Bishops – An Evangelical Viewpoint Submitted from within the Third Province Movement*, 2002, p. 2.

35 Banting, 'A Submission to the Rochester Commission', p. 76.

36 N. Atkinson, 'Scripture and Tradition', in *A Presentation from Reform*, p. 8.

37 D. Banting, 'Scripture and Reason', in *A Presentation from Reform*, p. 10. Emphasis in the original.

38 Bray, 'Bishops, Presbyters and Women', p. 17.

39 Toon, *Reforming Forwards?*, p. 35.

40 Toon, *Reforming Forwards?*, p. 36.

41 Sandom, 'Scripture and Good Practice', p. 6.

42 D. Gillett, 'A Fresh Hermeneutical Lens on the Ordination of Women to the Episcopate', HBWE (03) 5, 2003, p. 1.

43 Gillett, *A Fresh Hermeneutical Lens*, p. 1.

44 Gillett, *A Fresh Hermeneutical Lens*, p. 2.

45 D. Atkinson, *The Message of Genesis 1-11*, IVP, 1990, p. 71.

46 M. Hayter, *The New Eve in Christ*, SPCK, 1987, p. 113.

47 M. Evans, *Woman in the Bible*, Paternoster Press, 1983, p. 32. When she says that 'women were not barred from leadership when circumstances required it' she is referring to cases such as those of Deborah (Judges 4-5) and Huldah (2 Kings 22.14-20/2 Chronicles 34.22-28).

48 Gillett, *A Fresh Hermeneutical Lens*, p. 4, quoting B. Witherington, *Women in the Ministry of Jesus*, CUP, 1984, p. 126.

49 Evans, *Women in the Bible*, pp. 129–30.

50 R. Campbell, *The Elders: Seniority Within Earliest Christianity*, T. and T. Clark, 1994, p. 138, quoting R. J. Banks, *Paul's Idea of Community*, Paternoster Press, 1980, pp. 157 and 160.

51 Campbell, *The Elders*, p. 54

52 For the argument for this reading of Romans 16.7 and for the wider role of Junia in the Early Church, see R. Bauckham, *Gospel Women*, T. and T. Clark, 2002, pp. 165–202. The opposite view is presented by M. H. Burer and D. B. Wallace, 'Was Junia Really an Apostle? A Re-examination of Romans 16.7', *New Testament Studies*, 47, 2001. They argue that Romans 16.7 means that Junia was regarded by the apostles as someone worthy of note, rather than that she was someone worthy of note as an apostle.

53 See U. E. Eisen, *Women Offieholders in Early Christianity*, Michael Glazier, 2000, pp. 50–1 and the references cited there.

54 Hooker, *The Laws of Ecclesiastical Polity*, VII.4.4, in *Works*, vol.II, pp. 338–9, citing Jerome, *Epistle 85*.

55 Hayter, *The New Eve in Christ*, p. 139.

56 P. Gooder, 'Headship: A Consideration of the Concept in the Writings of Paul', in H. Harris and J. Shaw (eds), *Women and Episcopacy*, WATCH, 2002, p. 13.

57 Gooder, 'Headship', pp. 14–15.

58 Gooder 'Headship', p. 15.

59 Thiselton, *The First Epistle to the Corinthians*, p. 820.

60 Thiselton, *The First Epistle to the Corinthians*, p. 821.

61 T. Hart, 'Headship or Subordinationism and the Consecration of Women Bishops', in the *Green Paper on Ordination of Women to the Episcopate*, Scottish Episcopal Church, 2001, p. 86.

62 Thiselton, *The First Epistle to the Corinthians*, p. 1158, emphases in the original.

63 G. Fee, *The First Epistle to the Corinthians*, Eerdmans, 1987, pp. 699–708.

64 C. K. Barrett, *The Pastoral Epistles*, Clarendon Press, 1963, J. N. D. Kelly, *The Pastoral Epistles*, A. & C. Black, 1963, G. W. Knight, *The Pastoral Epistles*, Paternoster Press, 1992, W. D. Mounce, *The Pastoral Epistles*, Word, 2000.

65 Hayter, *The New Eve in Christ*, p. 143.

66 Aune, 'Evangelicals and Gender', pp. 88–9. Italics hers.

67 The most thorough argument for this position is put forward in R. C. and C. C. Kroeger, *I Suffer Not a Woman: Rethinking 1 Timothy 2:11-15 in the Light of the Ancient Evidence*, Baker, 1992.

68 For the range of interpretations of 1 Timothy 2.11-15, see C. S. Keener, 'Man and Woman', in G. F. Hawthorne, R. P. Martin and D. G. Reid (eds), *Dictionary of Paul and his Letters*, IVP, 1993, pp. 590–2.

69 J. Wijngaards, *No Women in Holy Orders?*, Canterbury Press, 2002, p. 130.

70 J. Shaw, 'Women, Men and Apostolic Succession', in Harris and Shaw, *Women And Episcopacy*, p. 23.

71 Shaw, 'Women, Men and Apostolic Succession', p. 21.

72 S. Sykes, 'Richard Hooker and the Ordination of Women to the Priesthood', in J. M. Soskice (ed.), *After Eve*, Collins/Marshall Pickering, 1990, ch.8.

73 Hooker, *Laws of Ecclesiastical Polity*, III.10.2, in *Works*, vol.I, p. 318.

74 Hooker, *Laws of Ecclesiastical Polity*, III.10.5, in *Works*, vol.I, p. 321. For a biblical argument for this position see Hebrews 7.12-19

75 Sykes, 'Richard Hooker and the Ordination of Women', p. 132.

76 F. Watts, 'Women and the Episcopate: A Brief Comment from the Perspective of the Human Sciences', HBWE (02) 23, 2002, pp. 1–2.

77 Watts, 'Women and the Episcopate', p. 2.

78 Watts, 'Women and the Episcopate', p. 2.

79 Watts, 'Women and the Episcopate', p. 3.

80 For this capitalized usage, see Chapter 3.4

81 Part of Newman's argument for the development of doctrine that we looked at in Chapter 3 was that there were aspects of Christian truth that only became explicitly acknowledged as part of Christian belief when an occasion arose that caused the Church to express its mind about them.

82 Gillett, *A Fresh Hermeneutical Lens*, p. 6

83 P. Avis, *Anglican Orders and The Priesting of Women*, Darton, Longman & Todd, 1999, p. 14. Acting responsibly would, of course, involve taking ecumenical agreements and relationships into account and acting with reference to Scripture and tradition. The point that Avis is making is that in a divided Church each individual church does in the last instance have to act on its own after taking all these factors into account.

84 Avis, *Anglican Orders and The Priesting of Women*, p. 15.

85 Women and the Church, 'Submission to the Working Party on Women in the Episcopate', 2001, p. 1.

86 Chelmsford Diocese, Barking Episcopal Area, 'Proclaim Afresh in Each Generation – A Submission to the Rochester Commission on Women Bishops', 2001, p. 11.

87 This material is taken from the minutes of the Working Party on 29 April 2002, HB (02) M2, pp. 6 and 9.

88 Letter to the Working Party from Amiel Osmaston, 19 July 2001, p. 2.

89 St James' Church, Piccadilly, 'A Submission for the Working Party on Women Bishops', 2001, p. 2.

90 Jones, *Women and Priesthood*, p. 68.

91 A. Loades, 'Women in the Episcopate', *Anvil*, vol.21, no.2, 2004, p. 115.

92 See 3.1.22–24 above.

93 A. Loades and C. Hall, 'Towards the Transformation of the Episcopate: Proposal for a Reinvigorated Process', HBWE (02) 15, p. 4.

94 Barking Episcopal Area, 'Proclaim Afresh', p. 13.

95 Barking Episcopal Area, 'Proclaim Afresh', p. 14.

96 For the issues to be considered here see Thiselton, *The First Epistle to the Corinthians*, pp. 812–23 and J. Gundry-Volf, 'Gender and Creation in 1 Cor 11.2-16: A Study in Paul's Theological Method', in Adna *et al.* (eds), *Evangelium, Schriftauslegung, Kirche: Gestschrift für P. Stuhlmacher*, Vandehoeck & Ruprech, 1997, pp. 151–71.

97 See 5.3.24–26 above.

chapter 6

1 Fee, *The First Epistle to the Corinthians*, p. 382.

2 Banting, 'A Submission to the Rochester Commission', p. 76.

3 Forward in Faith, *By Their Fruits*, pp. 10–11.

4 Toon, *Reforming Forwards?*, p. 35.

5 A. C. Thiselton, 'Comments on 1 Timothy 2.8-15', HBWE (02) 22, 2002, p. 7.

6 Although strictly speaking the term 'Roman Catholic' does not include the Eastern rite churches in

communion with Rome the reference here is intended to include them since there is no other convenient shorthand to describe the churches in communion with the see of Rome.

7 This term is used to cover both the Chalcedonian and non-Chalcedonian Orthodox churches, neither of which accept women as bishops, priests or deacons.

8 *Catechism of the Catholic Church*, Geoffrey Chapman, 1994, pp. 353–4. The quotation in the first sentence is from Canon 1024 of the *Codex Iuris Canonici* of 1983.

9 *Ordinatio Sacerdotalis – On Reserving Priestly Ordination to Men Alone*, CTS, 1994, p. 6.

10 *Ordinatio Sacerdotalis*, pp. 6–7. For the most detailed exposition of this position, see the 1976 declaration by the Sacred Congregation for the Doctrine of the Faith, *Inter Insigniores*, in *Women Priests Obstacle to Unity?*, CTS, 1986, pp. 3–19.

11 For the full text of the statement, see *Anglican-Orthodox Dialogue: The Dublin Agreed Statement 1984*, SPCK, 1985, Appendix 2, pp. 58–60.

12 Bishop Basil of Sergievo, *The Ordination of Women to the Priesthood*, HBWE (03) 12a, 2002, pp. 8–9.

13 *Women Priests Obstacle to Unity?*, p. 48.

14 *Women Priests Obstacle to Unity?*, p. 50.

15 *Women Priests Obstacle to Unity?*, p. 52.

16 *Ibid.*, p. 61. It should be noted that Cardinal Willebrands was referring to the proposal to ordain women as priests. He was not referring to the issue of their ordination as deacons.

17 *Women in the Anglican Episcopate*, Anglican Book Centre, 1988, Appendix IV, pp. 143–4.

18 H. Meyer and L. Vischer (eds), *Growth in Agreement: Reports and Agreed Statements of Ecumenical Conversations on a World Level*, WCC, 1984, p. 52.

19 Women and the Church, 'Submission to the Working Party on Women in the Episcopate', p. 1.

20 Osmaston, letter, p. 2

21 Lambeth Conference 1988, Resolution 1, text in R. Coleman (ed.), *Resolutions of the Lambeth Conferences 1867–1988*, Anglican Book Centre, 1992, p. 193.

22 E. Behr-Sigel and K. Ware, *The Ordination of Women in the Orthodox Church*, WCC, 2000 pp. 144–5.

23 U. Von Arx and A. Kallis, 'Common Considerations: The Orthodox-Old Catholic Consultation on the Role of Women in the Church and the Ordination of Women as an Ecumenical Issue', *Anglican Theological Revue*, Summer 2002, vol.84, no.3, p. 503.

24 It should be noted, however, that the consultation also made the point that:

> With regard to the preservation of communion in each church respectively, and to the union we seek, dogmatic-theological arguments – however important they may be – are not of sole importance when dealing with this question. So-called non-theological factors determining the pastoral action of the churches in each place also play a role. This and the responsibility of each local church for the communion of the churches also need to be borne in mind when local churches are making decisions. (Arx and Kallis, 'Common Considerations', pp. 505–6.)

25 N. Lash, 'On Not Inventing Doctrine', *The Tablet*, 2 December 1995, p. 1544.

26 Wijngaards, *No Women in Holy Orders?*, p. 154.

27 Wijngaards, *No Women in Holy Orders?*, p. 154.

28 Wijngaards, *No Women in Holy Orders?*, pp. 154–5.

29 Wijngaards, *No Women in Holy Orders?*, p. 155. For other books arguing a similar position, see C. Stuhlmeller, *Women and Priesthood: Future Directions*, Liturgical Press, 1978, and E. M. Tetelow, *Women and Ministry in the New Testament*, Paulist Press, 1980. In addition to the work of individual theologians there are also groups such as the Catholic Women's Network, We Are Church (www.we-are-church.org), and the Campaign for the Ordination of Women in the Roman Catholic Church (www.womenpriests.org), who are campaigning for the Roman Catholic Church to change its position.

30 *An Anglican Methodist Covenant*, Peterborough and London, Methodist Publishing House/CHP, 2001, pp. 49–50.

chapter 7

1 Geoffrey Kirk, for example, puts forward this argument in the March 2004 edition of *New Directions*: 'Options – Back to the Future', *New Directions*, vol.7, no.106, March 2004, p. 16.
2 See 5.2.21-29 and 5.2.46-47 above.
3 See 5.2.19-20, 6.2.1-6 and 6.2.16-34.
4 See 5.2.25, 5.2.49-50 and 6.2.8-9.
5 5.2.17.
6 John 17.20-21.
7 See 6.2.1-34 above.
8 6.3.1-2.
9 See 6.3.13.
10 As we have noted, this reading of Galatians 3.28 is itself contested – see 5.2.38-9 and 5.3.16 for contrasting readings of this text.
11 See 6.3.13.
12 Women and the Church, 'Submission to the Working Party on Women in the Episcopate', p. 2.
13 V. Faull and J. Tetley, *Women in the Episcopate – Options for the Way Ahead*, HBWE (03) 6, 2003, p. 8.
14 They specify women in senior professional roles and in civic roles such as mayors, high sheriffs, and lords lieutenant.
15 Faull and Tetley, 'Women in the Episcopate', p. 8.
16 Faull and Tetley, 'Women in the Episcopate', p. 8.
17 Forward in Faith, 'A Submission to the Rochester Commission', p. 14.
18 Forward in Faith, 'A Submission to the Rochester Commission', p. 11.
19 Forward in Faith, 'A Submission to the Rochester Commission', p. 14.
20 Banting, 'A Submission to the Rochester Commission', p. 76.
21 Coleman, *Resolutions of the Lambeth Conferences 1867–1988*, p. 194.
22 *The Official Report of the Lambeth Conference 1998*, p. 395.
23 *Priests (Ordination of Women) Measure 1993 Code of Practice*, General Synod, 1994, Appendix A, p. 1.
24 *Priests (Ordination of Women) Measure 1993 Code of Practice*, p. 1.
25 Faull and Tetley, 'Women in the Episcopate', p. 9.
26 Scottish Episcopal Church, *General Synod 2003 Agenda & Papers*, p. 87.
27 Women and the Church, 'Submission to the Working Party on Women in the Episcopate', p. 2.
28 Anglican Church of Australia, *Women Bishops in Australia? If so, How?*, 2001, p. 8.
29 Anglican Church of Australia, *Women Bishops in Australia? If so, How?*, pp. 8–9.
30 Anglican Church of Australia, *Women Bishops in Australia? If so, How?*, p. 9.
31 Ovey, 'The Economy of Salvation', pp. 66–7.
32 Ovey, 'The Economy of Salvation', pp. 67–8.
33 Ovey, 'The Economy of Salvation', p. 55.
34 Ovey, 'The Economy of Salvation', p. 55.
35 Ovey, 'The Economy of Salvation', p. 68.
36 *Women in the Anglican Episcopate*, p. 31.
37 *Women in the Anglican Episcopate*, p. 32.
38 Faull and Tetley, 'Women in the Episcopate', p. 2.
39 For details of their stance, see their leaflets *The Third Province Movement – Questions and Answers* and *Policy for The Third Province*.
40 G. Kirk, 'A Pertinent Proposition', *New Directions*, January 2003.
41 Faull and Tetley, 'Women in the Episcopate', p. 1.
42 Faull and Tetley, 'Women in the Episcopate', pp. 5–6.

43 The problem of a parallel jurisdiction not being in communion with the church of which it was a part and the issue of the potential non-interchangeability of ministry was the reason the Eames Commission warned against the creation of parallel jurisdictions for those opposed to women bishops. See *Women in the Anglican Episcopate*, pp. 30–1.

44 Forward in Faith, 'A Submission to the Rochester Commission', p. 16.

chapter 8

1 K. Ware, 'Man, Woman and the Priesthood of Christ', in P. Moore (ed.), *Man, Woman and Priesthood*, SPCK, 1978, pp. 81ff.

annex 1

1 The tenth General Synod of the Church of Melanesia agreed in 2003 to the amending of the Church's Constitution to allow women to enter into any of the ordained ministries of the church. The decision was passed without dissent by the General Synod, but this does not mean the church can proceed with ordination as yet. The amendment must first be approved by the eight diocesan synods of the church before the constitution can be changed.

2 Hong Kong has long been ordaining women as deacons and priests. At present, there are five women priests serving in three dioceses of the Hong Kong Sheng Kung Hui, but it has not started discussing the issue of women bishops. However, according to the constitutions and canons, clergy from Anglican Churches, which are in communion with the Anglican Communion (no gender is mentioned) are eligible to be nominated as candidates for the episcopate. From this perspective, the HKSKH could, in principle, have women bishops.

3 Ireland: a.) Canon Law (1990): 'Men and women alike may be ordained to the holy orders of deacons, of priests, or of bishops, without any distinction or discrimination on grounds of sex . . .' b.) No women as yet ordained as bishops. c.) No bar to women being appointed as deans, though none appointed as yet. Some cathedral chapters include women as canons.

4 Women bishops are canonically possible, but none are ordained as yet.

5 Women bishops are canonically possible, but none are ordained as yet.

6 Women bishops are canonically possible, but none are ordained as yet.

7 The General Synod of the Scottish Episcopal Church (SEC) voted to accept women in the episcopate, in 2003.

8 Provincial guidelines to provide for conscientious objections to the ministry of women as priests are in place. Similar guidelines in the event of a woman being ordained as bishop are being produced. Women bishops are canonically possible, but none are ordained as yet.

9 The Episcopal Church of Sudan agreed at its General Synod in February 2000 that women could be ordained deacon, priest or bishop. To date there are deacons and priests in a number of dioceses, though as yet no women bishops.

10 The ordination of women as deacons and priests has been canonically possible for nearly thirty years. There is currently one woman bishop and one woman dean.

11 In 1973 the General Synod voted in favour in principle of ordaining women to the priesthood, referred the question to the Church for further study, and then the 1975 General Synod agreed to ordain, with a conscience clause to protect those who disagreed. The first women were ordained priest in 1976. In 1986 the General Synod agreed that women could be ordained to the episcopate.

12 The enabling canon for the ordination of women to the presbyterate and the episcopate applies to all dioceses. Informal episcopal arrangements can be made to protect the conscience of an individual bishop.

General index

General index

Rose, Judith 2
Royden, Maude 119
Rufinus of Aquilea 270 n.51
Runcie, Robert, Archbishop of Canterbury 128–9, 190
rural/area deans 59, 129
Rusch, William 104

sacraments:
  and episcopal ministry 46–7, 63, 147–8
sacramental assurance 144–6, 181, 204
Sagovsky, Nicholas 74
St James, Piccadilly 175–6
Sandom, Carrie 150, 156
Savoy Conference (1660) 33
Sawyer, Deborah 92
Sayers, Dorothy L. 271 n.13
Scottish Episcopal Church 183, 186, 211–12, 279 n.7
Second Vatican Council, and the Bible 77
self-evidence, argument from 66–7
sensus fidelium 197
Sex Discrimination Act 1975 124, 174–5, 177
sexuality:
  female 167
  and human nature 74, 140–41, 228–9, 233
Shaw, Jane 168–9
South Africa, and women bishops 186, 218
Southern Baptist Convention (USA) 192
Stansgate, Lady 119
Stanton, Elizabeth Cady 92
Storkey, Elaine 118, 122–4
Stott, John 274 n.29
subordination, functional 149–51, 170, 176, 179, 182
Succession, Apostolic 37–9, 50, 63–4, 145, 191–2
  in Early Church 19–20
  in ecumenical agreements 33, 44–5
  and English Reformation 29
  and mission 51
  and women 168
suffragan bishop 25, 43, 56–7, 224–5
  responsibilities 245–6
Suffragan Bishops report 57, 58–9
support, argument from 67–8
Sykes, Stephen 169–70

Tait, Archibald, Bishop of London 117
Tanner, Mary 68–9
teacher, bishop as 14, 18–19, 45–6, 63, 242
Teams and Groups Measure 53
Tertullian 12, 18, 19–20
Tetley, Joy 206–7, 211, 216–17, 220
Theodore of Mopsuestia 10, 11
third province 6, 135, 155, 218–23, 241
Third Province Movement 152–3, 218
Thirty-Nine Articles 30–31, 46, 60, 108, 217
Thiselton, Anthony 110–111, 163, 164–5, 186
Tillard, Jean-Marie Roger 196
Timothy, and leadership of the Church 1–32, 38
Titus, and leadership of the Church 12–13, 38

Toon, Peter 97, 106–8, 155–6, 185
Towards a Theology of Vocation 68–9
tradition:
  bishop as guardian 18–21
  and development of doctrine 100–102, 168–9, 230, 231–2
  and interpretation of the Bible 84–8, 93
  and reception 106–8
  and women bishops 2, 86–8, 93, 102, 137–9, 168–72, 180–81, 189, 200, 202
Trible, Phyllis 83, 93
Trinity:
  development of doctrine 94–5
  and functional subordination 149–51, 179

United States of America *see* ECUSA
unity, bishop as focus 41, 61, 63, 154, 172, 243
  in Early Church 9, 11, 15–18, 40, 64
  and ecumenism 48–9, 58
  and episcopal teams 226
  and heresy and schism 49–50
  and suffragan bishops 57
  and women bishops x, 146–8, 181–2, 184, 192, 202–5, 206–7
Ussher, James, Archbishop of Armagh 32

validity of orders 109, 145–6, 181, 204, 208
Vincent of Lerins, St 94
Virginia Report 77, 88
vocation of women:
  and domesticity 91, 114–16, 229
  and priesthood 68–70, 72, 102
  and sisterhoods 116–17
Von Balthasar, Hans Urs 143

Walsingham, Master and Guardians of the Shrine 142–3, 146, 147–8, 203
Ware, Kallistos 17, 195, 228–9
WATCH *see* Women and the Church
Watts, Fraser 170–71
Webster, John 40–41, 89
Wenham, Gordon 273 n.25
Whitby, Synod (664) 27
Whitgift, John, Archbishop of Canterbury 31, 34
Wijngaards, John 167–8, 180, 197–8
Wilcox, Thomas, *Admonition to Parliament* (1572) 31
Wiles, Maurice 98
Willebrands, Cardinal Johannes 128–9, 190
women:
  in the Bible 81–2, 99
  clergy 129
  as deacons 126, 129, 133, 153, 164, 195, 197–8
  invisibility 114
  lay workers 121, 122
  ministry in Church of England 1, 68–72, 100, 102, 114–35, 167–8
  and religious communities 116
  seen as intellectually weaker 87, 101, 167, 169–70
  social role and status x, 1, 66, 91, 118, 122–4, 170

Index of biblical references